HOW TO WRITE
WHEN YOU'RE NOT A
WRITER

THE 4 PILLARS
of Becoming a Better Business Writer

BY

ALIA COSTER

CONTENTS

INTRODUCTION

Would you expect to sit down at a piano and instantly start playing like Mozart? Of course not. Well, unless you're a classically trained pianist, that is. So why are you expecting Roald Dahl to fall out of your fingertips?

1

Writing is more than putting pen to paper and creating pretty sentences. When you use it well, it can be the difference between scoring that sale, putting your foot on the ladder towards your dream job, and getting what you want. You can develop your writing today through four simple pillars, taking your performance in your professional life from good to great.

What so many people don't often realise is that writing is a discipline like any other. Would you expect to sit down at a piano and instantly start playing like Mozart? Of course not. Well, unless you're a classically trained pianist, that is. So why are you expecting Roald Dahl to fall out of your fingertips? It takes time, effort, and consistency. It's an individual journey with your own goal, and you need to handle it in your own way, in your own time. And you can start right now.

Drawing on my experience, I want to give you a toolkit to elevate your content and communication in the working world. It's why I created my four pillars of writing success: research, structure, writing, and editing. No matter your industry or role - whether you're struggling to produce impactful content or communicate effectively with others - these core concepts form the backbone to improving this vital skill.

What this book isn't is an in-depth grammar lesson. Writing isn't about being grammatically perfect. There's a whole layer of psychology you're potentially overlooking. I know, you'll want to get to writing as soon as possible. But spoiler alert: writing is the easy part. You simply write. That's all there is to it. But it's only one piece of a bigger puzzle. At some point in our lives, we developed this belief we should write elegantly. To be that great writer you want to be, it takes research, structuring, and editing. It's about looking not only at *what* we're writing, but also *how* and *why*. And that's what you'll develop through the four pillars.

Despite opinions that surround the 2022 Oscars, one of my absolute favourite motivational videos is by Will Smith. And he has the best piece of advice I can relate to writing:

> *"You don't set out to build a wall. You don't say 'I'm going to build the biggest, baddest, greatest wall that's ever been built.' You don't start there. You say, 'I'm going to lay this brick as perfectly as a brick can be laid.' You do that every single day. And soon, you have a wall."*

Writing follows a similar pattern. You don't sit down and write the perfect proposal, the most fantastic presentation, or a captivating email straight off the bat. It's a process. One that you commit to and work through until it's where you want it to be. There'll be plenty of top tips and exercises throughout the book to help you grow along your journey. Sticking with these over time will empower you as the unofficial writer that you are.

I'd love to hear your thoughts and what resonates with you the most. Let's stay connected. Drop me a personal line on LinkedIn: Alia Coster. Or, you can join the community over on Instagram and LinkedIn at @thefourwritingpillars. In the meantime, I hope you enjoy this book, and I wish you every success in becoming the writer and communicator you strive to be.

Alia Ayshea Coster

WHY READ THIS BOOK?

> You're an unofficial writer whenever words are
> involved in your professional life and aren't explicitly
> getting paid for them. If you're the boss putting
> something together for the website, you're an
> unofficial writer. If you're emailing both colleagues
> internally and customers or leads externally, you're
> an unofficial writer. If you're putting together
> presentations, proposals, pitch decks, tenders, or
> letters, you're an unofficial writer. If you're writing
> your CV for a new job... I think you get the point by
> now. If this in any way describes you, you're in the right
> place.

U nofficial writers come in all shapes and sizes, but, typically, there are two main types:

One - You can't stand writing. You want to be better at it ASAP so you can stop wasting time and energy trying to get it right. The thought of being asked to write a blog makes you want to tear your hair out.

Two - You love it, and you're good at it, but you want to improve where you're at. Either because your current process isn't sustainable and could be a bit more efficient, or because you simply want to get better. You love being given a writing task, but there's likely some perfectionism or fear stunting your progress.

Both are perfectly normal. And no matter where you fall on the Marmite scale between love it or hate it, it's vital for you to know that you're not alone. And I'm so glad you're here to learn. With your writing, these are the pillars that will guarantee your writing success:

- Research
- Structure
- Writing
- Editing

So, where do you even start? Without the fundamentals in place, most people write how they talk. But we don't read how we listen. Often, there's a huge disconnect.

We're approaching our writing from the wrong place, wondering why it's not serving us how we'd like. Using the four pillars as our framework, I'll teach you how to bridge the gap and transform your professional writing and written communication from good to great.

Most people understand that a crap website or a waffly email is terrible for business. I'm glad we agree with that. However, many people miss the connection between poorly written communication and other crippling effects on professional performance and success. When you look at it in the big picture, written communication is the glue that holds your career together. Done successfully, everything flows smoothly. But failure to communicate properly can create problems that are difficult to fix. These failures with the written word can vary from obvious to subtle, and we should address them with the respect they deserve. Some much-needed reflection is necessary to get to the root of written communication problems within your working life.

Trust me, the reward for fixing them is well worth it.

THE TRICK TO BEING A BETTER WRITER

Our writing - despite contrary belief, isn't only about us. Being able to write something and understand it doesn't mean everyone else will. That's what becoming a better writer is about.

M ost people's writing is serviceable. It's perfectly fine. It - *in part* - says what they want to say, and improving it isn't an urgent concern when there's so much else to do. Other matters such as business development, profits, and productivity take centre stage instead. So our written communication takes a backseat. And that's okay. But our writing isn't only about us. The fact we can write something and understand it doesn't mean everyone else will. That's what becoming a better writer is about and - I'm assuming - why you picked up this book in the first place. Because you know there's a benefit to being better, whatever that means to you.

When we focus on what we think of our writing, we can miss the potential problems it can cause. We might mean well when we write down every piece of information we know about something. But it could lead to you being the person who fills someone with fear when they see waffling paragraphs slide into their inbox at 4:57 p.m. on a Friday with the header "Can you just... " It's all too easy to accidentally hit a roadblock with our communication. Staying on emails, did you know 65% of businesses use emails as their primary way to communicate with clients? That's great if you already do that, but are you being mindful of how you're communicating project information? Is it easy to find or buried in a thread with 10 other people CC'd into it? In short, are you thinking about how your message is coming across?

That's the trick a lot of people miss. It isn't necessarily what you're writing, but how you're writing it. I often see

LinkedIn posts clearly dripping in passion. The author speaks long and lovingly about their product and how much of a game changer it was. I always love seeing that in people. But I had to reread their post 10 times before I got any of that. With a slightly different approach, they could have had a much more effective message.

We have to remember that when communicating through email or text message, a lot of the context disappears. In face-to-face conversations, we often take cues from someone's body language, facial expressions, or tone of voice. But in message form, these are absent. We can quickly misinterpret someone's mood or misread a joke and take offence. And this is precisely how connection, relationships, and morale can become strained. If we ignore the format of how we're communicating, then we can't be surprised when someone takes us the wrong way.

These seemingly subtle problems often persist and quietly exacerbate confusion, doubt, and bad feelings within a company. They can degrade morale, delay projects, or burn essential bridges between colleagues or clients. And it often happens without us even realising it. Because, at the end of the day, some people are fine with what they've written. They don't see the consequences as, well, consequences. Studies of professions ranging from professors to drivers have shown that most people rate themselves as doing above-average work - 90% in some cases. It's statistically impossible for most of us to be above average at any skill or task, yet some people believe they are.

Writing is something most of us have done practically every day since we were children. It should feel like second nature and something we all excel at. But with poor communication at the heart of many problems in a working environment, is illusory superiority to blame? The first step in improving? Having the self-reflection to know you **can** improve. And you've already done that! The fact you're reading this book is proof that you know you can write better. It's OK to accept that we're not the best at something. Isn't that the healthiest way to be? Acknowledging and embracing all the space we have left to develop?

Naturally, no one wants to be the person confusing others. We want to be the one whose courteous, quick responses always get to the heart of the question. The one who people genuinely enjoy working with professionally. Someone who gets the job done seamlessly and productively. By ensuring your written communication is up to scratch, you build a foundation for loyal customer relationships, forging a positive reputation for yourself and becoming more credible to your audience. As a result, you can increase your customer base and become more influential in your industry. Add more tangible value to your audience through informative, well-written content and, in return, receive more custom and business growth.

CAN'T I USE GRAMMARLY OR AI?

For many of us, it's been a little while since we've been in formal education - *not that I'm trying to show my age.* So while we probably get a lot of writing practice without realising it through our work, it's been a few years since we've brushed up on the rules. That's where spelling and grammar tools like autocorrect come in handy. But it's not something you should take without a pinch of salt. Technology isn't always your friend. It won't know what you're trying to say, and sometimes it's better to trust your instincts.

Good communication means more than knowing when to pat yourself on the back after successfully placing all your apostrophes. It's about saying what you mean. And that what you say makes sense to people without them scratching their heads. It's about adjusting your tone of voice to meet the situation. To leave the cryptic messages at the door. I've already listed many ways in which your writing might hold you back. That being said, what I'm not here to do is turn you into a robot. That's what online tools are for and - to be honest - even they're not perfect.

We're beautifully flawed as human beings, and it's our ability to show empathy and tell stories that separates us and makes us truly unique. But relying on spell check or jumping on the likes of Grammarly, while it can help catch silly mistakes, threatens to take a lot of your writing's meaning away. And that's something that will not change any time soon, no matter how hard developers try. The same rules apply if you're looking for technology to write for you. There's a delicate balance to strike between technically

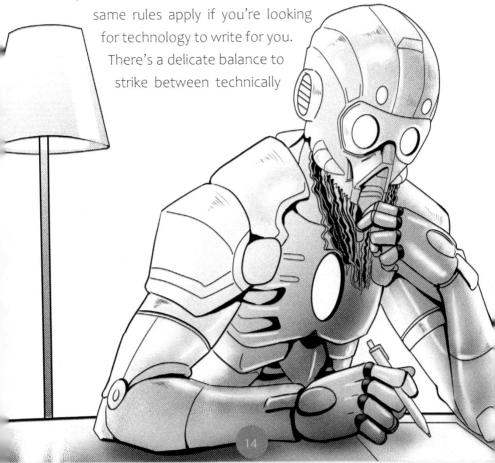

perfect writing and writing that's impactful, meaningful, and authentically yours.

I'm not raging against the machine here. Technology is fantastic; machines leave us free to upskill and enhance our creativity. And sure, there might come a day where a robot can sit in a lamp-lit room, twiddle its beard, and channel past trauma into a 15-page poem about leaves like a human being can. But that's not today. The problem with using artificial intelligence to improve your writing is that, despite its name, it can be dumb. It can follow instructions perfectly, but only **particular** instructions. And you have to be specific. If you want any form of creative interpretation of the instructions you give AI, you can forget about it. Everything is literal.

I asked one of my team to trial a 'blog writing' app heavily advertised on Instagram. Our test piece: an article on horse riding in the UK. Although it didn't start that way. The original blog on 'horses' wasn't specific enough for the software to comprehend. Fair enough. So, she changed it to 'horse riding' - still no good. Then she settled by adding 'in the UK', much to the app's delight. It got to work crafting the exciting blog we were so ready for. When the loading bar finally hit 100%, here's what our new robot friend had to say on the topic:

> *"It's your breeches on account of the manner of such horse riding equipment, but your pair of breeches can act as your insulating material layer over a pair of thermal tights in the event that your legs actually feel the cold beneath the first parts to feel the chilly and cause you the most distress when."*

What??? This paragraph was poor enough, but the robot followed up with:

> *"In addition, do not forget your feet."*

Not only is this article completely nonsensical, but to insinuate that the reader may leave their own feet somewhere other than the bottom of their legs was one step too far. Pun intended. All Grammarly had to say about this particular section of text was that five words needed a bit of a change-up.

- CONCISENESS

~~in the event that~~ → `if`

The phrase **in the event that** may be wordy. Consider changing the wording.

⑦ Learn more   🗑 ⋮

Don't want Grammarly to check quotes?   ✕
Change this in Editor settings.

- **actually** · Remove the phrase

- **the chilly** · Change the article

- **poor** · Choose a different word

- **In addition** · Change the wording

All of this to say that there's writing software out there to help you, but it doesn't *replace you*. It maintains coherence between various documents. Software keeps aspects like language, tone of voice, and style the same across your content and spots minor mistakes you might miss on a proofread. But if your message is landing badly in the first place - like our excellent horse article - you're not improving the value of what you're writing. You're simply polishing a turd and rolling it in glitter. Yes, it's grammatically correct, but it stinks.

While technology can produce or edit a 500-word piece of content with impeccable spelling, it still doesn't know who it's targeting. It doesn't know who it's representing, the correct tone of voice, any references or statistics to back up what it's saying, or how not to speak like an alien sent to find out more about their 'fellow humans'. Unfortunately, these are all the elements that matter the most in your written content. You need that touch to provide original thought. A message that considers the readers. That's empathetic and feeling. In short, that's **human**. Telling people not to forget their feet won't cut it. Let's turn off the robots and roll up our sleeves with the first pillar of becoming a better business writer.

PILLAR ONE:

RESEARCH

It's essential to be super clear about who you are and how you want to come across. Whether or not you're conscious of it, a personality is shining through your written communications. It's wise to make sure it's one you want representing you. We're all different, so by first understanding who you are and how you can best adapt to different situations, you'll find it easier to hit the mark with your messaging every time.

A s with everything in life, to create something, you need the right combination. For water, you need two parts hydrogen to one part oxygen. To build the perfect fire, you need fuel and a spark. For the perfect pizza, you need that thin base, glorious spread layer of tomato sauce, and a heart-stopping amount of cheese. You get the point. It's life 101: to create something, you need the right elements. The business world is no exception. To be successful at communicating, there are three fundamental tenets. There's you, your message, and the recipient. Becoming a better writer won't happen by writing alone. There's work to be done before you can pick up your pen. Before we start, we need the bread and butter for our writing sandwich.

For your message to hit the mark, we also need to delve deeper into you and your reader. Writing, no matter the format, isn't a sales pitch; it's a story. And like creating any good story, we have to start at the beginning with some research and exploration. A common misconception is that researching is strictly for content that's looking to teach an audience something. Such as a blog or whitepaper. Why should you care about research when you simply want to write tenders more effectively? Or stop rubbing clients up the wrong way? Or smash your CV and get the job of your dreams?

We change this perception by exploring what research even is. I'm not talking about Googling facts or reading around a topic. That's a given in certain situations. Our first pillar refers to understanding the two key players with any piece of content: you and the reader. If you're not clear on your tone of voice, your inconsistency will confuse people. Not taking the time to formulate what you want your message to be will cause you to waffle. Without a clear understanding of who you're communicating with, your message isn't landing. The list goes on. To get into the habit of consistently creating compelling content that gets you what you want, you first need to pause and reflect.

So I'll ask you... Who are you?

WHO ARE YOU?

From ancient Greece and its philosophy of "know thyself" to The Who classic (otherwise loved as the CSI theme tune) and beyond, we've had it instilled into us the importance of knowing who we are. And for a good reason. To best interact with others and the world around us, we first need to get to grips with who we are, what we believe in, and what we stand for. When did you last take the time to understand your communication style? Or how you handle your emotions? Do you know what ticks you off when talking to others or which personality traits send you over the edge?

This understanding of yourself will become the backbone of your writing. Once you make sense of how you communicate and react in conversation, you can assess if this is working. When you can be honest about what does and doesn't work for you, you can improve your communication skills.

For example, suppose you consider yourself an efficient emailer who gets to the point quickly so that you can move on to the next task on your never-ending list. This might help you identify that your one-liner emails are possibly landing as rude to others. Or you think full stops and paragraph breaks aren't a big deal. In that case, you'll learn throughout the following pages how this is inconsiderate to the reader. It can hold you back, and now you know about it, you can handle it differently. At the end of this chapter, there's space for you to work through this exercise.

It's essential to be super clear about who you are and how you want to come across. Whether or not you're conscious of it, a personality is shining through your written communications. It's wise to make sure it's one you want representing you. We're all different, so by first understanding who you are and how you can best adapt to different situations, you'll find it easier to hit the mark with your messaging every time.

Who you are goes a lot deeper than how you communicate. So, where do you even start when researching yourself? You could journal, work with a coach, or take any number of steps on this journey. However, personality profiling has been the fastest and most successful way I've seen for unofficial writers to develop a strong baseline for themselves. Personality profiling is something you might've come across, be it through psychometric testing or psychological profiling. A rose by any other name in this case. Essentially, it's where you measure what makes you **you**. I use profiling as an effective way to recruit for my team and strengthen our bond, and it's critical when writing content or forging new client relationships.

Think of it this way, if you don't realise you clash with certain types of people, and you're not tailoring your communication effectively, you're going to keep clashing left, right, and centre. Or if you have too many creatives in your leadership team, perhaps you're finding that projects aren't coming together as quickly and efficiently as they could be. There are hundreds of personality profiling routes you can take. I love them all in their own way. What convinces me is all the research and science that underpins them. For figuring out ourselves (and others), they're perfect. I'm not saying they reveal 100% of who a person is, though. It's important to remember that we are complex, fallible creatures that won't ever fit perfectly into neat little boxes. All we can do is recognise we're on a scale, identify where we fit, and adapt ourselves accordingly.

My favourites are the ones I find most relevant to becoming a better writer. These are the Myers-Briggs personality test and the colour system. The colour system - with all its variants - is brilliant when looking for an easy way to understand your audience and communicate in a considerate way to them. As it's a broader profiling tool, it's easier to apply to a stranger. Whether they're red, blue, or sometimes even an animal depending on the test, it's great for quickly identifying other people.

For yourself, you have a lot more time to dive into what makes you tick. That's why the Myers-Briggs test is one I always recommend. It uses a series of in-depth questions to determine your best fit out of 16 personality types. Because it's so deeply personal, it's not one you can use on others. It would look a little weird if you asked your prospective new employer whether they agree or disagree that they spend a lot of their free time exploring various random topics. Or if seeing other people cry makes them want to cry too.

Why does any of this matter to your writing? While no profiling is perfect, it gives you an indication of what kind of person you are, and it's a stark reminder that *your* way isn't the *only* way. So let's look at the Myers Briggs - otherwise known as the 16 personalities system. Through a series of questions, you'll learn where you sit on the scale between Extroverted or Introverted; Sensing or Intuitive; Thinking or Feeling; and Judging or Perceiving.

Let's consider the scale of Thinking vs Feeling: This refers to our decision-making. Whether someone is more thinking - considering situations objectively, harnessing logic, and maintaining a cold, rational view. Or if they're more feeling - acting subjectively and passionately, listening to their instincts, and considering the feelings of others when making a decision. If you're a feeler, your communications are going to reflect that. But if your reader is a thinker, your fluffy, emotive ramblings aren't going to be to their taste.

By first understanding your type, you can analyse how you're communicating with others. Then, as you get more confident with the profiling systems, you can adapt your tone accordingly. For example, I'm a textbook ENFP type - a people-centred creator focusing on possibilities and contagious enthusiasm for anything novel. I'm led by how I feel, trust my strong intuition, and tuned to my empathy. Suppose I'm conversing with another feeler over email. In that case, I could gush over how super cool their recent marketing campaign was or comfortably chat at length about our dogs, sharing cute pictures. I know they're likely to be on my level. If, however, I know I'm talking to someone that sits opposite me on the spectrum and is a fact-based individual, I would scale myself back, get to the point quickly, and present facts succinctly, losing the waffle and personal chat.

By considering these personality types ahead of crafting your communication, you can ensure both parties will have their needs met. It's when you switch the two around that you step into tricky territory. If your written communication doesn't always land as you hope, it's likely you're not communicating in a way that works for the specific personality type you're talking to. And that's an easy problem for you to fix. No matter which personality profiling method you use, figuring out the type of person you are is the first step. All the traits and beliefs that define you make you inherently biased in everything you talk about. In your CV, you list the accomplishments **you** are proud of. Sales pitches are likely to centre around the benefits **you** think are essential. In an email, you talk about the subjects **you** think are critical. But effective communication isn't about you. Once you break down all that makes you who you are, you can write across all formats more authentically, according to your own values and code of conduct in a way that lands well for the reader.

There are other benefits to better understanding who you are; you can also learn what doesn't work for you. Not every job is for us. Not every business opportunity that comes our way is the right fit. Not every client will be our type of person. Every year, my team and I sit down to evaluate who we are, where we've been, and where we want to go. The core of all our planning is what we bring to the table as individuals. We draw on what makes us unique and who we work best with. We've cultivated a list of buzzwords that make up our ideal client. And we draw more of these people out by addressing the things they think about in our content. The cliche of "your vibe attracts your tribe" works as well as "your words attract your herd".

When you know what you don't want, you can tailor your writing to attract what you do want. Take the qualities of the people you don't want and flip them around. Tactically turning off the readers you know aren't your people. They won't want to work with you if they don't feel you represent them. And that's exactly what you want. I welcome change. I believe innovation is the lifeblood of business. If you're not growing, you're dying. However, traditionalists would disagree with me. They like the world the way it's always been and have no intention of reinventing the wheel because they believe if it isn't broken, don't fix it. That's cool for them, but it doesn't work for me. And I know that can lead to some tricky situations and conversations later down the line.

I can filter traditionalists out by talking about breaking the status quo breathing life into new, exciting ventures. That sentence is honest enough to terrify the people that don't work for me (and I for them) and captivate the attention of those that love my approach and want to work with me. Say you're looking for a new job. Then think of your CV as being your personal recruiter. It's looking for roles that fit your vibe.

It's important to understand that this is not an aggressive or obnoxious way to be. This is you being your authentic self. It's a common misconception that we should try to please everyone. But let's look at this logically: if there are supposedly 16 personality types on one system, four colours on another, and many, many more systems out there, how on Earth are you going to please all 7.6 billion people on this planet? Why would you even want to!? Give yourself a break. Inauthenticity makes you sound generic. A lack of self-awareness means what you write ends up sitting on a page like white noise. In short, a sure-fire way for your content to fail you.

Instead, figure out who you are, who you align best with, and target your content towards these people. Then, let your content do the work for you.

Personal reflection exercise

Take the time to think about what you notice when communicating with others. Consider how you react when face to face with someone or communicating digitally. As this is your book, this is your safe space with no right or wrong answers. There's no one you have to worry about offending. If you feel confident enough, it's worth asking people you trust to give some genuine feedback on how you're coming across to them. You'll use these later on in the book when you have a better understanding of who you're communicating with, and how these styles might clash.

Take some time to answer the following questions. I've left examples to give you some ideas:

What's my communication style?

I have a light-hearted, friendly tone.

I'm not afraid of sarcasm or making jokes when appropriate.

I approach negative situations with compassion where possible.

_____

_____

_____

_____

_____

_____

How do I handle my emotions in communications?

I have a habit of saying the first thing that comes to mind, so in person, I have to work hard to bite my tongue and take a minute if someone is rude or passive aggressive with me. I find this in my writing too. So often, what I end up sending isn't what I first wrote.

Which triggers tick me off and why?

I don't like when people talk to me like I'm their mate down the pub.

I roll my eyes whenever someone writes a big wall of text with no punctuation or paragraphs.

One-word replies annoy me. What does "K" even mean?

Which personality traits send me over the edge in communication, and why?

There's nothing worse than speaking and not being listened to.

I'm not fond of people talking over me.

I can't stand when conversations jump between email, WhatsApp, Twitter, and Telegram. I prefer consistency, so I'd rather know which form of communication that person is comfortable with and stick to one method.

How do I need people to communicate with me?

Being listened to and heard is critical for me. If someone repeats back the opposite of what I meant or wasn't listening in the first place, it makes me switch off.

In a business setting, it's important to me that people know what point they're trying to make, and they get to it.

Any other reflections I notice when talking to people/listening to others?

I don't enjoy small talk with strangers. In a business setting, say a cold call, I'm too distracted by what they want before I'm comfortable to relax into a two-way conversation.

What does my personality profiling teach me about the way I communicate?

I'm a textbook ENFP type. A people-centred creator with a focus on possibilities and a contagious enthusiasm for anything novel. I'm led by how I feel, trusting of my strong intuition, and exceptionally tuned in to my empathy.

_____

_____

_____

_____

_____

_____

_____

_____

_____

_____

_____

_____

_____

_____

_____

WHAT'S YOUR STORY?

I love that intrigued head tilt people pull when I tell them I used to co-own a Muay Thai gym in North Thailand. I also lived in four countries, used to teach sports, have started five businesses total, and have a decade of various other weird and wonderful random work experiences. I've flip-flopped throughout my career, working from grassroots up to C-level and everywhere in between. I've worked in jobs I've loved and ones where I've gone home crying. I've worked with leaders that I idolise and bosses that I clashed with so hard I don't know how we both lasted so long. I've LOVED my journey.

Every decision I've ever made has been a learning experience for the businesses I have today. I learned I was a lover, not a fighter, and wanted to do something that made an impact. Something that set my soul on fire every day, even on the shit ones. Something that hit my passion: helping people achieve their goals. That's it. That's all I want to do, day in, day out. That's my founder's story, and I'm happy with it. Above and beyond learning who you are, when was the last time you sat back and reflected on your personal journey?

> So often in the professional world, you see
> the term "be original". But a beautifully
> passive-aggressive meme that I adore would
> add the quip "...just like everybody else".

The reason marketers keep telling their clients that originality is key is that so many businesses aren't. So instead, they follow the mindset of, "our competitors are doing this; we need to start doing that to keep up". But no one likes a copycat. The idea of competition is to set yourself apart using your best attributes. Even in sport, if your competitors are stronger, faster, or bigger than you, the only way to win is with a better strategy. If you launch a new carbonated drink brand, you haven't (I'm assuming) got the £3bn Coca-Cola spends on marketing every year to establish your brand. You can't compete with their brand recognition. You need to find a different angle to sell your drink. If you're going for a £70,000 a year job, but you only have one year's official experience on paper - but you have the proof you can do the job better - you have to be creative about how you show this to your potential new employer.

No matter who you are, you have to delve deep to uncover what value you add that's different to others. Otherwise, you risk looking like a knock-off, or worse, becoming overshadowed by someone else. The only way you can do that is by telling a story that's so unique to you that it's impossible to look like someone else's cast-off. Not only does it make you stand out, but it'll attract those that can relate to your journey.

When I write out all the jobs I've ever had, I can see the times I should have been a writer. I can see times my attention was on someone else's job. I was obsessed with storytelling. Even when I was told to stay in my lane, I would creatively divert back. It doesn't matter how much or how little experience you have. Your whole story, the value you've collected over the years on that journey, that's what matters. It's what makes you uniquely you. Whether you're a business owner, a founder, a professional, or looking to break into this world for the first time, your founding story is all the wonderful, unique ways that you bring something different to the table. Celebrate your differences, don't hide them.

You don't need to have a world of experience to be different. You don't have to be the most talented, 'naturally gifted', or the best in your field. Not being Elon Musk doesn't make you an unworthy industrial designer. Not being Deborah Meaden doesn't take away your credibility as an entrepreneur. Will Smith - putting personal opinions from the 2022 Oscars to one side - beautifully captures the essence of this. While talking about life lessons, he explains that the greatest misunderstanding is that to be someone who achieves, you have to have great natural talent:

"Skill is developed by hours and hours and hours of beating on your craft. I've never viewed myself as particularly talented. Where I excel is in my ridiculously sickening work ethic. While the other guy is sleeping, I'm working. While the other guy is eating, I'm working. There's no easy way around it.

"No matter how talented you are, your talent will fail you if you're not skilled. If you don't study, if you don't work hard and dedicate yourself to being better every single day, you'll never be able to communicate with your artistry how you want. The only thing that I see that is distinctly different about me is that I'm not afraid to die on a treadmill. You might have more talent than me. You might be smarter than me. But if we get on the treadmill together, two things are going to happen. You are getting off first, or I'm going to die. It's that simple."

What is your treadmill? Find it, and you have the cornerstone of what makes you unique.

Personal reflection exercise

Let's go on that journey together. What is it that, when anyone goes toe to toe with you, you're confident you'll beat them at? Think back to all the jobs you've had. All those wild, random, or seemingly inconsequential decisions that you've made over your lifetime that gave you brilliant, unique stories you have that no one else can compete with.

I started by making a list of where I've lived and worked in my adult life and delved deeper into what each experience gave me both on a personal and professional level. Old jobs taught me strengths and things I don't enjoy. My businesses have given me insight into the inner workings of a variety of industries, helped me carve out much needed solutions, and introduced me to countless new and wonderful (sometimes not so wonderful) mindsets. Now it's your turn. By reflecting on the stages of your journey, you might find insight that makes you uniquely you that you hadn't thought of before.

Lived:

Worked:

Lesson/experience:

Lived:

Worked:

Lesson/experience:

_____

_____

_____

Lived:

Worked:

Lesson/experience:

_____

_____

_____

Lived:

Worked:

Lesson/experience:

_____

_____

_____

WHO ARE YOU TALKING TO?

How you write could make Terry Pratchett misty-eyed with pride and be absolutely on point technically. But if it's not landing for the reader it's intended for, your written piece will only ever be 'meh'. Writing for your audience is the most important lesson of the book. And I'm pre-warning you, I'm going to keep reminding you. Your content can land flat for two reasons. First, you're not writing in a way that works for their personality style. Second, what you're writing isn't interesting to them. Profiling helps adapt your tone, style, and content to suit them. Otherwise, you're not appealing to what they care about. When you finesse the balance between matching your personality with a message your reader gives a damn about, it's an absolute game changer.

I remember an old job of mine where this was a struggle. Many moons ago, I worked for a global publishing house - I'll not mention who. The content in this one particular magazine was compelling, informative, and perfect for learning more about the industry. If only it were for the right reader. They were massacring the magazine's performance because they were more interested in who they decided the audience should be rather than who they truly were. When they conducted market research, they discovered the assumed target audience was not the target audience at all. They thought the demographic was middle-aged ABC1 men *(writer's note: that's affluent to you and me)*, earning £40k or more, and interested in luxury brands, science, and technology.

While the latter half of that belief was correct, the audience was 60% female - women who, according to the data, were passionate about gardening and cooking. Knowing the customer here would have paid off massively. Using that data, the magazine could have appealed more to their actual readership, delving deeper into the topics they were passionate about. The magazine didn't do this, so its success (or lack thereof) continued to reflect their ignorance.

Make sure you take the time to familiarise yourself with your customer and their habits through research. Don't assume. Even with substantial budgets, the magazine couldn't force people to read. They needed to either earn their new audience through their content or accept the people who supported the magazine and tailor their approach more to them.

Figuring out what kind of people your audience are doesn't have to be complicated. A super easy way to profile them is using the colour system I introduced earlier. While it's impossible to label anyone fully, there will always be a primary colour type we fall into when in our different modes. For example, who I am at the office is entirely different from who I am when I'm home relaxing with the dog. It's crucial you take the version of the person you're trying to reach in the business environment you're both coming from. The colour system I work with uses four colours to categorise a person's personality: green, yellow, blue, and red. Let's break down each one.

The green personality

We've all got that one friend we know we can go to when something breaks. Chances are they have the manuals stashed somewhere alphabetically. Not that it matters because they know the whole thing cover to cover in all the languages. For me, it's my best friend. And she's brilliant at details. Typically, your greens are systematic, detail-oriented individuals that work with data and love it. Think of the engineers and analysts of the world that take a systematic approach to all that they do. Those with a meticulous thirst for knowledge who like to break things apart to see how they go back together again. Their end goal is to seek understanding.

To others, they can seem analytical and distant, when in reality, they are a blinkered horse on a well-defined path to seek the truth. They're easy to spot in conversation, as they'll be asking lots of questions about seemingly inconsequential yet precise details. Green personality types are typically in roles that revolve around accuracy, working with numbers, science, or problem-solving professions. Of course, as the (not-so) common phrase goes, personality is in the eyes of a beholder. If you're reading this and thinking 'this is me', a fellow green will come across to you as someone that is rightly cautious, precise, deliberate, questioning, and formal. If you're not green, you might find them stuffy, indecisive, suspicious, cold, or reserved. As a methodical person, a green personality processes information slower and speaks in a more hushed, controlled way - something they share with the more relaxed yellow-type personality.

The yellow personality

You know the kind of person who personifies the word 'nice'? And you're not even sarcastic; they're that lovely. You want to put them in your pocket because of how cute they are. They usually put other people first. They're always caring, kind, and happy to be a shoulder to cry on, radiating a warm glow that can only be trumped by the sun. Everyone loves a yellow and wants to be their friend.

Typically a family- and friend-oriented person, the yellow personality type has a gentle approach to achieve their ultimate goal of harmony. They're not looking to pick fights. They want balance and equality for all, living to help and support others humbly. Yellows thrive in caregiving roles. They're the most helpful people you know and always put others' needs ahead of their own. Usually, this might be a parent, carers, teachers, or nurses.

To a fellow yellow or an equal lover of the slower pace - a green - a yellow will come across as caring, encouraging, sharing, patient, and relaxed. However, an opposing personality type, such as a red or a blue, could perceive these behaviours as docile, bland, plodding, reliant, slow, or stubborn.

The blue personality

Do you remember those wind-up teeth toys? You know the ones where you let them go and the mouth moves a million miles a minute? Now take that same toy, introduce it to the Tasmanian Devil, and picture that combination in human form. Enter the blue personality. Also known as the life and soul of the party, AKA, the social butterfly.

Great at starting tasks, but not so much at seeing them through, the blue personality is the unsmarmingly charming crowd-pleaser in any social setting. Well placed in a relationship-building, people-centred role, the blue thrives on recognition and brings a zest for life to any room. They're the vibrant storytellers, gestating like a mfkr to a crowd of tuned-in listeners. Blue personality types are as you'd expect them to be. Naturally charismatic and capable of lighting up a room when they enter. What they do, others follow. They're typically infectiously excited, fun, and inclusive in all that they do.

To a fellow blue or red, they come across as sociable, dynamic, demonstrative, enthusiastic, and persuasive. They think fast and talk faster. But they can appear excitable, frantic, indiscreet, flamboyant, hasty, too casual, and

overbearing to a slower-paced green or yellow. To them, a blue's lack of focus can feel frustrating.

The red personality

Mohammed Ali, Emmeline Pankhurst, and Beyonce come to mind. Reds are the furthest from a meek wallflower you can get. Absolute A-type go-getters that exude confidence and sheer dogged determination. The real "ask for forgiveness later" types that roll through closed doors like a juggernaut until they achieve what they want. Reds are natural-born leaders. They are the GOATs of the world. They're likely to confidently take charge, make decisions, and control the direction of tasks and projects.

They see objections as a challenge, maintaining the attitude of "I was born ready" and wanting everything done yesterday. To a fellow red and the social blues, they will appear competitive,

51

demanding, determined, strong-willed, and purposeful. They live to achieve and have to be constantly propelling themselves forwards. However, their poor listening skills and pushy nature can come across as overbearingly aggressive, controlling, and intolerant to a slower-paced green or yellow personality type.

So what does this all mean?

Naturally, the above descriptions are playing into extreme stereotypes. We all know a few people I have described to a T, but in everyday social situations, people you meet will only show a few of these characteristics, and they're probably going to be more subtle. I like to visualise the colours at an awards ceremony. It helps me keep these personality types in front of my mind and quickly align the people I meet with their respective categories. The reds are likely those up on the stage accepting awards and giving speeches. The blues are easy to spot as they flutter from table to table, making sure everyone is having a good time. The yellows are likely helping the staff, volunteering to lend a hand whenever they can. And the greens are probably sitting in a dark corner somewhere avoiding the blues, counting down the minutes until the last award so they can get into their pre-booked Uber.

Once you know who your audience is, you can write directly to them. A yellow doesn't have any interest in how you can transform them into a CEO in three years. And a red isn't going to want the spreadsheet breakdown of how you're going to make them a success. They simply want proof it's possible and pay the greens to comb the data. *'Who are you?'*, you can be more aware of the conversations you have. By understanding who you're speaking to, you can make sure that whatever your message, you're sure it appeals to the right audience. So, how do you get under the skin of a stranger?

Well, the good news is, you don't have to join the X-Men, become Professor Xavier, and develop the ability to read people's minds to make the research pillar work for you. Thankfully, it's a simple case of digging. Without looking like a psycho and putting your audience through rigorous personality testing, you can learn about them by simply focusing on what they talk about and how they communicate with you. There are many ways you can do this. But first, there are two factors to consider. How to better communicate with people you already know, and considering new people you are yet to engage with. The process is similar for both.

Ideally, having a real interaction with someone - even if it's a five-minute chat - is the best way to figure them out. If they're speaking to you at a million miles an hour and are bouncing around, they're likely red or blue. If they're slower, quieter, and exhibit more relaxed body language, then chances are they're green or yellow. Face to face, this is typically easy to ascertain in seconds. Even over the phone, you can go off someone's verbal mannerisms and place them that way. If you're looking to improve conversation with existing customers or people you already know, this will be an easy process for you. First, look back through previous interactions. Think about conversations you've had in the past and when they appeared more relaxed.

But what about when you don't have any previous reference points? Or even a voice or body language to go off? You always have their digital presence to fall back on. Do they have an IGTV or a YouTube channel? Are they on social media? Is there a way you can hear them speak or follow the content they're producing? Even an email is a great starting point. All you need to do is look at how people communicate. From here, you can extract what's important to them. The rules apply the same if you're reaching out to a specific company or an individual: you look at the appropriate channels to find their personality. For a company, you might look at a business website. Casual and non-invasive, non-creepy social stalking works better on an individual level.

There is one hard and fast rule you can be certain about no matter who you're writing to, and I'm going to pull off the plaster quickly here... your audience doesn't care about you. They genuinely don't. They're not interested in being moved along a sales pipeline. They don't care about your monthly targets. Or why you're #1 nationally or that you won the blah blah award again. Ultimately, you aren't writing for yourself. Let me shout that louder for those of you at the back. **Nothing that you write is written for your benefit** - *if you want it to succeed, that is.* You're writing for someone else to read your piece. To ensure someone else enjoys, engages with, and takes value from what you have to say, you must put your reader in the driving seat. Once you consider who they are, you can begin to think about their:

- Goals
- Pains and gripes they want to avoid
- Gains and improvements they want to strive towards

These three facets are essential as they drive everything you write. What's the point in focusing on products, services, or benefits that won't appeal to your audience? Once you've taken the time to understand them, you can set to work planning the content piece you want to send them. For this, you'll need our second pillar: Structure.

Personal reflection exercise

With these personalities in mind, take some time to think about the people in your life. Going through each colour, who do you know is a green, blue, red, or yellow personality type? Consider your family, friends, loved ones, and some people in your professional career. What's your type, and what's theirs?

Who do you know who is a:

- Blue
- Red
- Yellow
- Green

And why do you think they fall into that colour? Now, look at the relationship between you. Can you identify where you can improve your communication skills by dialling more into their personality type? Think back to your list in the "who are you" section.

What colour would you attach to the behaviours that annoy you? And list the behaviours.

How do you think YOUR communication lands for each of the colours? And what events can you pinpoint that might have been down to a personality clash?

_____

_____

_____

_____

_____

_____

When you strengthen this muscle for identifying people's personality types, you can start to communicate with them in ways that work best for them. If you want to put this to practise, try to go back to a conversation that's been uncomfortable or landed badly for you. Then, see if you can change the outcome into a positive one by writing to match their personality and writing for your recipient.

If you're trying this exercise with someone that knows you intimately, you're going to look a little weird as they know you inside out. So try it with a conversation that you're not too sad about the impact as a practice exercise.

PILLAR TWO:

STRUCTURE

Writing business content that works is so much more than simply articulating your point well. You also need to ensure you structure your writing right depending on its format.

sn't it mad how much pressure we put ourselves under to write perfectly from the first draft? Even though we all know that's never going to happen? Writing isn't wam, bam, and done - it's a process like any other. Imagine you worked in a factory making birdhouses. In the office is a designer. They pass the designs onto someone else who gathers the necessary materials. These materials get given to the next person who builds the birdhouse. Then it moves along to the quality assessor, who passes it to the distributor and finally to the public. It sounds like a good system, right?

Now imagine that at every step of this process, the staff are making minor mistakes that, when combined, turn into pretty significant problems. If your writing isn't working for you right now, that's all that's happening. You're not doing anything 'bad' or 'wrong'. Let's clear that up straight away. You merely have a few steps to take to optimise each stage of your writing process or are missing out key steps altogether. Depending on where the faults are, the results can be different. The likelihood is that many challenges you may face at the moment are down to not writing for your audience. That's something you've been able to address in the first pillar. The next challenge is perhaps the design you're using isn't working for you.

In terms of your writing, the research stage was you gathering your materials. With your newly formed understanding of what you're writing (you, your message, and who you're writing to), you've already ensured you're working with top-notch materials. Your structure is your design. Sitting down to write is your build. Editing your work is the last piece of the puzzle, the quality assessment. At this pillar, we've still not put pen to paper. Because without the proper structure and understanding of your chosen format, your content will always fall short. No matter how well it's written and edited.

NOT ALL CONTENT IS BUILT EQUALLY

Writing business content that works is so much more than simply articulating your point well. You also need to ensure you structure your writing right depending on its format. Typically, in the professional world, there are four drivers behind communication:

- Results
- Information
- Persuasion
- Negative

Results

This is when you're looking for instant results from your content. Typically, you're writing to clients or colleagues. It's a quick message to the WhatsApp group or an email to your team. They are informal messages sent off the cuff, either requesting information or completing an action. You can recognise results-driven content by its concise nature.

Unfortunately, these are often the statements that lend themselves to miscommunication and inefficiencies. When writing result-driven content, it's important to remember to ask for what you need concisely. Not only will this make the job easier for the recipient to give you everything you need in one go, but it also prevents the conversation from snowballing into a game of email tennis.

Information

Informational content is often the response to results-driven content, or found in outbound materials such as reports, social media, and marketing. Information communication relies on clarity, brevity, and adding value to your audience.

If you're replying to response-driven content, it's your job to make sure you're covering all bases and that you've understood the brief correctly. No one wants to chase you for the missing details. But if you're posting information communication to be educational, ensure you're not leaving the audience wondering "so what?" But for more on that, see pillar four: editing.

Persuasion

As it says on the tin, persuasive writing is when you're attempting to pull at the heartstrings of your reader. It's any piece of content that requires you to prove why you deserve to win the reader over to your way of thinking. Typically, persuasive content is in sales proposals, tenders, sales copy, landing pages, award submissions, and CVs.

I could sit here and talk to you all day about how to sell, but the reality is a huge part of sales and persuasion is identifying what somebody wants and speaking to that. This is what we've uncovered in the research pillar. Is it money and success that drive the reader? Something that's going to make their work more efficient? Is it helping people on a wide scale? When you uncover what drives the people you're writing for, you're no longer in 'sales' mode. You're having a conversation about what appeals to them and looking for the sweet spot that hooks them into what you're offering.

No matter what that is, you're always selling something. Be it a product, service, or simply selling yourself. It isn't sales in the traditional sense - this is a book about content, after all - but the insights learned in the research pillar will allow you to nudge the conversation in your favour.

Negative

Let me tell you something you already know. The world of content ain't all sunshine and rainbows. It can be a mean and nasty place, and I don't care how tough you are; it'll bring you to your knees and keep you there if you let it. OK, it's not precisely Rocky VI extreme, but sometimes we have to be the bearer of bad news. Whether that's delivering unpopular news, or any criticism and feedback. Being the bad guy is never comfortable. But there are plenty of ways to deliver the much-needed blows tenderly, without appearing unsympathetic or leaving the recipient scarred for life. Always remember there's a human on the receiving end of what you've got to say. Using the principles learned in the research pillar, you can land your message impactfully with the least damage.

Every person reading this book will have different writing needs in their professional life. Perhaps you're looking for help with your business plan, or you write all the content we cover. Each format of content will require a different structure from the next.

THE A-Z OF STRUCTURE

've created this A-Z guide so you can find the tips most relevant to you. Make no mistake: we're still not ready to write. You need to know some rules about each type of content before you can make a start. But trust me, you'll be glad to have this advice under your belt.

Whether you're a business owner, leader, salesperson, marketing professional, working in customer service, or whatever your role may be, feel free to thumb through the following pages and find what's most relevant to you. Then, once you've read the sections that are appropriate to you professionally, we can move to the next pillar, where it's (yes, finally) time to put pen to paper.

Together we'll go through:

- Ad copy
- Award submissions
- Blog and social media strategy
- Blogs
- Brochures
- Business plans
- Business proposals
- Case studies and testimonials
- Cover letter and CV
- Emails (marketing)
- Emails (ecommerce marketing)
- Email funnels
- Event promotion
- General written communication
- Handbooks
- Headlines
- Infographics
- Internal documents

- Job adverts
- Landing pages
- Leaflets
- Letters
- LinkedIn
- Long-form content
- Menus
- Negative content
- Newsletters
- Online courses
- Packaging
- Pitch decks
- Presentations
- Press releases
- Product descriptions
- Property listings
- Reports
- Signage
- Social media posts
- Tenders
- Website content

AD COPY

So much to say, so little time. Creating first-class ad copy that gets people to notice you can feel like attempting the impossible. Once you've applied the four pillars and made your website irresistible - not to mention the enviable social media pages - how do you stand out from the crowd on digital channels that are overflowing with brands and businesses just like yours? In a matter of a few words, you need to win people over… fast.

It's all well and good having an inspiring landing page waiting to greet your primed and ready leads, but if no one is reading it, it won't serve you at all. Ad copy will often be your very first interaction with a potential customer or client. And we *all* know the importance of a good first impression. You want to stop them in their tracks, mid-scroll, and make them *need* to find out more.

Consumers aren't always trusting of businesses. Or the whole concept of advertising, for that matter. Back in 2019, public trust in advertising hit a low of 25% - down from 48% in 1992. So when your intended audience are cold readers with little faith in random companies, how do you begin to build momentum?

Let's look at how to take your ad copy from good to great. Scratch that, from good to *exceptional*. The whole premise of ad copy is to intrigue your audience. To tear them away from their doomscrolling and get curious about your brand. To click on **your** website. One of the key ways to pique customer interest aligns nicely with the nature of ad copy: brevity. The best ad copy walks a fine line between giving enough information to entice your reader in, while leaving enough gaps in their knowledge or understanding to encourage them to find out more. You might have heard this referred to as a 'curiosity gap'. There's such a thing as too much information when it comes to your ad copy. Large chunks of text only run the risk of you contributing to the white noise clogging up your audience's screens and minds. And that's a first impression you can't come back from. In short, you want to leave your reader with a question only you can answer.

Now, no matter what platform you're writing for - be that Google, Facebook, Instagram, Twitter, or anywhere else - here are some tips for creating awesome ad copy.

Do show your personality

We've talked about the fact you can't be **the best** at everything. But there will always be something that sets you apart. What's the difference between your business and another selling the exact same product or service? In such brief communication, your unique brand personality will go a long way in enticing your reader and leaving a lasting impression.

Don't lose your cool

No one likes the smell of desperation in a business. You know you add value. And your ad copy's job is to clearly demonstrate that value to a reader, and entice them to engage with you further. That's it's only job. Let the website, landing page, or whatever it's pointing to do the next part of the process. Don't look desperate by trying to do too much at once or over complicate your ads. It's not sexy.

Do research the different ad platforms

All ad platforms will have their own restrictions, limitations, and expectations. It's worth doing extensive research into any platform you'll be using to avoid becoming *that* business known for unethical advertising. Or simply the business approaching Facebook ads in the complete wrong way.

Don't underestimate the power of emotion

Nothing encourages a reader to take action like a strong emotional response. Anger, fear, and disgust are common ones for ad copy. Get your reader onboard about the inconvenience of mowing the lawn before introducing your remote robot mower. Take advantage of the common pains we all relate to and reverse engineer them to paint your business as the saving grace.

Do start strong

Of course you want to be crystal clear throughout the ad, but your opening needs to be strong and impactful otherwise why would anyone read on? Especially with the likes of Facebook, where only the first two lines will be visible before your reader has to choose to see more.

Think of how quickly we scroll through social media. Research suggests that humans now have an attention span of a mere 8 seconds - down from 12 back in 2000. We're simple, impatient creatures, and only getting more impatient as the years go by.

You don't have the time to not be powerful and impactful from the get go. How can you stop your audience in their tracks? You want to hook them in and you can do that by addressing their needs. What works better: "our product is designed to help make cleaning your home easier" or "are you tired of wasting your precious free time cleaning?" In the latter, you're hitting on a problem people feel and drawing them in with a question. Remember to talk *to* them, not *at* them.

Don't forget to to follow through

Whatever dream your ad sold to your reader to encourage action, make sure it's immediately available on the click through. You want to make it easy for your audience to get what they want. They've already clicked your ad - don't make them jump through any more hoops to book that demo or download that digital guide.

Do keep your call to actions clear

Guide your audience to the next steps effortlessly so they know what you want them to do next. It's all well and good telling them in what ways you can change their life, but if you just leave it at that, then what are they supposed to do? Twiddle their thumbs?

Your call to action should give them clear instructions. And I don't mean just telling them to "get in touch". That's a bit on the vague side. Give them a telephone number, email, or contact form. Take it one step further so they can simply click and it dials or opens an email. The less effort they have to make to get in touch with you, the more likely they will take the leap.

Don't underestimate a little trial and error

One of the great bonuses of ads is you can easily measure and evaluate your results. You can try different approaches. It's not as simple as throwing a few ideas at the wall and seeing what sticks, but testing between two well-thought-out options is a solid strategy.

Trial different ad lengths or openers. Mix it up for the various platforms and focus on the ones that bring the greatest return on investment. If something isn't working, change something and go from there. You should always be analysing and tweaking your approach.

Get creative and quirky with your copy. Allow your ad to live, breathe, and evolve as your brand does.

AWARD SUBMISSIONS

There's nothing quite like the satisfaction of knowing that years of hard work have paid off. That after such hard graft and commitment, you and your team have been deemed the best of the best. That real humans - *outside of your organisation, I might add* - have seen something brilliant in you.

When they are genuine, business awards can be great for exposure and provide much-needed validation for years of hard work. They can work wonders for strengthening a brand's reputation and credibility, boosting internal team morale, or giving younger businesses that incredible "I've arrived" moment. There's a whole pint of serotonin purely in that "you've won!" message waiting for you.

Depending on your industry, there will be countless award opportunities available to you, and all will vary slightly in process and criteria. Let's break down some top tips for award submissions as a whole.

Choose award opportunities carefully

It's easy to fall into the trap of wanting award wins under your belt at any cost. Surely entering more awards means a higher chance of winning? While, probability-wise, this might be correct, it has its downsides and can actually prove counterintuitive to the cause.

First of all, entering awards can be expensive. Both in terms of time spent crafting your entry and any expenses associated with the awards ceremony itself. Can you really justify burning through piles of cash just to maybe win an award you were only lukewarm about in the first place?

Hear me out. Instead of entering anything that will let you, identify awards that align with your business's goals and are in keeping with your individual voice and story. Similarly, drill down into what exactly you hope to gain from winning an award. Will it help your reputation? Boost sales? Bring in new recruits? Whatever it is, identifying your goal will help you whittle through the masses of different awards out there to find one that actually promises to add value in the way you want.

Read the award's criteria

When you decide which awards you want to enter, study the criteria like you used to pore over your notes the night before an exam. I want you to be able to recite what the awards board is looking for before you even begin crafting your entry. Only kidding. But it is important that you play by their rules. If you make a mistake, they won't hesitate to cut you, so keep focused on what the entry's asking of you. No more. No less.

You can even do one better. Reach out to previous winners and pick their brains. The more insight you can gain into what's expected of you, the more thoughtful and tailored your entry will be. With all this in mind, here are some quick dos and don'ts to think about.

Do get everyone involved

This doesn't have to be a one-person job. In fact, I recommend you actively avoid making it one. Your colleagues may have examples or perspectives you haven't thought of. And asking for their help or advice will likely result in a more well-rounded entry.

A business is so much more than one person. To accurately capture your message, story, and experience, you want to look at it from as many angles as possible. Even if your business is just you, asking your clients for their two cents can similarly prove fruitful.

Don't leave it until the last minute

It takes a fair bit of time to compile all the information, gather the best examples, write everything down, craft a story, and rework it. This ties into the last point; getting other people's opinions is useful, but you know how slow some can be!

Do use strong, confident language

Think 'will' and 'do' versus 'can' and 'may'. The winner of an award is confident, self-assured, and certain of their value and successes. If you're not completely sure of yourself, the judges won't be either.

Don't be a robot

I'm not saying this is the place for all your best jokes. But this also isn't about stifling your voice and being overly formal. You're selling your business to a judging panel. And your personality will be a large part of what makes your organisation so unique compared to the competition.

Judges will be attracted to businesses or individuals who are unapologetically, authentically themselves. So sprinkle that personality like parmesan over a good carbonara.

Do keep it simple

You'll probably want to talk about every good point you think of. Every project, every pro-social action, every happy customer. But if you wrote about all that, you'd be sending in a tome that no one has time to read. So keep it simple and focus on the prime cuts. Which particular projects exemplify exactly why you're good at what you do?

Don't just list off facts about yourself

You want to tell the readers a story. This shouldn't just be a list of what you're good at; build up a strong narrative that takes the reader on an impactful journey through your business's life. Every company has its ups and downs. Simply talking about that isn't enough. Harsh, but true.

So it's up to you to make these stories special. To instil personality, heart, and passion into your writing. To explain how the challenges you've faced over the years have contributed to who you are now. Create a story the panel has never heard before. Make sure that when they walk away, they remember who you are.

Do explain yourself well

You may know your business like the back of your hand. But the chances are whoever's assessing you won't. Approach your award entry as if you were one of the judges. Always assume you're selling yourself to someone who doesn't know your business. Without being patronising or condescending, of course.

If you make the task of reading and understanding your entry easier for the panel, you increase the chances of them taking in what you have to say and share. If you don't make your answer's count and don't make the reading experience a pleasurable one, you run the risk of not even making it over the first hurdle.

Don't forget the evidence

You know when people make grand claims with no semblance of evidence to back it up? Frustrating, right? Don't be that person in your award entries. Link back every statement and claim to cold, hard fact. If you say you go above and beyond for your customers, give an impactful example of when you did just that. If you say you've got loads of really exciting works in the pipeline, give a little taster of what those might be. If the statements you're making aren't supported by evidence or statistics, any panel will see right through them.

Do seek external feedback

You - or anyone else that's close to your business - are never going to be the best judge of an entry. You're biased and far too close to the subject matter. With this in mind, always find an unbiased third party to give feedback. Their opinion will prove invaluable for trimming any bloat or ego-related oversharing. Ask them to go full savage mode in their judgement. The more honest they are, the more likely you are to make the appropriate changes.

Don't forget to use award wins in your marketing

Remember when I told you to drill down into *why* exactly you want a certain award? Once you win an award, now's the time to make those results happen. You may as well have never entered your business for an award if you aren't sharing your victory after the fact. A pat on the back is great, but it's not worth the stress and expense of award prep.

I don't mean for you to start using the term 'award-winning' after every mention of your business. That's just obnoxious. But celebrating your win on social channels, your blog, or through a press release can be incredible for furthering the momentum of winning. After all, if your goal was to secure new clients, you actually need to let your audience know that you won an award for it to have any impact on their future decisions. So own that win. Shout it from the rooftops and ride that wave of praise.

Trying to win an award is already stressful enough. If you're like me then you just want to win so badly! The last thing you need is worrying about getting the submission right. So don't worry about it. Follow these tips, put your best foot forward, and whatever happens, happens. Best of luck to you!

BLOG AND SOCIAL MEDIA STRATEGY

In an age of social media and constant connectivity, the internet can feel like a cacophony of noise that's hard to cut through. So, in an effort to attract attention, you might think quantity over quality is the way to go. *Posting anything is better than nothing, right?* Wrong. We all know that's not how the saying goes.

Not only is it going to stress you out constantly worrying about what to post or write, but it'll also take much more of your time. And, quite frankly, a lot of the content you produce will probably be shit. It won't relate to the core pain points of your audience or reflect the current times in your industry because you haven't given yourself the space to think what that is.

It doesn't matter if you're representing a brand or if you're the brand yourself, writing blog or social media content without a well-thought-out strategy is like shooting a gun with your eyes closed. You're taking a big risk and there's only a small chance you'll hit your target.

The Content Marketing Institute found that strategy issues - including a lack of one altogether - are the third greatest factor leading to stagnant business success. Yet 49% of companies still fail to follow an adequate marketing strategy. By first creating a blog or social media strategy, you can carve out exactly what you're going to post and when. This doesn't always need to be as granular as what each post every day is going to be. Although if this works for you, be my guest. It might simply be themes you want to cover over a given time period to make sure you're offering your readers some variety.

Having a plan gives you a sniper that guarantees you'll hit the target every time. You'll know that each piece of content you produce will in some way relate back to a common pain point your audience has. It keeps you both focused and motivated, and working both proactively and reactively. Doesn't that sound fantastic?

Working proactively

Being proactive means planning weeks, if not months, in advance. It's about anticipating what your audience will need from you and planning educational, high-quality content to suit. This could mean planning around upcoming events or holidays, such as a new product launch or the Christmas holidays. You want to look at not just the one day, but the lead-up to it. Your proactive strategy will include the types of posts you want to publish, as well as any core themes you want them to address. But more on that later.

Looking ahead also gives you the time to write up the content. If you know what you'll need, you can pace yourself without taking on too much at once. This also has the knock-on effect of giving you time to think about what you've written and adjust if needed. And what else can you do with that time? It leaves you free to handle more spur-of-the-moment, reactive content.

Working reactively

Reactive content is self-explanatory - you're reacting to the world. This might be a social media post that makes use of a popular new meme, or a blog responding to some breaking news story. It doesn't even have to be something in the public zeitgeist. It could be something as simple as a conversation with a colleague that sparks an idea. Since you've already given yourself the breathing room, you have the ability to react to this idea and get it out into the world.

Without a strategy, it can feel like you're in a constant state of white noise with no idea what to say or where to focus. And so often what will come out is an amalgamation of not much at all. You'll also default to the subjects you feel the most comfortable with, which means you'll give your audiences no variety.

A great strategy will marry together proactive and reactive marketing. You need to create a plan that will chart your posts for the near future. Consider weekly or daily themes to keep your content fresh. For example, Monday you could post a thought-provoking question, Tuesday a behind the scenes look at your business, and so on. Combine that with a reactive presence. If a customer asks something on Facebook, then respond. If people engage in discussion on your LinkedIn blog, then join in and keep it going.

So, how do you get started creating your own social strategy?

Where to start?

It's all well and good telling you to make a strategy, but what should it include? Thankfully, it doesn't have to be complicated and all you'll need is a spreadsheet. Simply lay out a calendar of every day of every month. Have a row for every new week and a column for every day. Then block out any days you're not going to post. Just going to stick with posting on Monday, Wednesday, and Friday? Then you don't need to worry about Tuesday and Thursday, or the weekend.

Then you want to populate your calendar with the content. As I said before, it doesn't have to be thorough. An idea of what it's going to be will do. My tip: create a matrix. List the topics and themes you want to discuss, and create a separate list for types of posts you want to use. So you might have something like this for a social media strategy:

Themes

- Productivity
- Staff wellbeing
- Efficiency
- Green practices
- Company news

Types of post

- Poll
- Quick question
- Longer thought-leadership post
- Industry trends
- Quote

And then combine each one with everything in the other group! Using those examples above, you'd have 25 unique ideas to post about - more than enough for a month of content. You can use that same matrix for every month, just make sure you write something different. So when it comes to writing, you'll see it's a poll about staff wellbeing. Then you can come up with a question to ask - such as, "what initiatives do you have to help your staff" - list a few options, and push people to engage in the comments. This is an example for social media, but it works for blogs too. If you want some inspiration, the *Headlines* section has some ideas for you to start with. The *Social media* section has a similar list.

Give yourself time to brainstorm some ideas and see what you come up with. Or, if you have a team to help, see what they can think of. If you put your heads together, there's no reason you can't come up with a theme list that has at least 20 entries - not too shabby! And this is just looking at it from a written content point of view. In reality, this can be a multimedia affair. Your strategy becomes so much richer when you start to add video, audio, and image content. All the other sections in this chapter? They can be a part of your strategy too. If you have an infographic, that can go on your LinkedIn page. Or do you have a new poster? That can go on Facebook.

Even if it doesn't directly fit onto a certain platform, it can be repurposed in other ways. No one on Instagram is going to read your 20-page white paper, but those statistics peppered throughout? They can be reworked into social media content. So don't forget about those when it comes to your strategy. Personally, I plan my blog and social schedule by the types of posts. For my Instagram, I like every third post to be a video. So I know if I'm posting every day, I need to plan out 10 subjects for my video content that month. For my LinkedIn, there are no hard and fast rules. I just know I want a variety. So I wouldn't put too many longer thought leadership posts in a row, for example.

If you want, you can add some more meat on the bones. This would be going more in-depth about what post or blog might be. For example, you could leave a link to a blog on industry stats to come back to later. You can also stick to one theme a month if you'd rather, giving some cohesion to your strategy. This works great if you've got something coming up you want to talk about. It's a lot to digest, so take your time thinking about this. While you do that, take a look at these dos and don'ts for your strategy.

Do shake it up to keep your audience interested

This is in terms of the type of content you're posting. If it's just post after post of you talking at them, it's not going to be engaging. On social channels, this might look something like a video one day, an educational post the next, then a quick quiz, followed by a funny meme, and then sharing a testimonial. You're keeping it fresh, mixing up media types, and keeping the audience on their toes. You can still focus on specific themes within that, but don't fall into a predictable pattern. It works the same for your blog. If you have a listicle one week, next could be an FAQ, then a how-to.

Who knows whose eye you might catch when you switch it up. When I was in the market for a new accountant, I got speaking to someone new. She was constantly posting about Xero, leaving out all the other bookkeeping softwares. She never crossed my radar because I wasn't interested in Xero. But when she mixed it up and spoke about something new - the convenience of not having to think about the numbers - she captivated my attention. Had she stayed small in the bubble of what mattered to her, she would have stayed in the dark in my eyes and we'd have never connected.

Don't forget to revisit it

You can do all the research in the world on your audience, but sometimes you don't know how your content is going to land. You might find that they don't engage with audio content and much prefer videos or images. Or that they're really into your tips and tricks. Monitor how well certain types of posts do so you know whether you could do with more or less of it. Then you can use this information to adjust your schedule, removing parts that don't work and maybe trying new ideas altogether. I recommend you revisit at least every six months, if not every quarter.

Once you have your strategy down, you can set aside regular time to actually write. It might seem like the hard part is still to come. But trust me, the whole process becomes far easier when you've already put the thought into what you want to say.

BLOGS

The humble blog. Like the elegant swan gliding peacefully across a spring lake, graceful up top, but very often, frantic chaos underneath. For most, maintaining a blog is an easy ticket to increased website traffic and sales. Or so they think. You see, it's one thing to have a blog and write a post. But it's something else entirely to do it right. The number one reason I see blogs fail is down to the author confusing a blog with a sales pitch. It may be on your website, but that isn't an excuse to write about how amazing you are and how you can solve all of the reader's problems. Can you? Of course, but that's not why they're there. It's a mistake to use it solely as a space to talk about yourself. You end up regurgitating information that could just as easily be found on your 'about us' page.

If someone's found your blog through your website, it's fair to assume they already have a sense of what you do, so let's not bore them. And if they happened to find you through Google, it's because they're looking for an answer to something, not for you to big yourself up. Instead, use your blog to become a fountain of wisdom. You've already spent time getting to know who your audience is. Now take that a step further. What are their pains? What gains are they chasing? By sharing expertise and insights into your industry, you offer genuine support and provide actual value. They leave your blog more informed, inspired, entertained, engaged - whatever your chosen goal is. And they tie that positive experience directly to **your company**.

Let's say you're a service provider like Squarespace, allowing businesses to build a website with ease. That's a great USP for the less tech-literate amongst us. You might think a great blog idea would be to talk about the importance of having a website. I'm sorry, but that's boring. Been there, done that, bought the T-shirt. Instead, go one step further and ask how you can add value. Some better ideas would be '5 ways to make your website stand out' or 'how to hold onto your audience's attention'. Do you see the difference?

Then, after you've added value, you simply use a quick call to action to snap your audience back into the room. You've solved their problem, they get to the end, and oh wow, would you look at that! You can help them. Isn't that a funny coincidence? Let's slow down a bit and look at it in more detail, starting with the structure.

Stick to a simple structure

Blogs themselves are easy to crack. So long as you have a beginning, a middle, an end, and a call to action, you're already halfway there. While this might sound glaringly obvious, you'd be surprised how easy it is to get this wrong.

A lot of articles I see have a strong middle, but they don't end. They just stop in the middle of the

There's no introduction to the concept, no closing statement, and no guidance on what the reader is expected to do next. You've basically walked into a room, spoke at someone as if you're halfway through a conversation, made your point, then walked out of the room. You look weird and the person you're talking to is left thinking, what the actual f...

Or they have a five-paragraph introduction that leaves little room for any actual value. Or the whole piece is made up of short sentences. Which is actually pretty hard to read. And annoying. And stops the chance of your reader building momentum within a piece. Or they go the complete other way and are made up of winding, esoteric sentence after winding sentence, all coming together to create a large, intimidating block of text that, frankly, nobody's going to want to even read, if they have the time for it in the first place; all in the name of just trying to look intelligent. You know the type we mean?

We're all busy people. And hard-to-read blog posts aren't respectful of an audience's time. 2-3 line paragraphs is a good rule of thumb for a blog, with some individual lines thrown in for momentum and emphasis. Let's break this general structure down a bit further.

The introduction

Your introduction can take a number of different forms, but whatever it is, it needs to get to the point. A good habit to get into is to start with a simple one-liner at the top: *"Male and female dogs need different foods to achieve optimal health. So why do we feed them the same?"*

Then, you can use your second paragraph to expand: *"Such a simple but overlooked fact is that, like humans, male and female dogs have different biological makeups and, therefore, need different nutrients. Female dogs have various hormones to be able to breed, while male dogs... "*

Other effective openers for a blog include:

- Storytelling surrounding a specific problem your audience face (one you will hopefully offer solutions for throughout the piece to follow)
- Ask a question - like my example above
- A surprising statistic

You want something that's exciting, different, and sets up the rest of what you have to say. How will you make them want to stay?

The main body

Now we're into the main body. This is where you're offering the juicy goodness. You can write a piece on the same one subject or give a number of tips. For a medium 500- to 600-word piece, you're looking at three decently fleshed-out points or five super quick ones. You can make five solid points in 1,000 words, and so on.

The conclusion

To close a blog, your summary should tie back into your introduction: *"Because of A needing B and Y impacting Z, it makes sense to choose a more tailored diet plan to create a long, healthy, and happy life for your canine friend."*

The call to action

I know you've been waiting for this bit, and now you can *finally* sell and talk about yourself in your call to action. Basically... we do what we just mentioned. *"Here's how to buy our dog food."*

It'll be a short paragraph at the end that succinctly summarises who you are and how you can help. It's the only part of a blog where you should be overtly promoting yourself. There are some exceptions - such as storytelling pieces or more casual, news-style blogs. But, for the most part, stick to this rule like glue.

Here's a call to action (or CTA for short) I made earlier: *"If your dog is showing any of the symptoms we've covered,* reach out today to get tested. For only £70 (£110 for two), you can take the first steps towards a healthier, more comfortable life for your pooch. You can order here (hyperlink your website) or reach out on Instagram."

Don't forget to include a link to any relevant pages or a contact number. Do not leave it up to people to find the right information themselves. People are lazy. If you don't make it easy, they'll head somewhere else and stop with the person/business that does make it easy for them. It's that simple. When you get into a habit of it, you'll find it flows so much quicker. Before we finish this up, let's run through some dos and don'ts for your blog.

Don't set off without a plan

However you decide to get your thoughts out on the page, a blog still needs some semblance of a strategy. As the famous saying goes, *"a journey of a thousand words starts with only one. It helps if that first one is in the right direction"*. Something like that anyway. Remember that not all blogs are business ones. I started my first because I liked the sound of my own voice, I'd committed to a big adventure, and I wanted to share it with the world. However, regardless of if you're writing for business or your own personal reasons, blog posts need a few non-negotiables to make them a success.

The planning stage is different for everyone. But you must have at least a loose idea in mind before you get typing (or writing, if you're old school). Writing without a plan is like trying to walk to Zimbabwe without a map. It usually helps to know:

- Where you're going
- Why you're going
- How you're going to get there
- How long it's going to take
- What you need to get there

That's for both your content and your walk. Don't forget your coat!

Do write in a way that suits you

The structure of a blog doesn't change. How you approach getting started is down to you. We're not all academically trained. And what worked for an essay in school won't always translate to a blog on what your dog's poop says about their health. Some people like to plan the structure of their piece, map out what they're going to say, and then flesh the content out. While others, like me, research the basic details and then think as they write. And then do a lot of reworking to make it legible.

In short, there is no right or wrong way to go about the process of planning an individual blog. So long as you're doing *some* thinking beforehand. To make sure you've got a valuable subject that's worth writing about, that it will be interesting or insightful to your audience, and that you have a basic sense of what the flow will be. From here, how you get these thoughts from your head to the paper are down to your own style and way of working. Then, simply stick to the structure. You do you, boo.

Don't underestimate the power of statistics

If you want your blog to have an impact, it has to be convincing. You can't just *tell* your readers something and expect them to believe it. Imagine you're writing for a bunch of the most sceptical and cynical people in the world. So back up your claims. When you want to hammer home your point, do it with statistics. Doing so shows there are facts behind what you're saying and instantly gets your reader on side.

For example, I might say, there are a lot of blogs out there, making for some fierce competition for you. On its own, you might think, "yeah, I guess, but so what?" But if I were to say there are 77.8 million new blogs posted every month on WordPress sites alone, you would be more likely to believe that, indeed, there is a lot of competition out there. It has much more weight behind it.

Statistics are effective because they make a point that much more real. It's a stone-cold fact that can't be denied and because of this, they're more persuasive. If you do use

97

stats in your blog though, make sure to cite your source as it is a) good etiquette and b) useful for SEO purposes.

Do use genuine, intriguing titles

I see a lot of people agonising over the titles of their blogs. But, unless you're writing with a specific SEO term in mind, you can save this for after you've written the piece. If you don't know exactly what you're going to write yet, how on Earth are you expecting yourself to elegantly summarise it? See the section on *Headlines* for more.

Don't get wrapped up trying to compete with the big boys

So often, I hear "we can't compete with the big boys". But you don't have to. Not everyone can be the 'best' in their field. A small renewable energy firm cannot compete with the buying and bargaining power of the Big Six. But it will have its own unique values and traits that you can't get with the larger corporations.

Be proud of what makes you unique. Take all the lessons learned in the research pillar about both yourself and your story and weave your personality, values, and ethos throughout your blog, allowing your individual brand to shine through and demonstrate why you're best aligned with your audience.

Do use subheadings

When you break those sections down, subheadings make big blocks of text more manageable. They keep the piece moving, breaking up the text. It's like when you're reading a book with short chapters - don't you find yourself so much more motivated to keep going? At a time where so many of us scan rather than actually reading, it also helps your audience to find the information that's most relevant to them, rather than clicking off in frustration. A rule to follow is no more than 300 words in any one section. For a 500-word piece of writing, 3 subheadings that pique interest and accurately summaries your points usually work a treat.

Just because anyone can write a blog doesn't make that blog instantly successful. By following these tips you'll stand out from the white noise you typically find online.

BROCHURES

A brochure is a fantastic way to reach more people, make more sales, and have something that looks good and lets people know you mean business. But only if you do it right. Let's be honest. A lot of brochures have way too much text in them. So these are the three golden rules:

1. Don't be boring
2. Don't go on about yourself
3. Keep words to a minimum

Something to consider is where will it go? Is it online-only or are you planning on printing it? If your brochure is solely for digital use, be mindful to limit your words. You'll want to keep it short and sweet regardless, but online content is even more likely to be scanned or overlooked entirely. Scouring through a mass of pages and words to find the information they want won't be ideal for your audience. But if you're printing it, you might have more room to breathe. The reader will be more inclined to sit down and put their attention solely on your brochure. That's not to say you can cram in a dictionary's worth of words - it still needs to be respectful of their time.

With that question answered, let's take a look at the layout.

100

Your brochure structure

Here are the sections you'll most likely want to include in your brochure, in this order:

- Headline
- The problem
- Products or services
- About us
- Contact details

Depending on your company, you might want to include extra sections or shuffle them around. That's totally fine. It is your brochure after all. But this is my bare-minimum suggestion. Let's run through each section.

Headline

Alternatively, you could call it the brochure's title. This will likely be on the very first page of your brochure, underneath your business name. You need to grab the reader's **attention**. Don't use cliches, generic language, or anything else that risks putting people to sleep. Make it unique and snappy. For example "Here to keep you safe: your one-stop-shop for PPE for your construction site". This instantly puts the reader first, tells them what you're selling, and even touches on a benefit they can expect from working together. See the section on *Headlines* for more information.

The problem

When I say "the problem", I mean the one you solve. Whether it's a product or service, what are you doing for the reader? You'll know this reason from the first pillar. Once your headline has them hooked, this keeps them there. This section doesn't have to drag on for pages, but it will switch the focus of the brochure from yourself to the reader. Talk about challenges that people/businesses like them are facing, and conclude in a way that invokes interest. "...We couldn't find a solution... so we made one ourselves."

Products or services

Once you've highlighted the pains of your audience, your services and products section answers the questions as to how people can go from where they are and improve with your help. Bullet points work great here. They save space and keep it snappy, but also allow the words to breathe. Ever seen a document where it looks like someone just kept making the words smaller and smaller until they fit on the page? It's a ballache to read. Try combining these bullet points with a paragraph or two that delve into deeper detail. That way, you cater to both the skim readers and the detail-oriented ones.

About us

It's important you stick to not talking about yourself because, frankly, people won't be bothered. They want to know what's in it for them, and the about section is purely to demonstrate that you're trustworthy enough for them to invest in you. Do you have any relevant qualifications, awards, or recognitions? Have you been in the industry for a significant length of time? If so, what have you learned in that time? What are your values?

Tell them in a way that matters to them. Saying I have X years of writing experience means bugger all. But telling you I've cultivated a way to get what you want by writing what you mean in four simple steps over those same amount of years paints a much more captivating story.

Contact details

An obvious but easily overlooked factor. They need you, they're in love with your mind-blowing product or service, and your expertise truly sealed the deal. They're foaming at the mouth with excitement and need to know what to do next. Tell them how they can take action. Include at least two contact methods - be it an email, phone number, website, or your business address. If someone has to source your contact information from anywhere else then you've lost the deal.

With your layout in mind, here are some dos and don'ts before you start writing.

Do talk about the benefits

Most people list a bunch of features and expect the audience to understand what this means to them. It's not their job to guess. When you've done the work to understand your readers, you'll be able to work out what's important to them. If they're looking for a new gaming PC, don't just say it includes a "high-speed SSD and 32GB of RAM". You want to say "the high-speed SSD allows you to get into the action faster than ever and the 32GB of RAM means you'll have the power you need to play the latest games for years to come". Shift the focus from yourself and all your fancy features to them and what they gain.

Don't separate copy from design

For anyone that's ever muttered "we'll just design now and fit the words in later", Somewhere the soul of a creative person was shattered. The two work hand in hand. When you write your content, you'll either find you have some empty space to fill and end up writing for the sake of it, or you have to spend your time cramming it all together. It wastes your precious time when you could just bite the bullet and fuse the two from the beginning.

Always keep the design in the back of your mind as you're writing the content. Maybe even leave notes for yourself along the way with how you envision the layout. "This part could be in columns and this bit could be a fancy infographic". The more you think about it, the easier it will be later on.

Do keep it snappy

If you need bullet points to keep the pages short and tidy, so be it. Short, simple sentences are a must, too. You only have so much space and time to win your reader over, so don't waste it waffling. Stick to key details. If they want more information, you can fill in the gaps with your website and blogs. Although, when it comes to design, don't just be lazy and actually use plain Jane bullet points; try icons or a mini picture to be creative. If you're talking about the benefits of ice-cream, use tiny cones. Simple swaps can make a huge impact.

Don't look like everyone else

That new Canva template looks the bomb, right? If you think that, so do countless others. Using bog standard templates and royalty-free stock images might make your life easier, but you're not the only one. If you're trying to stand out, don't follow the crowd and do what everyone else is doing. Not everyone can afford flashy photography or paying for a graphic designer, but if you're going to do it yourself, at least take **inspiration** from standard templates, but don't tie yourself to them.

There's no denying templates can save you time, money, and energy. But they also inhibit your ability to stand out. Using them is one of the key reasons you're potentially separating copy from design in the first place. Take a look at picture and layout styles, find ideas that you like, then you can plan your content with your design in mind.

No matter the topic, your brochure is likely going to be a professional, thorough dive into your brand. So make sure everything about it sings.

BUSINESS PLANS

I nvestors play a key role in the success and growth of a business. But to get them on board, your business plan needs to electrify them, putting them in a position where they feel they simply can't pass up the opportunity. Alas, so many business plans are lacklustre. Less 'hyped and ready to go', more 'lethargic and kill me now'. You can't excite your readers if you, the *owner* of the business, sound like you'd rather be watching paint dry. They'll get bored, switch off, and chances are they won't be giving you any money.

Instead, let's look at what a business plan should be to have them throwing their cash at you. Now, before I get into it, I will say I'll be focusing on writing for investors in this section. But the same logic applies even if you plan on keeping this document for internal strategising and planning only. Right, back to the business plan. It needs to include:

1. Executive summary
2. Business overview
3. Operations plan
4. Market analysis
5. Products and services
6. Sales and marketing
7. Management team
8. Financial plan

Let's run through each one and the dos and don'ts for them.

Executive summary

In short, the executive summary is the most important part of the entire document. No pressure. It should be able to stand alone as a separate document, outlining the key takeaways to be found in each section to follow. It's, you guessed it, a summary of the entire plan. It should include:

- A one-line summary of what your business does
- Why an investor should be interested in giving funds to your business
- Why their money will be well spent
- Why you do what you do
- Key points from each section of the business plan

Here are some dos and don'ts to keep in mind when writing your executive summary.

Do keep it short....ish

First off, you want it to be concise. You're looking for somewhere between one and four pages. Or around 10% of the entire document. You have to remember that the executive summary is only the start, too. They have much more to read. But that's only *if* they decide to read on. To keep it short and to the point, consider using bullet points. These keep your page looking neat, tidy, and scannable. It's not lazy; it's being respectful of your reader's time.

Don't write it first

Most people try to summarise their business plan before they've had a chance to write it. Unless you're gifted with foresight, it'll make your life so easy to write it at the end of your process. There's nothing wrong with working backwards.

Do be confident

It isn't difficult to sense a lack of confidence in writing. Our current mindset directly influences everything we do. This includes language choice. So there's no hiding. If you're having an off-day, come back to it later. A lack of confidence is a trait investors will flee from.

Don't use unsubstantiated claims

This should go without saying, but don't make claims you can't back up with evidence. Investors want cold hard facts. This also goes for anything that's not directly related, or of interest, to your investors. Don't let random waffle take up precious space. If you can't back something up for good reason, it probably doesn't have a place in your plan.

Business overview

Sometimes referred to as the company summary or description, your business overview gives the reader basic information and background on your company. It should contain the following:

- The basics, including the company name, business structure, and location.
- The type of business.
- A breakdown of who owns the business and how each owner is involved, shares, and names and roles of the management team.
- A mission statement; a succinct description of the purpose of your business.
- Business formation history.
- How you'll conduct business (online, brick and mortar stores, etc).
- Your product/service and who your customers are. Save the numbers for later in your business plan, though.
- Your goals and vision for the business.
- The legal structure.

To make your overview as impactful as possible, here are two golden tips.

Don't go on too long

Like the executive summary, keep it short and sweet. Especially if this is an internal document being used by people who are already familiar with your business. That's not to say certain elements aren't important, but decide what's top-line information or what can be saved for other parts of your business plan.

Do write the sections that come the most natural

As long as you finish with the structure we've outlined, it doesn't mean you have to write them in that order. Starting a plan with a summary is counter intuitive. That goes for the rest of the document. Write the sections you feel the most comfortable and knowledgeable about and put them all in the right order later.

Operations plan

Now we're starting to get into the meaty parts. The executive summary and business overview are the fluffier, more passionate parts of the document containing need-to-know info. But now we're delving into the *how* and *why*. The operations plan is where you'll explain how the business will function, including the setup and how different teams and departments will contribute to achieving your goals. You want to outline the day-to-day tasks that'll keep your business up and running. This should cover departments such as recruitment, marketing, finance, and anything else you think is critical to the function of the business.

You'll want to include (for each department):

- What tasks need to be completed.
- Strategies you'll follow.
- Who's responsible for these tasks and strategies.
- What the time frames for the tasks and strategies are.

Once you've visualised these critical tasks and responsibilities, it becomes easier to set goals and research the steps needed to achieve them. You should look to answer these common questions:

- What's the department budget?
- What's the current condition of the team?
- Where does the team need to be in the future, including in the next month, quarter, and year?

- What steps will be taken to get them there?
- What KPIs will be used to measure progress?

Next, you need to plan how your money will be spent. After laying out your goals, map out the finances needed for all the outlined projects, tasks, and activities. This should come from the department's annual budget. As for some specific dos and don'ts, keep these in mind.

Do be thorough

As mentioned, this is the part where we really start to get into it. You'll want to dedicate a lot of time to this as it could be make or break for your entire business plan. There's a lot of detail to include here, so find the best way to structure that information for yourself first before writing it all out.

Don't go too far with the personality

I'll always advocate for bringing your brand's personality into everything you do. It's how you stand out, after all. But there's a time and a place to turn that dial up to 11. The operations plan isn't it. You'll want touches of it peppered throughout to break up the monotony of the serious info, but don't start cracking jokes every line. There could be a lot of money on the line, and investors aren't likely to part with it if they don't think you're taking it seriously.

Market analysis

Strap in, because we're going to dive in deep here. Market analysis reduces risk and shows investors you've done your research on what the market is like and what it demands of your business. This is going to be a **thorough** analysis of your market. Look at the industry as a whole, producing specific data, charts, and graphs. You'll define your target market and reveal your plans for how you'll cater to your audience. Cover:

- The wider industry within which you sit
- Your target market
- The market value
- The competition
- Any barriers to entry
- Regulation

The wider industry - Where is it headed? Is it in decline or is it on the rise? This section should look at:

1. The size and state of the industry and where you see yourself within it.

2. Your product's life cycle - discuss the research and development, and the launch, growth, and decline.

3. Your projected year-on-year growth.

114

Your target market - Who are they? You can't sell to everyone. Discuss your target market and how you'll adapt your product/service and approach to appeal to them. Look at this in depth and create customer personas.

Market value - This is great for any greens who might be reading your business plan. Make sure your numbers are thorough. To estimate, you'll do a top-down analysis. You can do a bottom-up analysis if you prefer, but top-down is easiest and still does what you need it to.

The competition - Every business has direct and indirect competitors. Unless you've created a time machine or something equally groundbreaking. Direct competitors sell the same product as you. McDonald's and Burger King are direct competitors because they both sell burgers. Indirect competitors don't sell the same product, but sell one that could be used in place of yours. KFC is an indirect competitor of McDonald's because they sell fast food. Dig into all of your competitors' strengths and weaknesses. Then cover:

- How big of a threat they are.
- How *you'll* cover *their* weaknesses.
- What better or different solutions you have to solve the same problem.
- How you'll use tech to improve the customer experience.

Barriers to entry - This stops you from making any legal or business mistakes. This part's crucial as it's of high interest to an investor. You might look at:

- Cost - Starting a business is expensive. Talk about employment costs, rent, and any other essential costs to your business you expect to navigate.
- Competition - How big of a challenge is it to open a business in your industry right now?
- Location - If you're opening a BMX shop, you don't want to open it in the countryside. You need a location where your target market is.
- Branding - Branding costs money but is essential to stand out from competitors.
- Technology - Will your product be useless in a few years' time due to the rapid development of tech?

Regulation - You must do this research. It's your responsibility as a business owner. This includes tax codes, employment and labour laws, advertising, privacy, and environmental regulations.

Products and services

This might sound simple. But you aren't just going to list what you offer here. Instead of rattling off a list of features, showcase the quality, value, and benefits. Now, this is an interesting concept because this isn't a client-facing document. You have three people to consider: you as the writer, the customers that will pay your company, and the investor reading the document.

So thinking about the personality colours earlier, if your customers are going to be yellow (caring about others and being super fluffy and helpful), but your potential investor is a red (thinking about the bottom line), then you need to appeal to both. You could talk about how your SaaS software helps care homes provide a better quality of life for their patients (which makes the yellows happy). Then include evidence of how many care homes there are in the UK with lacklustre technology and what the potential for profit is (which makes the reds happy). You'll also want to include why it fills a gap in your market and how it'll compete against similar products while considering both parties. Include:

- Descriptions of your products, bearing in mind your readers' level of knowledge.
- Pricing.
- A comparison against your competitors' products.
- Sales content. This includes marketing materials and how your website will contribute to sales.
- How you'll handle purchases, like processing orders.
- What tools or systems you need to handle an order. How will you deliver your products? Do you need specific software?
- Intellectual property (like trademarks) or legal issues you need to address.
- Ideas for future products.

Here are some key ideas you should consider.

Do explain why your product is needed

This is especially important if you're venturing into something unique or something that hasn't really been done before. If you're selling software, is it easier to use? Cheaper? Does it have valuable features that others on the market don't?

Don't forget to focus on the benefits

Benefits usually land better with a reader than features. You can tell me your camera has 64gb of memory. Or you can say it has enough space to hold over a year's worth of photos. The latter is the benefit. Investors won't necessarily be experts, or even knowledgeable, in your chosen field. So instead, tell them how a feature fixes a problem they can relate to.

Sales and marketing

Unless sales and marketing are genuinely your area of expertise, it's a good idea to plan your strategy with a consultant for this section (*wink* *wink*). Using the first pillar, you can highlight all the audience types you're appealing to and why, and identify the appropriate channels to reach them. As well as this, you should also include brand messaging, marketing assets, budget, and create a timeline of what you'll do and when. Assess how your competitors market themselves and detail what response that generates from your target audience. Show that you're aware, informed, and prepared to learn from their mistakes or successes.

Don't feel you have to use every channel

When it comes to driving new business, you don't have to succumb to using every possible marketing channel for the sake of it. For my dog food business, I use Instagram, my website, and ads as that's where I see the most success. But for my marketing agency (and consultancy), I use LinkedIn and my website, as those are where the biggest portion of my audience are. I don't waste my time or energy on other channels as I don't need to. In some cases, they serve as a great secondary form of marketing to build brand presence, but are not, and will never be my primary source of income, and so aren't of importance to me personally. But that's your call for your own situation.

Management team

Your business is only ever as strong as the weakest person on your team, so it's important that your investor knows about everyone working with you, not just you. You can detail qualifications, past experiences, and any other relevant information about your team that showcases their strengths. It's best to keep this section short. One paragraph per person should do. Ask yourself: what do investors *need* to know about your team? What does each member bring to the table? Keep it relevant. This isn't the time for John or Sarah's X Factor audition.

Do showcase their greatest strengths

By this, I mean the ones that are most relevant to the business. Someone might have over 20 years in the industry, but how will that play into your organisation? Do they have particularly good management skills, for example? Include the details that show investors they'll be a good fit in **their** role.

Financial plan

This is a forecast of the future. It's not the same as accounting. Don't go crazy with the details. But do keep it realistic. While this section is important for you, it's also something investors will want to see. Start it off with a sales forecast. Use a spreadsheet to project your sales over the next few years. For your first year, set up columns for each month. Each year after that, set up quarterly columns. This is to calculate your gross margin. Then create an expense budget, a cash flow statement, income projections, and a breakeven analysis. Anyone who's considering investing in you needs to know this information.

Do include your personality here

Just because you're talking about cold, hard numbers doesn't mean they have to be bland. A bit of your brand colours and signature font go a long way in making the figures that bit more engaging.

And there you have it. Now you have a complete, detailed, but somewhat concise and clear business plan. Treat yourself with something nice. You deserve it.

BUSINESS PROPOSALS

You know your product or service is next level. Your existing clients know it too. Your client base is growing each month, which is great. But you have a hunch it could be growing faster... So you decide you need an amazing business proposal. One that outlines your value and screams, "if you don't work with us, you're missing out". But where's the line between a bog-standard proposal and one that really shines? Well that's the million-dollar question I'm here to answer!

An excellent proposal won't just talk about your offering. It won't even be a fantastic sales document. No, it has to do more than that. Remember, the person reading it might have zero familiarity with who you are. So this proposal has to anticipate the reader's questions before they even ask them. It has to make you sound not only like a valuable service, but a valuable **partner**.

I should also make a distinction between solicited and unsolicited proposals. While the type you're writing won't hold much bearing on the content of the proposal itself, it will influence specific tone and word choices. Solicited proposals are requested by the customer themselves. Perhaps you've already had a call and they're intrigued to know more. Or sometimes businesses will post on social media that they're interested in receiving proposals from certain service providers. Either way, this is a customer who's already in the market for a specific service. Their request will often be accompanied by a description of the problem they need solving and any specific formatting requirements for the documents. With this insight into the business you're pitching, you'll be able to hone right into their unique pain points and be more specific about how you can help. Your proposal will end up a lot more personalised for it.

Alternatively, you might want to send unsolicited proposals to cold contacts in the hopes of gaining their attention. These will be more general as you might never have spoken to the business before. As such, you don't know what specific challenges they face. Although you can make an educated guess. Or shine a light on a problem they might not even realise they have yet. Since the recipients of unsolicited proposals might not know your business from Adam, these may require some more foundational information about your wider business too.

So keep that in mind as you work on your proposal. It goes back to the first pillar and knowing your audience. With that in mind, where do you start?

Plan your structure

Like I said, no matter the specifics of the proposal you're writing, the structure will be similar. There are certain elements that are expected in one, so by following the format, you give the reader what they're expecting. The non-negotiables to include are:

Title page - A simple front cover featuring your logo, business name, and contact details.

Table of contents - Every customer will have different priorities when it comes to choosing service providers. Providing a table of contents allows them to flick through to your services, prices, or whatever else is a top priority for them.

Executive summary - In just a few sentences you want to explain who you are, the service you provide, and **why** you're the perfect choice for your reader. Speak less about yourself and more about why this would be the ideal partnership for them. Why should they choose you over anyone else? What will be the long-term outcome of investing in your services?

The problem - This is where you'll bring in some storytelling. What problem are you addressing for the reader? Depending on whether you've spoken to the recipient before, you might know this for a fact and be able to get really specific. If not, you might want to take an educated guess, or be more general about common issues faced by similar businesses in their industry.

Propose a solution - How can you help them overcome this challenge? Your best bet is to pick one service to highlight here. Talk about what the service involves and what results can be expected. You might also want to explain what the onboarding process looks like and how the service can be scaled as the business grows.

Brief overview of any other services - Just because you're highlighting one service here doesn't mean others won't be relevant. It never hurts to spend a little time showing your reader some of the other ways you could help them towards a stronger, more successful business. But keep these brief. They won't have all the time in the world.

Qualifications - What makes you qualified for the job? This is about providing evidence of your authority and skill in the space. What success stories have you had with this service to date? Do you have any relevant credentials or experience that will help to increase trust?

Pricing - Money is a big factor in a prospective customer becoming an actual one. So you want to be giving your reader all the information up front. How much do each of your services cost? If there's flexibility, say so. But at least provide a ballpark estimate.

Terms and conditions - Again, the T's & C's of working with you might be a dealbreaker for some businesses. Say you require a six-month notice period but that isn't realistic with their current finances. By laying your terms out upfront, you weed out the bad fits. This saves both your time and theirs.

This structure is great to follow as it ensures you don't miss any vital details. I recommend laying these sections out on a document and creating a bullet-point list of talking points for each. Just get your initial thoughts out there before going back and expanding. Get it done one section at a time and it won't seem so daunting. And now for some dos and don'ts of writing business proposals that always hit the mark.

Do say more with less

Time is money and you're writing for professionals or business owners who are very likely to be time-poor. Especially if they're openly requesting proposals, they might have **a lot** to get through. The more you can simplify your writing and provide a lot of information quickly, the better. Bullet points, statistics, charts, and graphs are all great ways to condense your message.

Don't over-explain

In a similar vein, don't feel like you have to throw every point at them. When we really want someone to choose us, it's natural to let them know how great we are. But sharing too much and over-explaining will only make you appear less confident and sure of yourself. Wherever possible, keep your sentences short, simple, and direct. You already know you're a catch.

Do avoid using 'can', 'could', 'may', or 'might'

Or any other word that sounds tentative and unsure. *'Our graphic design services will help your business achieve its goals'* sounds far better than *'our graphic design services could help your business achieve its goals'*. An exception to this rule is if you literally can't make guarantees for legal reasons - such as in law, financial services, or healthcare. Have some faith in what you offer.

Don't forget about the benefits

A feature of your service might be more leads. But what does this actually *mean* for the customer? Going one step further and explaining how more high-quality, relevant leads will lead to increased revenue and help them to achieve X and Y goals helps put your value in the context of their business. It makes everything feel more tangible and relatable.

Do include testimonials

It's normal for people to feel sceptical when faced with a person or brand they've never heard of. After all, I could tell you I was once a Michelin-star chef - it doesn't make it true. Including credible testimonials helps build trust and authority. They show you're not all talk. These are actual businesses who have become stronger thanks to your input. By including these, it becomes far harder for people to be sceptical or distrusting of your value.

Don't forget about your call to action

You've put in a hard graft winning them over, but how does your reader now act on their interest? You want to lay out those next steps. How is it best to get in touch with you? What can they expect once the ball starts rolling?

Do inject your personality

Ideally, you should present yourself consistently from initial meeting through to long-term working relationship. You don't want to start with a proposal that's stuffy and professional, only to switch it up and let your personality loose once you've sealed the deal. If you're a fun, energetic brand, let that be known in your proposals. By letting your personality shine, you'll be able to attract more of the right clients, and turn off many of the wrong ones.

The needs of your business proposals will vary depending on the nature of your services, and the types of businesses you're reaching out to. But by taking a customer-focused, personalised approach, and being direct about how you will add tangible value, you'll be gaining new clients in no time.

CASE STUDIES AND TESTIMONIALS

You can talk about how good you are until you're blue in the face. But the people reading what you've written don't know you from Steve or Susan. It's the foundation of why case studies and testimonials exist. And you're right to want to get some of them on your website. There's nothing stronger than proof of what you're good at, or positive words from another customer or client.

Testimonials aren't written by you, so for the purpose of this book, you can pre-empt what's said by sharing with your customers what you'd like their feedback on to make the testimonial valuable. Typically, this could be how you helped them, what key differences you made, and how they found the whole experience. Of course, not everyone has perfect spelling and grammar, so you might want to at least proofread - *leaving the piece in their own words* - to take out any glaring mistakes.

Case studies, however, I've got some thoughts on. They shouldn't just *tell* your audience what you do, but also *show* them what that actually looks like. You want your case studies to include what the brief was, any challenges, how you overcame them, the end results, and what the client's views are. By doing this, you're displaying actual proof of what you're capable of, which is far more effective than just telling them how great you are.

So, how do you write an impactful case study?

Put some meat on the bones

Case studies are opportunities to tell a story. They're not just a dispassionate list of events that happened during a project. Don't waste them with one-liners that don't offer any value to the reader.

"We did a project that delivered X."

"We did it well."

"The end."

Flesh out the story to provide evidence of your organisation's skills over and above your actual service offering, such as problem-solving and determination. Think of when you're reading a great novel, and your attention is captured by the twists and turns. You want to evoke this same feeling in your audience. Admittedly on a lesser scale - you're writing a case study after all, not a bestselling murder mystery.

If you ran into hurdles, it's ok to talk about them. No one is expecting everything to run smoothly, especially if it was out of your control. Perhaps there were issues with the budget. A global pandemic came and scuppered construction for months on end. Or something didn't quite go to plan, but your team worked tirelessly to overcome it. Find the story that will help get your reader invested. Be authentic and show that not only did you face challenges, but you overcame them. There's just as much value in someone learning what you did in the face of adversity then there is in knowing all the factors you got right.

And once you've got this nailed down, it's time to work out the structure. Most successful case studies go like this...

Introduction

Lay out a basic overview of the project. What was the goal/task at hand?

Background

This is where the research on the client comes in. Who were you working with? Where did the project start? What problem were you solving? Did you anticipate any challenges ahead of time? How did you prepare for the project as a whole? A quote on why your client believed you were the business for the job would be especially powerful here.

Evaluation

This is usually where a challenge or problem comes up. You need to discuss what worked, what didn't, and explain why. If a project went swimmingly, explore why this was. What did your team do to ensure smooth sailing? Where did you go above and beyond?

Solutions

You said there were problems, now we need solutions. What did you do to fix any issues? How did you tackle any hurdles? Support your choices with solid evidence. This may include personal experiences or research. Say you're a construction company. You might write: "National lockdowns pushed the project back by seven months, leaving us unable to hit the original time frame. In response, upon being allowed to carry on, we did X, Y, and Z, maximising productivity on site, while keeping to strict government guidelines on social distancing. This enabled us to keep the project running smoothly and allowed us to finish the project within the newly agreed timings." It makes you look cool, calm, collected, and in control.

Results

What was the finished product? Include percentages and hard facts if applicable. Perhaps even pictures if there's something tangible to show for your efforts. What were your clients thoughts on the job you did? Is there anything you wish had gone differently and are taking forward as a lesson learned? Try to always be radically transparent in your reflections. Before you hit the ground running on writing up your case studies, here are some dos and don'ts for you to refer back to as you go.

Do be specific

Details make your case study more credible, interesting, and will help to answer any questions the reader may have. The more vivid a picture you paint in your reader's mind, the more engaging and impactful your piece will be.

Don't underestimate the power of testimonials as part of your case study

Your audience is far more likely to believe an unbiased third party than they are you. Can you blame them? It's human nature to be untrusting. A business is *obviously* going to think of themselves as great. Sharon from Kent, however, has got nothing to gain from fibbing. So testimonials can work wonders for sealing the deal on potential new business.

Do share the stories of the customers you want to attract more of

Like attracts like. Similar potential customers with problems that they can relate to will want you to achieve the same for them. How did you overcome adversity? What might seem an impossible challenge to the audience can paint you in a glowing light if they can see how you helped someone else in the same boat. Something to encourage relatability for your reader. "This company is just like me! This is exactly what I want! I better get in touch right away!" Okay, they might not be quite so hyper and enthusiastic, but you catch my drift.

Don't write a case study just because the brand you worked with is well-known

Although it's tempting to have a big household name linked to your business, if there's no story or it isn't a particularly impressive example of your work, it's not going to make for a great case study. Visitors to your site will know straight away if you've included a name simply for clout. Case studies are more about what *you* achieved, rather than *who* you achieved it for.

Do organise case studies on your website by benefit or result

Visitors should be able to filter through case studies easily. Not every example you give will be relevant or interesting to every reader. For example, cases that resulted in an improvement in sales should be kept separate from cases that resulted in higher employee retention. Demolition case studies should be kept separate from interior fit-outs. You get the idea. Visitors to your website need to be able to find what they're looking for quickly, otherwise you risk your case studies sitting there gathering metaphorical dust.

If you follow all of this guidance, you'll find yourself with a selection of case studies that grip your readers' attention and successfully demonstrate your company's experience and skill.

COVER LETTER AND CV

Writing a CV can be tricky. You're essentially writing an advertisement for yourself. And it's difficult to remain objective. When this document is what's standing between you and a job you really, really want, it's easy to get frustrated and give up the task entirely. You *know* you're perfect for this job. But *how* do you put this into words on a page? While some people are capable of bigging themselves up, others find it feels unnatural and end up selling themselves short. Writing a CV requires us to speak highly of ourselves and notice our positive traits. To some people, winning the 100m sprint against Usain Bolt seems like the easier challenge.

Mind over matter

It all comes down to mindset. Let me introduce you to a concept called "confirmation bias". Confirmation bias means that whatever you tell yourself, your brain tries to find evidence for. Why is this relevant? Well, if you sit around telling yourself you're shit at everything, you'll only think about all the times you messed up. Whenever you make a simple mistake, your brain will latch on to that as proof and reinforce the idea you're not good enough. Every. Single. Time.

The reverse is also true. If you step back, lean away from this mindset, instead telling yourself you're a great team leader and fantastic at creative problem-solving, your brain will search for evidence to prove this. Your brain follows the path you set it on. So choose wisely. You can't write a good CV if you're in the wrong mindset. Biologically, you'll be unable to see the positive traits amongst all your perceived 'bad' ones.

Your mindset will leak into your writing itself. No matter how hard you try to separate it. If you're uncertain or nervous, people will be able to tell because it affects your word choice and sentence structure. If you've been rejected from five jobs and sit down on a Sunday with an "I can't be arsed" mindset, do you really think you're going to create an engaging CV that's going to win over prospective employers? Doubtful, right?

So first of all, look at what you think about yourself. Save this task for a time where you're feeling more positive, objective, and open-minded. When you finally sit down and let it all out, cut the BS and be real. I recommend writing a list for yourself that's honest, full of your good and bad work traits. Then just write about it.

Don't worry - no one will see your unfiltered thoughts. It's about taking your qualities, such as being "shit at working in a team", and changing your mindset on them. So you're not "shit at working on a team". You're "An independent worker who thrives when given a challenge and is adept at problem-solving". For a position that's work-from-home and doesn't require much micromanagement, you've suddenly become the front runner. In short, say something meaningful.

The cover letter

Now, before I tell you what to include in your CV, I want to touch on the cover letter. A lot of people hate writing them. You already have a CV; what else is there to even say? But the truth is that CVs in and of themselves are relatively cold and impersonal. There's a set criteria we all know we need to hit, and it leaves very little room for individual creative thought or personality. Cover letters, however, can be a fantastic opportunity to properly introduce yourself, show your enthusiasm, and back up your CV. You have the chance to really sell yourself here and stand out from everyone else. A CV is only as strong as its cover letter.

But don't fall into the trap of trying to create a generic cover letter to save yourself time. I know how tempting it can be to just change the company name and send out the exact same letter for each vacancy. But you'll have a far greater success rate writing ones tailored to the role. And that's mostly because people can often tell when you've just swapped the company name in. This doesn't mean you have to completely rewrite the whole letter every time. Perhaps designate a paragraph or two to inject some more personalised information. There will always be certain points you can address in the letter that were mentioned in the job ad. But we'll come back to this later.

I can't tell you exactly how to write a cover letter, because it largely depends on the role. But here's how to get started…

Research

Research in this sense means finding out what the company does, their ethos and mission, who their competitors are, who their target audience is, what the job involves, and what skills you will need to succeed in the role. This will help you tailor your cover letter to them and match your language to theirs. Are they a modern and bubbly company looking to challenge the status quo? Then they'll want to hear from people just like that. Also, it'll help in the interview stage; no one wants to be that person that freezes up when they ask "so why do you want to work with us?"

Now onto the structure. Here's a good plan to follow.

Paragraph one - Why are you applying?

You should be to the point. Explain that you're applying for the role of X that was advertised on Y. Then explain that your CV has been attached.

Paragraph two - Why are you suitable?

Describe your professional and academic qualifications, and any other experiences relevant to the role. In the job description, there will be a list of skills needed and a list of ones desired for applicants. Touch on as many as you can, but also try to keep it brief. The reader can always find more details in your CV.

This is why you shouldn't use the same cover letter every time. Different roles prioritise slightly different skills. And you want to position yourself as perfect for this individual role. You don't want to just make this a list. Put them into context. So you're a team player? When has that come up in your professional life and why is it relevant? If they're looking for a leader, demonstrate your success as a leader. The ten years you spent in sales prior to that have no place here. That's not the reader's focus.

Paragraph three - Why will the company benefit from choosing you?

This is where you'll really sell yourself. You should outline your career goals, keeping them relevant to the position, and expand on some relevant points from your CV. Stats and figures are perfect here too. Did customer experience improve 22% due to the changes you implemented? Include that in this paragraph, as long as it's relevant. This helps the reader visualise the benefits of having you work for the company. And it's harder to dismiss cold, hard, irrefutable facts.

Paragraph four - Restate your interest and why you'll be the perfect fit.

Think of this as a conclusion. Using the paragraph before, reiterate why you'll fit the role. Explain that you have had all this success in previous roles and you want to bring your expertise and knowledge to this new one. Sign off by thanking the reader for their time and for considering you for the role. Mention that you look forward to meeting them to discuss your application. Then close with "yours sincerely" if you know the name of the hiring manager, or "yours faithfully" if you don't.

Now you have an idea of how you're going to do this, it's time to cover some quick dos and don'ts of cover letter writing.

Don't just regurgitate what's on your CV

If your cover letter is good, they'll check out your CV. So, instead of repeating what you say in that, use this space to expand and inject some of your personality. When you get to writing your CV, you'll notice how quickly you run out of space. The recruiter has given you the opportunity to basically extend it, so don't waste it.

Do be human

I know you're trying to be professional, but being overly formal can make it difficult for recruiters to relate to you. They're human, you're human, have a human conversation.

Don't apologise for your lack of experience

Sentences like "despite my lack of experience in..." just highlight your, well, lack of experience. Instead, put a positive spin on it. "My natural charisma and fantastic communication skills make me a great candidate for this role" is much more powerful and focuses on the positives. This tip goes for your CV, too.

Do ask someone close to you to check it

Those who are close will be more blunt with you. They're more likely to point out grammar mistakes, tell you that something doesn't read right, or straight up let you know when something sounds arrogant or you're selling yourself short. If someone knows you well, they'll be able to offer a lot of valuable insight during this process. Make sure you ask someone who is more confident as a communicator, as not all advice is equal.

Don't be overenthusiastic

Of course you want to sound enthusiastic. Otherwise, they'll think you don't want the job. But too much enthusiasm can make you sound desperate. If you're excited, you can say so. But steer away from intensifiers like really, very, and extremely.

That's the cover letter sorted. Now it's onto the CV.

The CV

First, we'll start with the structure. Your CV should include:

- Contact details
- Personal statement
- Key skills
- Employment history
- Education
- Achievements
- Hobbies

And they should be in that order.

Contact details

Your contact details go below your name at the top of the page. You'll need your full name, email address, phone number, and, in some cases, your address. If you're unsure about whether or not to put your address, the city you live in should be fine.

Personal statement

This is where you'll introduce yourself. Yes, you'll introduce yourself a bit in the cover letter, too. But this will be the introduction in the context of your CV and the role you're applying for. Just as you tailor your cover letter to each role, you should adapt the personal statement on your CV to each role too. Use it to provide an overview of who you are and your suitability as a candidate. If you were applying to be a social worker, for example, and love helping and talking to people, put this here. You should touch on your passions, traits, and strengths. The ones that made you want this job in the first place and would make you well-suited to getting it. But keep it short. This section should only be around four or five sentences.

Key skills

Again, ideally you want to tailor this to each role. Look at the ad for the position you're applying for. Just like with the cover letter, you're focusing on what they need and desire in an applicant. If you have them all, that's great. But chances are you won't. You're not Superman, so don't worry. What's important is that you don't lie. Instead, focus on your strengths. And if you have skills that aren't related to the ones the role requires, explain how the skills you do have are transferable or how you can learn from them.

Maybe in a past role you learned how to use complex software in a short space of time. This shows you're a fast learner. Although it may not be the one the company you're applying for uses, you could probably pick up their software as quickly as this one. And give examples. I can very easily say I have great customer service skills, but so can everyone else. Not everyone can say that they handled a frustrated, upset customer with care and patience, resulting in them leaving with a smile on their face and a table booked for the following week. Examples like this make you that much more believable and personable.

Employment history

Add your work experience in reverse chronological order. You can set each role as a subheading to keep it clear and easy to scan. Here's an example:

"Best Company Ever LTD, 2017 - Present, business development manager"

This way, the recruiter can easily scan through your past experience and see what you did, where, and when. Below each, you'll need to cover the "what". What did you do, what were your duties, and what did you achieve? Any notable experiences that link back to your key skills? Use bullet points to keep it neat and so you can fit in more information. You don't need to go in as much detail for your earlier roles though. If you're applying for the job of business development manager, what you did when you worked in a bar as a teen isn't really relevant anymore. You can still mention it, as you don't want to leave any gaps in your employment history,

HOW TO WRITE WHEN YOU'RE NOT A WRITER

just don't go too deep into it. Otherwise, you're robbing yourself of precious space on the page.

Education

This should look similar to the employment history section. State the name of the university or school and the years you were there. Below, list what qualifications you achieved and at what grade. Again, there's no need to go into too much detail. No one cares what you got in primary school Spanish if you're applying for an IT job. Keep it relevant, omit unnecessary bits, and bring attention to the qualifications that matter.

As a rule of thumb, the more employment experience you accumulate, the shorter this education section will become. For example, if you've been in an extremely relevant job for the past five years, you can most likely leave out your GCSE and A-Level results, focusing solely on your university studies and employment experience. If you didn't go to uni, state your most advanced qualifications and leave it at that.

Achievements

This is a great chance to show off what you can do. If you helped a past employer achieve a goal, add it here. Discuss successful projects that you were a part of. Did you win an award? Are you certified in something? As long as it's

148

relevant, share some of your most notable achievements here. Include what you did, when you did it, and where.

Hobbies

You wouldn't believe the hobbies some people list on their CV. A lot of people take it far too literally. The employer probably isn't interested in the fact you enjoy watching movies or hanging out with your friends. Everybody likes that. The recruiter is looking for signs that your personality ticks the right boxes. For example, if the job requires working in a team, mentioning that you play team sports is perfect. It's relevant. If you're applying for a role that requires great written communication skills, mentioning that you write a blog is a nice boost.

Traditionally, a CV would end with references or "references available upon request". But, nowadays, everyone assumes you have references at the ready and will just ask if or when they need them. So save that space for the more valuable, relevant information about you.

And that's all the core content to include in your CV. Now you've got the basic structure and content down, let's cover some dos and don'ts to make it the best it can be.

Do focus on what you can do, not what you can't

Everyone's list of what they can't do is bigger than the list of what they can. So focus on all that you can do. You're selling yourself after all. And that's all the employer cares about. So what are you good at? Shout about it. Make a song and dance of it. Especially if it's a powerful soft skill, something relevant to the role you're applying for, or if it's difficult to learn.

Don't waffle

CV is short for "curriculum vitae" which translates to "course of life". Despite this, employers don't actually want to read your entire life story. Cut out the waffle. The cover letter should be one page of A4, and a CV should never be more than two.

Do avoid bland, cliche, or overused language

Are you a flexible, motivated, multi-tasker with a strong work ethic? You might be. But so is everyone else apparently. There are some words that seem to be on every single CV ever written. It's boring and unoriginal. But if you really are a flexible, motivated, multi-tasker with a strong work ethic, you'd never say that aloud. Please choose different words. No one talks that way. Here are some of the most common culprits:

- Detail-oriented
- Hard worker
- Self-motivated
- Independent
- Multi-tasker
- Strong work ethic
- Enthusiastic

- Reliable
- Conscientious
- Natural team leader
- Self starter
- Creative
- Results-driven

So you don't want to say "detail-oriented". Switch it out for another, less abused word like "accurate". Google is your friend. All you need to search is "synonym for X". It's a really simple way to sound a bit different while still saying what you need to say. Or, better yet, instead of claiming you're detail-oriented, show them why. Give an example. Let them be the judge.

Now you know how to create a CV that will dazzle all potential employers, along with an engaging, well-thought-out cover letter to match. All that's left for you to do is to go out there and smash those interviews.

EMAILS (MARKETING)

*For this section, we're covering emails sent
for the purpose of converting business.
For general day-to-day conversations, see
general education written communication.*

We all have a love-hate relationship with our emails. They can pile up on us and be a nightmare to fight our way through. But they can also be the easiest way to communicate and digest information. It's a little bit masochistic, right? There are some undeniable benefits that make them so good. Email is 40x more effective at acquiring customers than Facebook and Twitter combined. Shoppers spend 138% more when targeted through emails compared to those who don't receive any. Despite how powerful it is and how long it's been around - at least compared to tools like social media - it still seems to be something many people struggle to get the most out of. An email isn't as simple as writing it, sending it out, and praying it works. If only it were like that. No, just like anything else, there are rules to doing it the right way.

Little mistakes get in the way of truly nailing an email, like not making the most of the preview text and not personalising them. Or using one of the many words that will get it sent straight to the spam folder. Seriously, it's longer than both my arms; you can find a list of some of these words in the *Newsletter* section. So how can you improve your open rates and identify mistakes that are killing your emails before you even click send?

Our advice can generally be applied to any type of email, whether it's a weekly newsletter, an introduction to a potential client, or even just a quick exchange between colleagues. They're also great for ecommerce and marketing funnels, but we'll get into that in the next section. Let's start at the very beginning. No, not the introduction. Not even the subject line. Who's it from?

Your name

It's easy to forget about, but your name will likely be the first detail the reader notices. And if they can find a reason to not click on it, they will. So you have to get over the hurdle of potentially being someone they don't know. We've all done it. "Who's this Dave guy? I don't know him." And then you swipe the notification away and crack on with your day. Unless it happens to be Beyoncé or Barack Obama. Using just your company name might also be a bad idea too. It comes across cold and impersonal. So a good medium is to use both. Keep it more personable and use [name] from [business name].

Now onto the subject line.

The subject line

Did you know that 47% of people decide whether to open an email based on the subject line alone? So it really goes without saying that writing an amazing subject line should be your number one priority. Without it, no matter how banging the body text might be, you're missing out on half your audience. Entice them. Lure them in. Give them an irresistible benefit right then and there. People want to know what's in it for them. This is especially important with emails. Most people have other, more important parts of their day to be getting on with. They don't want to be reading through junk mail.

Here are some top tips for getting your subject line spot on.

Do keep it short

You only get so many characters for your subject line. And while you obviously don't want to be cut off, the longer it is, the more the reader has to digest. So keep it snappy. Aim for around 30 characters, if possible. Also, be mindful that most people check their emails on their phones or other small-screen devices. You want to be certain they can read and appreciate your killer subject line in all its glory.

Don't spam

By this I mean watch your language. There are dozens of words that trigger spam filters. Words like 'free', 'now', and 'call us'. As well as pound signs, excessive punctuation, and even words in all caps. When it comes to punctuation, you don't want more than three per subject line.

Do personalise it if possible

Adding the recipient's name is an easy way to increase the chances of them opening your email. You can also personalise based on their location, send promo emails for their birthday, anniversary of their membership, and more. If this sounds a bit too much for you, personal pronouns like 'you' or 'your' are incredibly effective too.

Don't forget to test your subject lines

Even the most minor of details can affect open rates. Testing your subject lines is the only way to figure out what resonates with your audience most. To do this, you can use a handy little trick that you might already know - A/B testing (you may also know it as split testing). For those not familiar with this idea, you create small variations to your subject line and send them out. Then you can compare stats like open rates and conversion rates to see if one works better than the other. If one does, then great! You can use this to make more tweaks and do even more testing. It's an ongoing process that will slowly refine your approach, so don't forget to do it.

The preview text

Next up, you'll need preview text that both tells your readers what's in the email while also getting them excited and intrigued enough to read it. This is usually about the first sentence. So you want to ensure it lands. Take some of the tips from the headline - how can you make it snappy? How can you draw people in? Two effective methods would be to use an interesting fact or a question that piques their interest. It's like the blurb of a book or the description of a film on Netflix. It helps you decide if this is something you might be interested in. Or whether you can swiftly swipe and delete.

Think of how many random emails you receive on a daily basis from all those companies you forgot you gave your email address to that one time. For your first-class email marketing to be recognised and given the time and attention it deserves, you have to cut through literally hundreds of emails in your readers' inboxes. To make the best first impression, you need to make sure you start your email *right*.

And try not to reveal *everything* here. Think of it like this. Your subject line's job is to stop your audience in their tracks and make them take a pause to peruse your preview text. That first sentence's job is to offer just enough value to encourage them to open your email. While your email's body text's job is to evoke whatever action you want from your audience. Speaking of which, it's time for that all-important body content.

The body content

This is the main bulk of the email. Unless your audience is an especially academic bunch, you'll want to keep it straightforward and to the point. Most people just want to know what's going on, why they should care, and how it can benefit them. Ideally, the start of the body content should be personalised. It doesn't have to be complicated. "Hi John" is perfect for more informal communications, while something like "Hello John" or "Dear John" would be more appropriate in more formal emails. In short, tailor the greeting to who you're writing to. For the rest of it, there are some formulas that are worth considering to see if they suit your style - namely, the BAB and 4Ps formula.

BAB stands for "Before, After, and Bridge" and looks like this.

B - Before

Start by detailing the reader's current situation. You want them to quickly relate to what you're saying and elicit some sort of emotion - frustration, anger, curiosity, whatever you want.

A - After

Then, you should focus on the benefits they'd experience if their problem was dealt with. How much more streamlined their business would be if they invested in a more intuitive piece of management software. How much money they could save by rethinking their office's energy supplier. You get the idea.

B - Bridge

You've wet your readers' appetites by outlining a problem they relate to and have painted a pretty picture of what the opposite could look like. Now, it's time to bridge this gap and offer your product or service as the solution they simply *need* to take you up on.

And then, we have the 4Ps:

Promise

Promise something that you know your audience will be interested in and that your product can deliver.

Paint

Paint the picture of what their lives would look like after you deliver on this promise.

Proof

Prove that you can deliver. Social proof works great here. Testimonials, case studies, or any other examples of how you've delivered on the same or a similar promise to a client, *and* how they've benefited from the very same benefits you've just described.

Push

Push them to take action. Not too aggressively, of course. Use a call to action that relates back to what you were just talking about and leaves your reader unable to say no.

These formulas won't work for every email, but can be helpful when you don't know where to begin. Now you've got the gist of it, here are some dos and don'ts for writing your emails.

Do make your emails clear and easy to read

In our fast-paced, modern lives, if something isn't immediately obvious, we drop it. And that includes the email you spent so long creating. So you want to make reading it as quick and painless as possible.

Don't annoy your audience

No one wants to feel bombarded by a business. If your audience feels like you're constantly in their inbox and aren't adding anything worthwhile, it won't take long for them to hit that unsubscribe button. You know the times you sign up for a company's newsletter and regret it when they send you 10 emails in 2 days? Yeah, don't be that person, I beg of you. Twice a month is usually a good place to start. And it's always great to give them the option to change the amount of correspondence they receive, or the categories they're opted in to, as this might make the difference between them staying signed up or unsubscribing entirely.

Do engage in a little trial and error

Similar to above, you want to view your email marketing as a fluid, flexible process. You shouldn't just settle on one approach and layout, sticking with that forever, regardless of whether it's working or not. To get the most out of your email marketing, you need to be open to trying new approaches and tracking the progress of every small change, learning and evolving as you go.

Don't send without testing

Test. Your. Emails. This isn't testing in the same way I told you to test your subject line. This is about making sure it actually works. Test to see if they look good in the inbox. Test to see if the layout looks good and is easy to read on multiple devices. Test for broken links. Emails don't always get to the inbox looking the way you expected them to.

Do optimise for mobile

Mobile opens account for 46% of all email opens. Yet, if I scrolled through my inbox, I bet I'd find a handful I wouldn't be able to read properly on my phone. And it's different for each device and email provider. Yep, an email in my Gmail will look different in my Hotmail. And it won't be the same on an iPhone and an Android phone. You want to make life easier for your audience, regardless of their email provider or device choice.

There are lots of tips, tricks, and factors to consider when crafting the perfect email. But if you master the art, it can be transformative for your business. The ROI for email marketing can even be as high as 4,400%. With potential like that, how could you not try it out for yourself?

EMAILS
(ECOMMERCE MARKETING)

B efore we jump in, let's separate your email content. In the chapter before this, we covered general guidance for crafting sales-driven, cold email content that encourages your reader to open the email and take action after reading. And the same advice goes for any and all emails you might find yourself sending. Ecommerce email marketing is a different kettle of fish. Typically, it goes hand in hand with automation software on an ecommerce platform. We're going to focus on the content side of this because, well, that's what this book is for.

Automated emails are probably the easiest way to stay on your customer's minds and, as a bonus, require little effort. All you have to do is set them up and you're good to go. Some of the most effective automated ecommerce emails include:

- Welcome emails
- Abandoned cart reminders
- Follow-ups
- Prompts to re-engage
- Upsell offers
- Educational content

But before we begin, I want to say a little something about segmenting your audience. This is a necessary first step to ensure readers receive the content they care about. And, more importantly, that people **don't** receive content they couldn't care less about. Imagine I own a pet shop and send out an email about a dog food sale to everyone on my mailing list. That would mean bird, fish, reptile, and cat owners all receive the email too. But they don't care. They don't have a dog. If this keeps happening, they'll eventually give up and unsubscribe altogether. Meaning Sally's no longer around next time you have a sale on fish food which would be perfect for her goldfish Mary.

Segmenting your audience helps prevent this. Just because you have a list of contact addresses doesn't mean you should make use of all of them. The more targeted you are, the more effective you will be. With this in mind, let's look at the types of ecommerce emails in a bit more depth.

Welcome emails

A welcome email isn't just a small but thoughtful gesture - it's become largely expected. It's your business's way of saying "hey, I see you! Thank you for investing in us." And it's quite like a warm, comforting hug that starts to build that invisible space for loyal, repeat customers. Typically, this is the first point of contact between you and a new customer. Nail the first step, and it could be the start of a fantastic relationship. You, sending automated email offers, and them, loving and buying everything you send them. Well, that's wishful thinking. But still, you need to get this welcome email right.

You don't want to go shoving all your fantastic offers down their throats straight off the bat. Rather, you're supposed to be confirming that they did in fact opt-in to receive your emails, that they've given you the right email address, and everything's in working order. Don't scare them away with hard selling before they've even settled. To strengthen your welcome email, add a cheeky offer or free trial. Such as 10% off their first purchase. In doing so, you'll build an association between an email from you and a benefit for them. They'll be more likely to open the rest of your emails and your conversions will increase. It's all psychology, really.

Also, include calls to action where appropriate to boost cross-channel engagement. A simple "follow us on Twitter" or "check out our latest blog post" can go a long way. Encouraging this can boost the amount of brand impressions they receive from you on a daily basis, making them more likely to remember you and choose you over a competitor. If it takes 5-7 impressions for people to remember your brand, the quicker you can get on their screens through a variety of channels, the better.

Abandoned cart reminders

These are the emails that catch most of us online shoppers out. We have a little browse, adding items here and there to our basket as we go. Then our senses come back to us. We realise we don't need all that, so we close the app and put our phones to the side. But then, a few hours later, we get an email that says "did you forget about all this amazing stuff you're absolutely dying for? Come buy it now!" And we do.

Abandoned cart emails are ridiculously powerful. So powerful that they can recover around 10% of your lost revenue. And they can win customers over using a few different tactics. They might use urgency: "6 people bought this item in the past hour and there are only 4 left". The reason they get so specific is because humans respond best to numbers. It feels more real than just saying "be quick, this item's running out". Especially when every store implies items are running out all the time. It also stirs up feelings of FOMO (that's 'Fear Of Missing Out'). So including countdowns, especially on abandoned cart emails that are being sent during a sale or promotion, can really push the reader to make that snappy - maybe even a little impulsive - decision that results in them buying what they originally had second thoughts about.

Another technique is to sweeten the deal. "We noticed your interest in X, Y, and Z. If you're still debating, have this 15% off code on us. Every little bit helps!" Throw in a "this code is only valid for 48 hours" and you can simultaneously tap into the FOMO I mentioned above.

Follow-ups

Social proof is everything to a business. People respond so much better to impartial opinion and recommendations than they will to a business tooting its own horn. So, post-purchase, why not ask for a review to help boost your reputation? Here's where follow-up emails come in. Keep them clean, neat, easy to read, and obvious. Start with a short but sweet preamble saying how you hope they're loving their purchase. Then, just ask them outright to leave a review on the item they bought. Or for the wider business. No beating around the bush here. And, while you're at it, make it *easy* for them to do you this favour.

Leave a link or a "click here to review" button. Humans are lazy creatures and if something requires even the smallest bit of effort, when we aren't in the mood, we simply won't do it. So hand-feed them. Do most of the work ahead of time. You can even throw in an incentive in the form of a discount code to win them over. At the bottom of the email, you can also add products similar to what they've already bought in the hopes of winning some repeat custom.

Prompts to re-engage

You've probably got more than a handful of customers you haven't heard from in a while. Customers who haven't been on the website recently or bought something once and have since disappeared off the face of the Earth. But even though you've not seen them for months, these customers are still warmer than those who have never bought from you at all. Research shows that it costs five times more to acquire a new customer than it does to retain an old one. Also, while the success rate of selling to a new customer stands at 5-20%, for existing customers, it's 60-70%. So don't go counting yourselves out yet. There's still a chance. Use prompts to re-engage existing customers and showcase some irresistible offer. You could use discounts, a free product, or a raffle. Pick a perk and then centre the email around it.

Upsell offers

Your customer has already bought X. But Y would make it so much better. So tell them about it! It's a simple way to get the most out of your existing customers and boost revenue. And it doesn't even come across as upselling; you're just helping them out. There are plenty of tools and apps out there that allow you to segment your audience and put them on different lists. From here, you can use past purchase history or web pages viewed to send targeted emails and offers about the products they're more likely to be interested in. This also ties in to the personalisation we spoke about in the previous chapter. The more targeted your correspondence, the more valued your customers will feel, and the more motivated they will be to buy.

Just don't go overboard. Too many choices can have the opposite effect. You don't want your readers feeling overwhelmed as they may just close the email. Also, tailor any recommendations to their spending habits on past purchases. If your customer spends £10 here and there, they are unlikely to buy the product that's on sale for £1,000, for example.

Educational content

Educational content is a simple way to enrich your reader's life. Tricks, tips, and hacks can add value to their lives, building up a relationship and increasing the chances of them choosing you over a competitor. Eventually, they become an unpaid brand ambassador who waltzes around singing your praises to everyone they meet. This type of communication also makes your brand look a little more human. It makes for a refreshing change of pace from the more salesy content, showing a more helpful, friendly side. In markets where a lot of brands can come across as cold and detached, putting your customers first every once in a while can work wonders.

Also, with what you'll be well-versed to teach them, your audience can learn to make the most out of the products they've bought from you. This improves their experience, makes them trust you more, and will even boost the chances of a lovely testimonial from them. And these emails can be sent out based on customer interests and purchase history to boost personalisation and relevance. Brilliant.

If you're anything like me, during the COVID-19 lockdowns throughout 2020 and 2021 (depending on what your country did), you spent a fortune. Buying clothes, shoes, perfume, even though you're not going anywhere. Why? Because there were all these sneaky, exciting emails catching me at just the right time. As well as the ones listed above, there's a whole ecosystem of emails to consider to support your ecommerce site:

- Account set-up success
- Cart recovery
- Change email
- Forgotten password
- Guest checkout
- New account
- New credit note
- New invoice
- New order
- New order for guest
- New shipment request
- Newsletters
- Payment failed
- Post-purchase thank you
- Sale announcement
- Stock alert back in stock
- Subscription success
- Unsubscribe success
- User notification

At every point of a sale, potential or otherwise, there's another opportunity to communicate with your customers.

So spend a little extra time making sure your email marketing is shit hot to maximise the value of each customer long-term. Here's a round up of my dos and don'ts for your ecommerce emails.

Do start off building rapport

Even if you don't plan on doing half of the options above, *always* start off communications with a lighthearted welcome email. You truly can't understate the importance of building rapport with your audience before you jump into selling and pushing for action.

Don't forget about your brand's personality

Short and sweet ecommerce emails are perfect for getting some of your brand's personality across. Inject some humour if it feels right. Include a funny meme that made the rounds of the office last week. Take a satirical view of recent events. If your brand prides itself on its personality, try to incorporate at least a little of it into your emails.

Do tap into the interests of your target demographic

While there will always be outliers and exceptions to the rule, your brand's audience personas (if you don't have these, refer back to the *Business plan* section) should give a fairly clear picture of the types of people you're reaching with your emails. This provides plenty of insight into ways to better connect with your contacts. Is Netflix and chill their favourite pastime? Is it summertime and you just know your audience can be found every night curled up on the couch watching Love Island? Are they into travel, good food, going out for drinks, watching sport, or reading good books? These are all very generalised of course. But these subtle notes of reference can be incredible for relating to your audience and establishing rapport. Sure, some references might fall flat for some people, but for others, it could add some significant momentum to the relationship.

Don't leave your mailing lists collecting dust over time

Spring cleaning your mailing lists ensures you're not left with hundreds of cold contacts dragging your statistics down. By regularly revisiting your lists, you can remove those who, despite your best efforts over the past few months, don't want to engage anymore. You want to keep your contact list as up to date and relevant as possible. If you've got a ton of contacts from before your brand underwent a seismic shift in personality and product, it's probably time to let them go. you.

And that's cold ecommerce emails! When you've mastered them, you should see a healthy uptick in your email-led sales. That sounds like a win to me.

EMAIL FUNNELS

I haven't got enough fingers and toes to count the number of times I've heard potential clients say their email strategy is basically one long essay of EVERYTHING their business has to offer, followed by a tirade of phone calls and a monthly newsletter. And each person always carries the same air of disappointment and confusion as to why it's not working. Let's put you in the reader's seat for a minute. When was the last time you read past the second line of an email you weren't expecting, let alone line 28,753,489,653 of self-indulgent waffle?

Sending one email and expecting results is like walking up to a stranger in a room that's casually minding their own business, spouting your life story at them for fifteen minutes, then finishing with, "so what do you reckon, want to get into bed with me?" You'd look mental, right? A far better approach is to gently introduce yourself. You have a light conversation and set up the next one. Over time, you get to know one another better, conversations get deeper, and eventually you may or may not seal the deal.

Your email marketing strategy should follow the exact same process. Metaphorically, of course. The chances are that what you're already sending is good to a degree. But don't say everything in one email; split it over four or five over a period of time. Instead of force-feeding them a buffet, drip feed your reader little bits to keep them interested. This is what's called an email marketing funnel. It may seem like a good idea to jump ahead. But life isn't that easy. There's a process for a reason. And a big part of that is because people don't trust businesses they've never heard of before. You need to nurture the relationship and give it time to grow more organically.

If you aren't familiar with marketing your business through an email funnel, you want to take your reader on a journey that follows four steps.

Awareness

The problem with cold emailing someone is there's a good chance they have no idea who you are. Either they've forgotten that one time they gave you their email or they just straight up don't have the foggiest. So your first priority is making them aware of exactly who you are. But how? The good news is a lot of the content you already have can be repurposed into a quick insight into your business. The about page on your website? A great opening paragraph. A blog about a problem you can solve? Fantastic for adding context about what you're all about. Words, images, and videos are all fine to use again.

These are perfect examples of raising awareness of your company amongst cold leads. And it means you don't have to create entirely new pieces of content every time your emails need a refresh. But it doesn't just save you time; it can help the customer too. We all learn information in different ways. Some of us have to hear it, some need to read it, some need to figure it out for themselves. By recycling your content, you can put it into as many forms as possible, helping your audience better understand you, and likely increasing your reach past a very select demographic. What's important in this opening email is that you don't sell a product or service. You're here to share your value and - more importantly - the benefits of what you provide.

Engagement

In your next email, you want to encourage the recipient to engage with your brand. Again, this isn't the time to sell. You want to create an interactive experience for them that either entertains or informs. Think downloads, quizzes, how-tos, or FAQs. Say you're a clothing company sending an email about this season's fashion. Maybe you could create a flowchart that helps them find what accessories they should wear on a night out. The topic is adjacent to what you do, but you aren't pushing anything. You're just helping them! You want them to engage with what you're doing and build a positive impression of you.

Consideration

You had their curiosity, but now you have their attention. It's time to ramp it up another notch. Now you want them to start considering buying from or working with you. Again, it's still not the time for the hard sell. You're on their radar and now it's time to use testimonials, case studies, blog posts, and more to help them understand your product and gently nudge them towards a decision. For example, if you have three different products that have the same purpose, create comparison videos. Or you might be a construction company who just finished a project - perfect time for a case study that shows them how much of an amazing job you did.

Purchase

Now is the time to push your contacts over the edge and encourage them to take action. Be that schedule a demo, call, buy from you, or come onboard as a client. Your final email is you at your most bold; you say what you mean and you do so with the intention of closing the deal. It's called a funnel for a reason. It starts very wide at the top and narrows as you go down. That's what you're trying to do with these emails. You start with general and light content that introduces the reader to who you are. You're not looking to overphase them with too much information. You want them to **learn** about you so they feel confident in who you are before committing to buying your product or service. You're educating them softly through different formats, and guiding them, hopefully, towards a purchase, or whatever action it is you're looking for them to take.

That's your general structure sorted. But now it's time to think about what to write. Before you begin, here are some dos and don'ts for your email marketing funnel.

Do look to add value to your audience

Like with ecommerce emails, sending an email funnel is *obviously* going to be centred around your business and service offering. But let's not forget about another critical component here: your reader. You want your funnel to add value to them, over and above handing them your business offering on a silver platter. Whether they come away a client or not, you want your mailing list to reach the end of the funnel with greater insight, awareness, and resources surrounding your industry or service.

Don't forget to revisit your funnel

As with anything, change is only natural. Your email funnel should never remain stagnant. Over time, your business will grow, you'll produce new, more relevant content you want to include, and how your audience best interacts with your brand might shift. Regularly revisiting your funnel and tweaking your approach ensures you're always getting the most out of your efforts - reaching the right people, at the right time, in the right ways. You want to evaluate every six months to a year, at least. This way, you can check if it's still working for you and what might need adjusting.

The funnel is your trick to drawing customers in and closing deals slowly. Keep this advice in mind and watch as your email strategy changes in front of your eyes.

EVENT PROMOTION

You heard through the grapevine that events are a brilliant way to build brand awareness, strengthen customer relationships, and generate new revenue. You even read that 31% of marketers consider events to be their most effective marketing channel. And naturally, you wanted to give it a go for yourself. But you're now a few events deep, and they just aren't achieving the buzz you'd hoped for. Let's change that.

The chances are this has very little to do with the events themselves, and more to do with how you're promoting them. When it comes to promoting events, you get back what you put in. While some established brands can do very little promotion and still secure high attendance, most of us don't have that luxury. We have to put in that extra effort to stand out in the ever-growing events space. Regardless of whether it's virtual or in-person, promoting them across your channels will look the same. So let's get straight to it.

Iron out your who, why, and what

Before you begin promoting your event, there are three important questions to ask. This will be an extension of the work you've already done to get under the skin of your audience.

Who? - Who is this event for? Who **isn't** it for? Who are the speakers (if any)?

Why? - Why should someone attend this event? What's in it for them? What about their current situation are you looking to improve? How will they be better off after attending?

What? - What will the event include? What subject matter will be covered? What format is the event going to take? What does the itinerary look like?

Answering these questions will help you approach your promotional content from the perspective of your audience. Showing people that you understand them, and demonstrating that you're in a position to help, is how you will get people excited to attend your events. And the more excited your attendees are, the more likely they are to share the invite around their own networks.

Go where your audience already is

You've already worked hard to build a following on Instagram, your podcast averages 100 listeners per episode, and your company blog has a dedicated following. Why waste all this hard work? Start integrating your events into your existing content strategies. Going where your audience already is allows you to profit off all the hard work you've already done. Rather than pitching your event to people who have no idea who you are, pitch it to people who already know and trust in your authority and value.

In the lead-up to your events, try adding one or two event-related posts a week into your social media strategies. The goal here isn't for event promotion to be the main takeaway. You want to add value first and be a tad self-promotional second. Pick a theme that's relevant to the event and create an educational, engaging post around it. Then, mention your upcoming event in the CTA as a way to find out even more. Why not publish a series of blogs to introduce some of the core ideas your event will tackle? These could go out weekly or monthly, depending how far away the event is. With these, you want to offer just enough insight to build trust and show people you know your stuff, while leaving enough unknowns to encourage event registrations.

By staggering this content over the weeks or months leading up to your event, you'll be able to catch people at different stages. Someone who missed your event announcement on LinkedIn might learn about it for the first time on your Instagram a week before. Another person might have planned to sign up when you originally announced but has since forgotten. Seeing an event-related blog post could be the reminder they need to sign up. Others might take a while to come round to your event. In this case, mentioning it consistently and adding value surrounding the event's premise could help win them over.

Create a landing page

Landing pages give you somewhere to send prospective attendees once you've piqued their interest. Whenever you're plugging the event, you can link people to a professional landing page to find out more. You can even include a registration form on this page to make signing up as easy and convenient as possible. You'll find full guidance on writing for landing pages in the designated section. But for the purposes of event promotion, your landing page should include the following:

- A snappy headline that conveys the core challenge your event will resolve. For example, *"Be a part of the pack: the ulti-mutt dog convention in the UK."*
- A brief blurb on what the event is about and how it will add value. Try to include some relatable storytelling to attract the right audience.

- The key takeaways your audience can expect. This might be a bullet point list of the topics covered.
- A list of speakers (if there are any). Include a brief blurb on main speakers - especially if they're well-known and likely to attract an audience.
- Event info - the when, where, and what of it all. Include an itinerary if you have one.
- Next steps. How can people sign up?

Use your mailing list

If you have a mailing list, it'll be a powerful tool when spreading the word about upcoming events. These are people who have already engaged with your business in some way. They will already have some degree of brand trust and awareness, making them far easier to win over. You have a few options when it comes to promoting your events through email:

- Newsletters - You could send out a stand alone newsletter dedicated to the event. Or you can set aside a single section of your monthly newsletters in the lead-up to the event, tackling a different angle or selling point each time. Check out the *Newsletters* section for more guidance.
- Email funnels - Email funnels can be brilliant at securing extra registrations. They give you multiple chances to win people over and allow you to drip

feed information to build anticipation. I usually find that three is the sweet spot.

#1 - Introduce the event. Include a brief synopsis of what it'll include. This might be sent a month or two in advance, or whenever you first announce.

#2 - A few weeks/days later, send a follow-up email. This will be similar to the first, but should dive deeper into the tangible value attendees can expect to gain. You might also include an announcement of any top speakers and the itinerary if this has now been confirmed.

#3 - Best sent a day or two before the event if virtual, or before registrations close if it's in-person. This is a final reminder. It's the perfect opportunity to create a sense of urgency. You can check out the *Email marketing* section for more guidance.

Another quick trick is to include a brief headline about your event and link to the corresponding landing page in your email signature. That way, whenever someone hears from you, they also get a little reminder. Now for some dos and don'ts to keep in mind while working on your event promotion.

Do focus on benefits

Rather than simply listing all the topics that will be covered during an event, you want to tell your reader why the insight gained will make their life or career better. Focus on the tangible benefits they can expect as a result of the knowledge or experience. Your event breaks down the psychology of communication? Great! But what will that mean for my business? Will I be one step closer to establishing a more engaged, productive business? Will I be able to take my leadership to the next level and set the foundations for a more compassionate work environment?

Don't miss out... on FOMO

As people, we hate to feel like we're missing out. And this can be a powerful emotion to tap into with your event promotion. By specifying how many people have already registered or how many expert speakers you have on board, you make your reader feel as if they're missing an opportunity by not attending. Sharing how many people attended a previous event or releasing testimonials that say what a great time past attendees had will have a similar effect.

Do be consistent

How many of us have signed up to a free online event that we never ended up attending? Mentioning your event consistently across your social channels helps keep it front and centre in your audience's minds. If someone begins to lose excitement, a new post will come along and reignite it.

Don't be persistent

That being said, you don't want to take this too far. Sending daily emails for the two months prior to an event or *only* posting about your event is one way to ensure people are over it before it's even begun.

Do plan ahead for future event promotion

With each event you host, you have an opportunity to increase the momentum of your next. By asking attendees to complete a survey after an event, you'll gain valuable statistics and testimonials to help hype up future ones.

187

A large network doesn't guarantee you event registrations. Neither does putting on one-of-a-kind events. It's how you promote and build awareness of your events that determines whether or not they're a raging success. Follow these tips and you'll be dominating the events calendar in no time.

GENERAL WRITTEN COMMUNICATION

We've talked about emails in general. We've covered ecommerce emails specifically, and walked through a marketing funnel. Now we're looking at general, near-instant written communication - such as emails, WhatsApp, and instant messaging. This is likely going to be with people you already know on a professional level, typically in a one-on-one situation. And how you can communicate with them effectively and cut down on those "what is this person on about?" moments.

When it comes to communication, we like to be spoken to how we like to speak to others. Anything else is never going to register as well. And the same goes for all faster-paced written communication. Be it emails between coworkers or among clients, WhatsApp messages, or instant messaging on any internal system, such as Slack. Using the colour system covered in the *Research* pillar, we already know that if you're a red, you're likely to send a straight-to-the-point message to save time. If you're a blue, chances are your message will be more on the chatty side. As a green, you're thinking you're being helpful by including **every** detail. And if you're a yellow, trying to book a meeting with you probably takes five or six messages (at least) because you're too busy trying to plan around the other person.

The challenge with these differing approaches to communication is that unless you're talking to another you, you're likely coming across in a way you're not meaning to, without really even realising it. But first, how many of these are you guilty of?

The one-liner response

In your mind, you're just being efficient. You've got something simple to say. In, out, jobs a good 'un. How you're landing is entirely different. For others that don't think like you, you look overly pissed off. Short, cold, and blunt, when they're used to communicating with warmth and friendliness. People might wonder what they've done to trigger you, spending the day worried and mentally scrolling back through past interactions to see if everything's OK. This obsessive anxiety on the part of your recipient is not only stressful, but it's taking time out of their day unnecessarily.

The super chatty, rambling essay

We've all seen these. Walls of text that don't actually say anything. Or, they do, but it's hidden underneath tonnes of ramble. They always tend to land when you're in the middle of juggling a hundred jobs at once, don't they? We're all busy people. If you're emailing someone who's already got 20 things on their plate, your rambling thoughts certainly won't help. Unless this is the norm for your communication with someone, it can be an incredibly inefficient way to talk. There's a fine line between friendliness and testing someone's patience. Based on these last two examples, it's safe to say there's a balance to strike between communication that's overly long or short. You want to say enough to actually answer someone's question and provide adequate help or support, but avoid wasting their time by sending over a block of text.

Ten messages when one would have done

Which of these would you rather?

Person A: I'm free Thursday if you are?
Person B: Thursday works, what time?
Person A: Most of the day I'm free!
Person B: Me too, whenever works best for you.
Person A: How about 3 p.m.?
Person B: Ah, I'm leaving early. Can we do 11:30 a.m.?
Person A: Tell you what, let's make it 11 a.m.
Person B: OK, perfect.
Person A: Can you put it in my diary?

OR

Person A: Sounds great, I'm free 11:30 a.m. on Thursday, if you are? I've put it in the diary just in case. If this works for you, great, otherwise I'm free after 3 p.m. Or I have 9 a.m. to 3 p.m. tomorrow or 4 p.m. Thursday. Just let me know.

Person B: *Diary invite accepted*

Why are we making life so complicated for ourselves? Now I'll admit, this second approach will come more naturally to a red or a blue character. For greens and yellows, it may feel a tad aggressive. But it's quite the contrary. By being assertive, trying to nail down a plan quickly, while still offering the recipient freedom of choice, you're saving them time and stress, and making your communication more streamlined. The average office worker gets around 121 emails a day. The more we can all do to minimise the amount of messages flitting back and forth, the better for *all* of us.

Death by facts

We're all familiar with the expression 'death by PowerPoint'. Find me one person (other than a green) that gets turned on by the idea of sitting through a 100-slide presentation. Sometimes, a lot of information can't be avoided. But, if it is required, you don't have to send an email long enough to cause RSI while the recipient scrolls through it all. Perhaps just pick up the phone or schedule a Zoom or coffee?

Or, if written communication (probably email in this case) is your only option, break it down into attachments and summarise with bullet points what the reader needs to know on the attached email. This way, they don't need a palaeontology degree to dig out your key points and can read the sections most relevant to them. You're giving them a choice, not smothering them in facts that are important to you, but not necessarily to them.

The message for message's sake

Most workplaces are slowly joining the 21st century when it comes to in-person meetings. Many are realising there's no need to waste people's time by having them sit in a room talking about something that isn't even relevant to them. Messages however, haven't quite caught up at the same speed. Unless you need something to have a paper trail, have some courtesy for others and stop clogging up their inboxes. No one likes coming back to 100+ messages after their weekend. Or even their lunch in really dire situations. And if we all pledge to stop being part of the problem, the world of professional communications will slowly become a better place.

Before hitting send on a message, think to yourself: can I find the answer out myself? Can I Google it? Figure it out? Or have I already asked this before and can refer back to my old notes? Is this *definitely* the person to ask? Or will they simply pass me along to someone else? Can I just go to that person directly? Just because it's quicker for you to ask someone else doesn't mean it's the right course of action. Be respectful of people's time and attention, just like you'd want them to be of yours. Your professional relationships will thank us for this tip later.

Sharing urgent, important messages via email

How often do you lose an email in your cavernous inbox? Perhaps you read it, thought "I'll pick that up after lunch", and never thought about it again. Or maybe you never even noticed it come in. This is exactly why urgent, important messages shouldn't take place in email inboxes. As a form of communication, it's become far too unreliable and concentrated with spam. What if an essential task gets missed and your business's productivity takes a real hit? If it's a time-sensitive or critical matter, leave it out of the inbox. Opt for a phone call or text message instead.

Replying to all when all don't need to see your reply

When you're working on a group project, or want to share information with multiple parties, CC'ing a lot of people can be necessary. But, equally, there are times we find our inboxes pinging over a thread we've never engaged with, and likely never will engage with or even read. Just because a lot of people are CC'd on an email doesn't always mean all these people need to see your response. Use your best judgement here, but avoid replying to all when really you're just planning a meeting with one person, for example. The same goes for any group chats. Ask yourself: is this really a group-appropriate message? Will everyone else benefit from it? Or is it best taken over to an individual chat?

Why should I care?

You might be thinking it's not your responsibility or concern how people receive your communications, but actually, it's precisely your job. As a writer (unofficially or otherwise), you should always be writing with your audience in mind, even in seemingly minor daily correspondence. You want an answer, some information, to schedule a meeting, to share feedback with your team, and that's cool. But you maximise your chances of achieving whatever your goal is by putting the other person or people first. How you do this in any instant correspondence is easy. It's a simple trick I learned from Tony Robbins.

To instantly build rapport with people, you need to communicate with them as they do. Going back to our subconscious liking of - or aversion to - certain people, if you interact with someone as they would with you, they're more likely to be receptive and give you what you want. They'll be far more likely to absorb what you're saying, and the whole exchange will become effortless. In the same fashion that we don't notice our heart beating - it just happens - when we start to build rapport, we subconsciously become more responsive to one another too. That's the crux of this advice in theory. In practice, this is about matching and mirroring the person you're speaking to.

In person, this might look like breathing at the same pace or sitting with a similar posture to build instant connection. When it comes to writing, our approach needs to be a little bit different as we have fewer cues to go off. You can't rely on body language and presence. But what you can do is look at how they communicate and match it. If someone is formal and starts every email with "Hello Alia", then respond in kind with their name and mirror their sign off. If they send you a single-line email, you know sending one back will be perfectly OK as they're clearly a red and you're matching them. If they're asking questions and circling around details, then they're clearly a green. In response, you can slow the aggressive sales tactics down and provide them the details they need, while remaining more subtly assertive. If they're blue and hit you with a wall of text, you don't have to do it back because that just wastes everyone's time. But the cues you can take are that it's fine to become a little more socially familiar and share anecdotes or pictures of your dog should the opportunity arise.

In short: give back what you get. Adapt your communication to meet that of your recipient. The structure of a text or WhatsApp message is relatively straightforward. They should resemble a Tweet. If you're sending a wall of text, stop and think: can you communicate this in a better way? Is this conversation better suited to a call? Or a voice note if that's more convenient? Perhaps, if you're finding yourself having the same conversations over and over, you can instead create a simple infographic to send, or an explainer video while recording your screen. When it comes to emails, the structure doesn't have to be complicated.

Greeting

Try to match the formality of their tone.

Quick, polite one-liner that links why you're there

"*I hope you're enjoying the sunshine! Following on from our call on Monday, please find our finished presentation attached.*" If you're talking to someone you're already familiar with, a quick sentence to add warmth can also be included here.

A short paragraph or two that summarises what you want

"In our presentation, you'll find both our X and Y range which are soon to launch. I think you'll love them." If you find that you're writing a wall of text again, the same applies as did for instant messaging. How can you convey this message more effectively and respectfully for your reader?

A polite sign-off that drives an assertive call-to-action

"Once you've had a chance to digest, let's arrange a call to discuss. I have Tuesday 10 a.m. available. How does that sound?" The exception here is if it's an in-and-out email that doesn't need this.

Finish the email

"Warm regards, [your name]." Try and avoid something short like "best", unless they're that way inclined.

It's a simple trick, but one that works well the majority of the time. By talking to them at their level, you'll be surprised how quickly they warm to you. Before we round out this section, here are just a couple of quick tips.

198

Do know when to take the lead

Emails and instant messaging are a simple waltz. If you want a perfect 10 from Craig Revel Horwood, let your partner lead the way. If you're the one messaging them first and you don't know what kind of communicator they are, dig into their online persona and see what you can find.

Don't be disrespectful of anyone's time

As a rule of thumb, imagine everyone you're in contact with is super busy 100% of the time. This way, you'll naturally challenge yourself to be as succinct and clear as possible. Whether it's an email, text message, or anything else, say what you *need* to say and nothing more. If you've got a lot of information to get across, think whether a phone call or Zoom might be better. Or attach the bulk of your information as an attachment and send a simple bullet point list overview in the body of the email.

By adapting our communication style according to who we're speaking to, we can save time, stop leaving people feeling frustrated or disrespected, and more effectively achieve whatever we've set out to. Everyone's a winner.

HANDBOOKS

At some point, we've all found ourselves screaming at our new wonky IKEA furniture that just doesn't look right. Why does it look like that? How can anyone follow these instructions? They're stupid. It doesn't look *anything* like the picture. What does *that* even mean? This makes no sense! You get the picture. Obviously, you don't want to frustrate or practically traumatise your readers with your handbook, so let's look at how to do one *right*.

Handbooks are there for the user to reference during times of need. They're for guidance. And they exist for just about anything and everything. Whether they're called a handbook, manual, or instruction booklet, at the end of the day, they all have the same purpose. Here are just a few types of handbooks:

- Product handbook
- Instruction manual
- Installation guide
- Troubleshooting booklet
- User manual
- Crisis management guide
- Employee handbook

Putting everything someone needs to know into words is a simple concept but a daunting thought. And to do it in a way that's easy to understand? You don't want to be like the wonky IKEA furniture. If the reader doesn't understand what you're trying to say, they'll either give up and have a poor opinion of your brand or waste your staff's time by calling customer support. Or in the case of an employee handbook, they'll work less efficiently or have to bug their manager. So your goal is to make something that's functional, clear, and usable. I'm just going to go over the two most common examples and the ones you're more likely to find yourself writing. But the tips can be applied to every type of manual or guide, so keep them in mind. Let's start with employee handbooks.

Employee handbooks

While these seem like a no-brainer, there are still ways to get them wrong. 43% of people don't read the entire employee handbook. And 11% don't even bother to turn the first page. Why? Let's be real, they're often boring, difficult to understand, or too long. Sometimes even all three. You want to create something that has a natural flow to it and explains everything staff need to know in the best way possible. But where do you even start? When you've created the company or been working there for a few years, you don't realise how much you just *know*. Someone new isn't going to have that luxury. So here are a few facts you might want to include:

- Company policies
- Terms of employment
- Paid time off
- Discipline
- Safety
- Dress code
- Social media and use of mobile phones
- Ethics
- Equality and discrimination

You might use just these, you might be able to think of more. That's down to your business, but remember to include what they would want to know. There are some areas - like equality, discrimination, and sexual harassment - where it isn't a joke. Remember to be tactful and in no uncertain terms make your policies clear. There's a time and a place for humour. When addressing topics like these, it's actually better to be transparent. Simply stating that you don't tolerate certain behaviours in a simple, conversational way will get through to more of your employees. They know what you expect and exactly what it is you don't tolerate. That's as clear as it gets.

And that advice goes for the entire piece. Use your handbook to speak to your staff like they're people. Because they are. Unless there's been a sudden rise in the robot population that I missed. You're telling them what you expect from them as valued members of your company, but also what *they* can expect from *you*. An employee handbook isn't just barking orders; it's letting your staff know what you do for them and how you're available to help. Achieving success is a joint effort. Now, let's look at some dos and don'ts for your employee handbook.

Do keep it short

This one's fairly straightforward. If you catch yourself writing a lot, just stop. It's that simple.

Don't bore your staff

What are the chances the handbooks that 43% of people don't read are plain white documents with pages full of text? I'd say it's pretty high. Some people seem to view their brand's image and tone of voice as something just for the customers or clients. But it should be for the staff too. The easy way to not bore them is to bring your handbook to life. Add some colour, images, infographics - anything to make it jump off the page. If you think it suits, a bit of humour will go a long way too. Whatever you write should reflect who you are as a company. This:

a) gives new staff a feel for the company culture, and
b) passively teaches them how they need to talk to customers.

Do make your handbook easy to understand

Again, the entire point of a handbook is to cut out questions and help employees understand something on their own. So don't go throwing in a bunch of big words because it looks good. Simple language makes your handbook accessible to all. Be clear. Is there an app that clocks your employees' hours? Tell them. Are they paid by the year and expected to work 9-5? Tell them. Putting the information plainly is key. Don't say "Here at X, we have a flexible work-and-have-fun style. You're always free to work how you want." Okay, so can I work in the evenings? On the weekends? How much room do I have?

Instead, create clarity by saying: "Here at X, we want you to work flexibly. As long as you log 8 hours a day on Monday through Friday in the online portal, we're happy." Do you see the difference? Clear instructions are much better and cut through the double-speak and waffle. This will be an ongoing project for you. When it's finished, make a point to revisit it every year to make sure it reflects who you are as a business, what you want your employees to be, and how your business works.

Product manuals

What does that button do? How do I change the time? What if it stops working? These are the kind of questions your users will undoubtedly ask about your product, and it's your job to predict what they'll need. So you'll have to do a bit of soul searching to figure out *exactly* what you're hoping to teach the user. Is it a manual for how to use the product? Or is it about repairing it? If it's a new microwave, run through all the features to ensure you don't miss any. Whereas if you try to write off-the-cuff, you're more likely to forget something.

Then you need to identify every single step you want the reader to take. For example, if your product is a piece of tech, you might start with unpackaging the product then list all the steps that get the user to the point of switching the product on. Or you might go further and guide them through the setup process. Here are some quick dos and don'ts to get you started.

Do use images

Sometimes certain steps can be too complicated to describe. This is where graphics come in. Imagine you were trying to explain to the reader that they need to flick the little switch at the back, but not the one they think, the other one. The one that's, like, next to the little knob, but not the red knob, the one that's kind of underneath, but not quite - do you see where I'm going with this? Words just won't do it justice sometimes. Pictures save you and your readers a lot of time and effort. They're especially useful if they're telling users how to build something.

Don't forget to test

Once you've written out each step, test your own instructions. Try it multiple times or, better yet, ask someone else to do it. Testing your instructions will always be the best way to see their effectiveness. And the more people that try it, the better. Everyone's brain works differently so just because one person thinks your instructions are amazing doesn't mean they'll work for everyone.

Do include an intro and conclusion

By this stage, you'll have written the bulk of the product manual. You'll have covered each step and developed appropriate graphics to make the manual as easy to understand as possible. But this is only the middle. You still need an intro and a conclusion. It might just be a simple manual, but like two bookends on a shelf, you need something to hold it all together. What you include in your intro and conclusion is up to you, but generally, the intro includes a thank you to the customer for buying the product and a general overview of the product. And the conclusion could include warranty details, details on how to get in contact with the company, and disclaimers. FAQ and troubleshooting sections aren't uncommon either.

Once you've got an intro and a conclusion down, you're done! Enjoy your product manual - and I'm sure your audience will too.

HEADLINES

Headlines can be the most important part of whatever you're writing. If they have one, of course. If it doesn't, then you might be lost. The section on packaging is *that* way. But back to headlines. Think about it. If you read one and it doesn't resonate with you, you won't click on it. And neither will your audience. In less than a split second (most of the time), we decide whether or not this piece of content is worth 30 seconds to scan through. More often than not, we'll come to the conclusion it isn't. Even if your blog post can solve all your readers' problems and add unprecedented amounts of value to their lives, they won't click on it if the headline isn't up to scratch. Unless there's an intriguing headline to hook their interest.

Many writers struggle to find the right balance. They either make their headlines as dull as dishwater - going a bit too literal with what the post is about - or it'll resemble a spam email subject line - "Change your LIFE right NOW". The latter just screams clickbait, which people have learnt to ignore, while the former gets much the same response.

Getting those clicks

Before we get into how to write a great headline, let's talk about clickbait for a second. Clickbait has been around as long as the internet has. Or, at least, the version of the internet we recognise today. The actual definition of clickbait is: "content whose main purpose is to attract attention and encourage visitors to click on a link to a particular web page." Personally, I don't think this is a great definition. Every piece of content wants to attract attention. I didn't spend three hours on a blog for no one to click on it.

Instead, clickbait to me is when a title or headline *over-promises or lies* to get clicks. So, if you're worried you've written a clickbait title, ask yourself if the "answer" to the headline can be found in the content and if the excitement the headline generates is matched. For example, a headline that generates too much excitement might be: "This new vacuum cleaner will BLOW YOUR MIND". That's pretty exciting, right? I know I'm excited. But how exactly will a vacuum cleaner "blow my mind"? You've over-promised. I'm expecting to be blown away by a common household machine that I've seen every other day for years. It just won't happen. But let's say this vacuum cleaner truly is mindblowing. Maybe it reverses global warming or cures deadly diseases or something. It still probably wouldn't be a good idea to use this headline. We're used to seeing headlines that promise the world, and have been conditioned to block them out. Too much enthusiasm and excitement brings out our inner sceptic.

We need to find a balance where we're hooking our audience and creating a buzz around our content *without* overselling it entirely. If you followed pillar one to a tee, then you should know what your audience wants to see. Right now, they don't *know* they need this blog, newsletter, or whatever you've written. So you need to convince them they do. One trick is to nail down the main benefit of your article. How will reading this add value to your readers? "This daily five-minute routine will help stop you from ever being late again". Okay, this headline is a little long, but you get the gist. It's specific - a five-minute routine. And there's a benefit - to never be late again.

Ideally, you should spend as much time as possible crafting your headline. It can be the difference between a post that gets your most clicks and shares ever or a post that goes straight to the grave. It's an art. And art can't be rushed. This is why so many people aren't any good at it. It's a skill you develop over time; no one's born a fantastic headline writer. It should also be the last part you write. How do you write an enticing summary for something that doesn't even exist yet? You can't. And if you try, more often than not, your piece will end up being something entirely different and you'll have to rewrite the headline anyway. Or your content will suffer as you try to cram it into a headline that doesn't quite fit. Save yourself the time, effort, and trouble and write it last.

If you need some help getting the creative juices flowing, I have a list of different types of headlines you can use, along with an example of how they work. Each one is enticing in its own way and, combined with the right words, can work extremely well.

The listicle
"5 ways to write an amazing headline"

The teacher
"Everything you need to know about headlines"

The how-to
"5 steps to improving your headlines"

The speedy how-to
"3 simple steps to writing better headlines"

The how-not-to
"5 things you shouldn't be doing in your headlines"

The contrarian
"Why your headline isn't as big a deal as you think"

The storyteller
"How I turned my blog around with engaging headlines"

The case study
"How one company improved their headlines"

The insider
"What you need to know about your headlines"

The outsider
"What the experts have to say about headlines"

The scientist
"What this survey tells us about headlines"

The sceptic
"Do headlines even matter anymore?"

The meerkat
"We compare which headlines work best"

The Q&A
"10 common questions about headlines"

The FAQ
"Headlines: an FAQ"

The dos and don'ts
"The 4 dos of writing headlines (and 4 don'ts!)"

The choice
"Short or long: what should your headline be?"

211

Let's be clear, there's no one-size-fits-all title that's instantly going to make your piece a winner. Without writing something actually good following our other advice, no headline can save the day. This alone will not guarantee an article's success. Take them more as an outline you can use and inject your own content and creative flair into. Playing around with different types of headlines can help diversify your content and keep your audience engaged. If an insider-secrets-style piece doesn't go down well with one reader, perhaps a comparison piece will. Mixing up headlines also means you can easily recycle your content. You can take parts of an old blog - say a simple "what is" piece - and use it in a new one, changing the angle to an FAQ.

Finding the perfect headline

So let's look at it a little bit deeper. You have the style of headline you want to write, now you just need to pick the right words. My advice would be to take advantage of human psychology. There are plenty of ways you can do this. First, try to make your headline emotional. But only when the time's right, obviously. Don't go writing emotional headlines about mundane topics. "Woman discovers heartwarming toilet-cleaning hack" just sounds insane. But if emotion *can* tie into it, go for it. Emotional headlines get higher engagement. Or add an element of mystery. Again, if it works for the content, withhold some information. If the headline tells the reader *exactly* what the story is, why would they click on it? We're naturally inquisitive creatures, use this to your advantage by leaving just enough unknowns to encourage those clicks.

Questions work well, too. Bearing in mind many people search using Siri or Google Assistant, the way we search for content online is changing. On a desktop computer, you might just type in random words that don't even make a full sentence. Like "best bars London". But, when we use assistants, we're more likely to speak in full sentences, such as "what are the best bars in London?" When you phrase your headline as a question, you're more likely to show up in the results. And did you know that headlines with odd numbers in them outperform ones with even numbers? For whatever reason, odd number lists outperform even ones by 20%. Maybe that's because we view odd numbers as more random or intriguing. If you have the headline "The eight best gin cocktails to try this summer", try to find another or take one away.

Once you've written your headline, there are plenty of online tools that will grade it for you. CoSchedule, Sharethrough, and Capitalize My Title, to name a few. They're just robots, so don't take their advice as gospel, but they can be quite helpful for identifying obvious areas for improvement. Now you've got the hang of headline writing, it's time to refine your skill further. Here are some tips to take your headlines from good to great.

Do write headlines that are eight words long

Okay, your blog won't tank if it's nine or even five words long. But, for some reason, eight seems to be the magic number. Headlines with eight words receive a 21% higher click-through rate than average. And a separate study showed titles with 6-13 words attract both the highest and most consistent amount of traffic. So keeping it around that number should help.

Don't settle for the first headline you write

Write a few. Play around with it. Mess around with the order of your words. You might think you've written the perfect headline, but after a few more tries, you write one that's miles better. Since this is the most important part to draw people in, don't just go with the first idea that springs to mind.

Do put your keyword at the start of your headline

You can use a colon to separate it from the rest of the title. Like, "writing headlines: what not to do". I Googled "what to blog about" and the top result used this trick. And I got a similar result when I Googled "keywords". It just works. The reader can see at a glance that your content is what they're looking for. It's more eye-catching.

Again, the perfect headline comes with practice. And even after writing a hundred, there's still going to be room for improvement. It takes time to master. But if you follow these guidelines, you'll be on track to writing killer headlines in no time.

INFOGRAPHICS

No matter who you're talking to with your content, one aspect remains the same. Everyone who views your work is human. And humans are visual creatures. Sometimes we really *do* like to read books with pictures. So often, audiences will scan through a webpage or social media feed in the hunt for eye-catching graphics and images, bypassing chunks of text entirely. We like the information we need to be delivered to us on a silver platter, easily digestible and concise. That's what makes something like Instagram so great - you can just scroll for hours in bed and still absorb content without reading. And would you look at that, it's 3 a.m. somehow.

It's why infographics work so well. They're incredibly powerful tools, and there are plenty of ways you can use them. Attach them to emails so you can draw attention to the important points. Or share them on social media to drive traffic towards your website. But a successful infographic needs to add value first and foremost. Reader's should come away thinking "I've learned something new". And with your business now on their radar. Add enough value over a period of time and you'll start to see more interest in your products and services.

What makes for a good infographic? It should accomplish two goals: it needs to be sexy and it needs to be clear. If it looks crap, people are going to scan right past it. If it reads even worse, you're not going to keep your reader's attention for long. It's a delicate balance to strike between the visuals and copy. Despite being a predominantly visual medium, it's still something that needs writing. Images and graphs only tell your reader so much. It's up to you to fill in the gaps, help your reader understand *why* they should care, and create a narrative. Which is why your accompanying copy needs to be up to scratch. Writing that's clear and easy to digest is the name of the game here. If your usual content (blogs, social media, website copy) is your 23kg packed suitcase, your infographics should be the hand luggage. It should be a basic, topline overview of your chosen topic.

Let's look at the basic structure. With each section, you're looking to secure your reader's interest enough to encourage them to keep reading the rest.

Headline

Like any blog or article, you need to instantly draw attention to your infographic with an engaging, relevant headline. You can check the *Headline* section for more help here. Just hop back a section and you'll find it.

Introduction

Below your headline should be a short, sweet, yet powerful introduction. Just a few sentences that serve as an extension of your headline explaining why this is a topic worth discussing and offering some context for the information to follow. Spell out in these few sentences what value the reader gets from your infographic. What common problem will it address? And how will the content solve all their woes? For an extra punch, include your most hard-hitting statistics here.

Main body

This will make up the bulk of your infographic, and will contain multiple sections. This is where you break down all the information, data, and insights you want to share. Take extra care when organising your thoughts and data. The best infographics tell a story, taking readers on a journey. Say you're a software company. And you're creating an infographic about the effects of forced downtime on businesses. Slow emails, dodgy systems, you know the culprits. You just so happen to have the best solution on the market. But your audience doesn't realise just how bad their problem is. So to reach them, you make an infographic. You might have sections following this structure:

- Addressing the issue
- Outlining industry data regarding the problem

- What impacts might these problems be having on businesses?
- What is best practice for optimising productivity?
- What specific solutions are out there to combat forced downtime?
- What are the pros and cons of some different solutions?
- Your top tips for moving forward

Since this is an infographic, your ideas (preferably) need to be supported by statistics. If you can, put this into a visual form, too - a graph or pie chart would work well. So you might say "50% of people believe outdated tech is hurting their productivity at work". That's sure to get their attention. Important to note however, is that sprinkling in facts and figures and leaving it at that isn't the goal here. Statistics can be excellent at backing up your thoughts and adding weight to what you have to say. But it's up to you to explain why your reader should care about them and what it means for them.

But including stats *isn't* always a non-negotiable. Sometimes, you simply won't be able to find cold, hard data to back you up, nor the time or resources to collect that data yourself. In this case, bullet points with iconography can be equally as effective. "How outdated tech could be slowing you down", for example. By doing so, you're still positioning yourself as the authoritative voice.

Closing thoughts

You have two options here. One: keep this generic and avoid a more transparent sales pitch. Or two: tie this back into your business and push a bit harder for your readers to take action. For the former, this will be a few sentences that mirror your introduction, tying together the points you've made and reflecting on what the data you've shared shows. The latter may involve this, too. But then you might introduce your own business as an essential helping hand for the problem you've addressed. Using the example above, you've shared why forced downtime can be so detrimental. Your software has been tried and tested to minimise downtime, boosting productivity and profitability. If you opt for the second choice, I recommend keeping this section small. It shouldn't make up any more than a fifth of the entire infographic.

Call to action

If you opted for the former choice in your closing thoughts, now is your chance to bring it back to your business with one simple sentence. This is your call to action - or simply your "CTA". You've successfully brought your audience all the way through your infographic. What do you want them to do now?

> "[Business name] helps organisations just
> like yours minimise downtime and become

*more profitable. Get in touch with us and
we'd love to schedule a demo."*

This might not exactly apply to you, but you catch my drift. You've successfully brought your audience all the way through your infographic. With this in mind, here are some quick dos and don'ts to consider when attempting your next infographic.

Do strike the perfect balance between images, white space, and text

First-class infographics are a balancing act. You want plenty of images and graphics. And you want compelling copy to help your reader situate themselves. But you also want some negative space to make your content more appealing to the eye. If you've got a graph, include a few sentences to explain what they're looking at and why they should care. If you've got a bullet point list of top tips, use iconography to make it more engaging. If you've got three hard-hitting statistics, make them into charts to lay out across the page.

Don't decide on your design last

In a similar vein, don't create your design and content separately. Infographics are primarily a visual form of content. This means even the best copy in the world won't be able to capture reader attention unless your design is equally brilliant. Rather than trying to cram pre-written content into a cohesive design after the fact, plan out both your content and design simultaneously. Decide which sections can afford to be a bit more copy-heavy, and how you can break these up with visual-heavy sections.

Do brand all your infographics

You want there to be no doubt that it's your business adding this value to your readers. And branding your infographics is key to this. Your logo should be somewhere on the page. Using your brand's colours is another way to align this content with your wider business.

Don't forget to include references

Not only is this just the ethical thing to do - sharing references for data you've taken from other sites or businesses - but you also want to make it easy for your audience to find your sources. You never know what inspiration a piece of data could generate in your reader.

Infographics are a brilliant way to get your creative juices flowing and create eye-catching, one-of-a-kind content to capture your audience's attention. As long as you're striking a good balance between visual images and written copy, are adding concrete value and insight to your audience, and are super clear and succinct with your information, go wild!

INTERNAL DOCUMENTS

For any business to thrive, your team needs to be on the same page. Jeff from sales and Sophie from accounting might not even know each other exists, but they still have to work towards a common goal. If they're working in opposite directions, then how can you expect to get anywhere at all? You just can't be a productive, profitable business this way. Not if most of your staff are unsure about what's expected of them. Or if the information they need is messy, scattered, or - even worse - non-existent.

Whether you've been in a role for two decades or two months, there's something comforting about knowing all the information you need is never more than a few clicks away. Sometimes, we just need a refresh on the way certain systems work. And other times, we might have to cover someone's role and need some clarification. When you need something like that, you'll turn to the company's internal documents. Done right, these can be a key way to maximise productivity, support your workforce, and streamline your business.

Note that this is different from a handbook. In a previous section, we talked about creating an employee handbook that provides new staff with all the information they need. Internal documents are that and then some.

It's about detailing every part of your company. They might be on a shared drive or in the cloud somewhere, and there might be a lot of them. In short, they're a written record of how everything works. A large bank of information that could be valuable for your staff to reference at a later date. From health and safety guidelines, daily checklists, and till systems, to IT support, project or team information, and HR regulations, it covers everything.

What you need, when you need it

Picture this: you've had an influx of staff members leave around the same time. It's unfortunate timing and now your brain has hit the panic button. You've got 10 roles to fill and Bob keeps emailing you because he doesn't know how to do all these new responsibilities he's had to pick up. And when they start, how the hell are you even going to train them all? But if you had a nice library of well-written internal documents ready to go, you wouldn't have to worry. Sounds great, right?

But did you know that 51% of employees have avoided sharing a document with a colleague because they couldn't find it? Or that nearly 60% of remote workers miss out on important information because it was communicated in-person? That's why it's so crucial to get these right. There are a few different types of documentation you might find useful across your business:

Process and procedure documentation - The steps needed to complete certain tasks, such as putting a sale through the till, locking up the offices, or using certain software. Resources for common processes that are likely to be repeated often.

Onboarding documentation - All the information you need to give new starters when they first appear all bright-eyed and bushy-tailed. However, this should also be readily accessible to existing staff, just in case they need a reminder.

Team documentation - This is where you'll find all team-specific information, like team goals, meeting notes, strategies, style guides, staff information, or timelines. Anything that helps them do their job.

Project documentation - Any information that's specific to particular projects - think proposals, project requirements, or design guidelines. And this will likely span *all* projects past, present, and future.

When it comes to onboarding, team, and project documentation, it's more about organising the masses of paperwork you'll likely already have. We'd recommend you go fully digital as it saves you money on paper and printing - not to mention the fact that it's just easier to find, read, and change. It's about making the important information readily accessible and frequently updated. When it comes to process and procedure documentation, you might want to take a different approach.

Identify the key processes

Not everything needs to be - or should be - documented. Don't waste your time writing up every single action. Only focus on the frequently repeated tasks that need some explaining. That being said, they don't necessarily need to be complex tasks. It could literally be something like the right way to get rid of the trash. Or about securing your PPE. They sound simple, but you have to ensure they're done *right*. Just use some common sense as to what needs spelling out. If it's an overly simple task that anyone off the street could do blindfolded, your time will be best spent elsewhere. If you're unsure, you can always ask your team. Seasoned staff will especially have some good insight into what they would have appreciated as a new starter.

Create a template

If you're not sure where to start every time, whip up a template. This will make it easier for you to create a new document and ensure you're including everything you need to. Your template might include:

- Why? - A brief description of why this process exists and why it's important to the business.
- Who? - The role responsible for completing this task. If they're absent, you also want to outline who needs to step up.
- What? - A step-by-step outline of how to complete the process.
- Misc - If relevant, include any products or equipment required for the job.

Now for some dos and don'ts for your organisation's internal documents.

Do take stock of what you already have

Before you spend any time creating new documents, explore what you already have to hand. Some businesses will need to start from scratch, producing new documentation *and* making it accessible and organised. Others may simply need to tweak existing documents to make them easier to read or simply need to reorganise all their documents into a more streamlined online system.

Don't rely on text alone

Visuals and diagrams can be a lifesaver for getting knowledge across. Sometimes, no matter how great you are with words, what you're saying just doesn't make sense.

You'll need to *show* your reader how to lock that fire door or where to leave the rubbish on bin day. They leave less up to the imagination. Your staff will thank you for the clarity.

Do write documents with varying audiences in mind

Imagine you're a new starter trying to figure out how to do a refund on the tills. You get to the relevant section and there's a brief overview of ten bullet points. That's it. Before you know it, you've given a customer a £2,000 refund instead of a £20 one. So you make sure it's super detailed. But now the person who's come back from maternity leave and just needs a refresh has to read 10 pages of size 8 font. Time to break out the magnifying glass! When you're writing, you have to anticipate *everyone* who might read it. And you have to cater to each of them. It's not as difficult as it sounds though; just rework what you have.

You might start each section with a general overview. Bullet points of the process, for example. This works great for Mary coming off maternity. Then you can go into greater depth with a thorough step-by-step explanation and accompanying visuals for Norman the new guy. Everyone gets the information they need in the way that suits them.

Don't make it hard to find

It's all well and good producing exceptional documents. But if staff can't access the information as and when they need it, what's the point? You don't want your staff going on a wild goose chase to track it all down. What you do want is for them to find it straight away. So consider putting it all in one folder on a shared drive or in the cloud. Part of this is ensuring the title tells them exactly what it is. Speaking of which…

Do consult with someone who isn't familiar with what you're writing about

It can be hard to gauge whether you're describing a process well if you're extremely familiar with it. You're likely going to skim through assuming you've gone into enough detail. After all, you know what you mean, so it must be right! In reality, you're meant to be writing for someone who has no previous experience. This is why it's never a bad idea to get a second opinion. Get someone with no experience to give it a read and see if they understand it. Ask them to describe the process back to you. If they struggle, you know it's time to add a bit more detail. If they say you're teaching them to suck eggs, you know you can strip it back a bit.

Don't forget these are living, breathing documents

There's no need to start a new document every time something changes. The last thing you want is 10 different versions floating around. That's just an invite for something to go wrong. The wonderful aspect of digital documents is that you can edit them in real time. The second something changes, you can go in and edit the document directly. From that point on, that'll be the only version available to your staff.

Do come back to them

You know when paperwork piles up on your desk and it seems to be doubling daily? Before you know it, you're overwhelmed and are putting off organising it because it's become such a big task. This can happen with your internal documents, too. Some of it might not be relevant anymore. Perhaps certain procedures are no longer needed, teams have been disbanded, or projects just never came to fruition. But now their relevant documents are still sitting on your database, gathering metaphorical dust and distracting your staff from all the still-relevant information. Get in the habit of cleaning out your documents. Perhaps quarterly. Delete anything irrelevant and make sure everything is filed in the right place.

Any business looking to keep their team organised and productive should make an effort to create a solid foundation of internal documents. After all, the more informed everyone is, the easier everyone's lives will be - and the more your business can thrive.

JOB ADVERTS

The Avengers. Mystery Inc. The A Team. All perfect examples of teams that know how to work well together. Each person plays their role beautifully. But if you want your team to be the same, you need to make sure you have the right people. All this to say that recruiting is hard as hell sometimes. You want to find the most talented and passionate people who can help your company grow, but sometimes that search is like finding a needle in a haystack. Except the needle is tiny. And the haystack covers a whole football pitch.

So what can you do to make the recruitment process more of a breeze? Well it helps to have an amazing job advert. If you want to attract the best, you have to show you're the best. Why should they want to work for you? What makes you so great? But just look at the majority of what's there on job websites right now. Either it's clearly been written in a rush and barely has the time to tell you what the job even is, or it's the same as every other job advert - 400 words of nothing. Gone are the days where you could throw a few nondescript sentences together and shove it on Indeed. It's time to get serious about how you're selling your business to potential candidates.

233

Can you afford to get it wrong? If it isn't enticing, people are just going to scroll past it. Even if it's perfect for them, they're going to pick the one that's at least clear and appealing. On the other end of the spectrum, you could attract the wrong type of person and waste your time interviewing them because, oops, you forgot to mention they need to know Photoshop. You've got a few hundred words to sell yourself. It's called a job *advert* for a reason. A big mistake people make is assuming they're doing candidates a favour by potentially offering them a job. But they're the ones doing you a favour. After all, they're giving their time and effort to make your company better. Your job is to make people want to take the time to apply.

Much like how you'd write to appeal to customers, you want to carefully create your job adverts to meet the needs of your potential applicants. Picture your ideal candidate; think about what drives them and what would entice them to your business. Do you think they want to hear the excruciating details about the company history? Or do they want to know what their day-to-day looks like? Do you think they want to know about how many awards you've won? Or do they want to hear about the benefits of working there? You get the idea. You want to grab your reader's attention. Fast. So try to always bring energy, warmth, and enthusiasm. Keep it brief and targeted. Make your organisation, and this particular role, seem irresistible. Let's look at the basic structure of a job advert.

234

Job title

Try to use common, recognisable keywords here. Now isn't the time to get creative and niche. Does anyone actually take the term "sandwich artist" seriously? You want this to be as clear as possible to catch people's attention mid-scroll and easily show up in search results. If someone is looking for a job as a video editor, those are the two words that are going to stand out to them.

Salary and location

This is the basic housekeeping that will quickly determine whether or not a candidate sticks around to find out more. You want to be open and transparent about what a candidate should expect, otherwise you're wasting both their time and yours. And please, no "competitive salary" nonsense. If it's so competitive, why aren't you boasting about it? Offer a salary range if you have to. But do mention some sort of salary information explicitly. 74% of people expect to find it on a job advert, so if it's not there, what's to stop them from just scrolling past?

Introduction to the business

The majority of people reading your job ads won't know the foggiest about your business. The exception is if your company has instant brand recognition. This should just be a short and sweet overview of your business. A few sentences should do. You want to describe your wider operation, purpose, and - importantly - let some of your personality shine through. If you're a modern, fun workplace, make sure it comes across!

Role and responsibilities

Now it's time to get more specific. What is the role? What can the candidate expect? What will a typical day look like? It also helps to put it in context within the wider company. What are they accomplishing in this job? Increasing sales? Boosting brand recognition? A sense of purpose is the fourth most important quality to applicants. So let them know how they'll be making a difference.

Key requirements

This is where you outline the qualifications, skills, and experience you expect candidates to have. You'll probably want to split this into required skills or qualifications, as well as ones which you'd prefer, but aren't a dealbreaker. You want to be thorough enough to give your reader an accurate sense of whether they're up to the job, without overwhelming them with requirements and putting off perfectly suitable candidates. Depending on your organisation, you may also want to include an **employee benefits** section to help sweeten the deal. This might include your benefits package, holiday allowance, on-site gym membership, health insurance, or anything else beyond the salary.

That's the layout sorted. It includes everything candidates will want. Now it's time for the content. Here are some dos and don'ts to think about when writing your job advert.

Do be clear and concise

The simpler and shorter you can keep your adverts, the better. Include **relevant** information only. And put yourself in the shoes of potential applicants when deciding what's relevant or not. Bullet points work great in getting this info across in the most readable way possible. They allow you to outline the key parts and keep it super clear and simple for your audience. But avoid jargon or buzzwords - people can see right through them. And while we're at it, regular bullet points might be too bland. Use a different icon - perhaps an arrow - to make it more creative.

Don't be vague about the role and responsibilities

Applicants will want to know exactly what to expect. Instead of saying they'll be "working closely with the marketing team", describe what they'll be doing with them. What are they going to achieve? The more information you can provide about the role, the more you'll ensure only relevant, suitable candidates apply.

Do end on a warm note

The close of your advert should leave your reader feeling like they can't wait to apply. They'll only do that if they feel like you want them to apply. So end with eagerness. Let them know that you can't wait to hear from them.

Don't forget to be human

You're talking to real people. So drop all the marketing speak and corporate nonsense. People don't want to work for faceless corporations. 80% want to work for places that fit their same culture and have the same priorities in life. Talk like a person and, above all, be authentic.

Do paint a picture of the process

Speaking of which, candidates will appreciate transparency in what they can expect in the process. Let them know the deadline for applications and whether or not they should expect a response if they're unsuccessful.

By describing what the interview process will look like, you can ease a lot of anxiety or uncertainty, allowing them to prepare well in advance. Even better if you can specify when interviews will happen so they can plan accordingly.

Don't use negative language

Avoid "can't", "never", and "must" at all costs. You're not the boss of this person yet. So don't go telling them what to do. *You* need *them* at this point, remember.

Do mention the working conditions

Since the 2020 pandemic, the world of work has changed massively. Meaning it's important to specify what this role will actually look like in practice. With many of us having become accustomed to working from home - some actually preferring it to being in the office - being transparent about whether or not the role is suitable for remote working could be the difference between an incredible candidate applying or not. Whether they'll be needed on-site full-time, part-time, or it's completely flexible, be sure you're letting applicants know straight off the bat.

Don't forget about other devices

Bear in mind that candidates will be viewing your adverts on a mix of phones, tablets, and laptops. Which would you prefer to see: a tiny phone screen with large chunks of text or short, sweet, and to-the-point bullet lists? View your job adverts on multiple different devices to make sure your formatting is accessible and attractive to readers.

Always try to keep it simple, relevant, and make as great a first impression as humanly possible. You've got this.

LANDING PAGES

S o you've got a document people can download. It might be a report, infographic, or information resource. You know what your next step is: creating a landing page for it. This is far from the only use for a landing page. Got an event coming up? Landing page. Want to welcome new customers? Landing page. Need something for a follow-through link on an email? You guessed it: landing page.

They're often quick and short, but that doesn't mean they don't deserve attention. And that's why you're here. The landing page will do a lot of the heavy lifting. There's no better way to turn intrigued website visitors into potential customers who are willing to invest more time into your brand and share with you their precious contact information. So what do you need to think about to make a good one?

What is its purpose?

The big question to answer first. Why do you want a landing page in the first place? This is for your benefit as knowing its purpose allows you to shape the content. Is it to make them download something? Get in touch? Buy a product? Each requires a different approach to make them do what you want. If you don't know the answer to this question, ask yourself if it's needed at all. There's no point wasting your time if you don't need the page.

Inspiring action

Unlike other pages, a landing page is quite transparent in what it wants. You're not necessarily trying to be subtle. If you want them to download your latest report, it's probably going to talk about how they should download this report. Does that mean you go for the hard sell? No. It just means your content is going to be more specifically tailored to the topic at hand. Say you have a report on your sustainability initiatives. It's going to talk a lot about the notion of sustainability, what companies should be doing about it, and what your report is about.

To cap it off, it needs a strong call to action that pushes them to do what you like. The good news is that if they're on the page, it's likely because they want to be. So any push should be well received. All you have to do is make the required action as easy as possible. If you want them to download something, make sure the button is big enough for them to see. And don't have them fill out a whole form; asking for an email address is good enough. And that's really all the advice there is when it comes to planning your landing page. You can find more specific details about creating web pages in the *Website content* section. As for the downloads and resources you might be pushing, there are specific sections for them too. To finish off, here are some top tips for engaging landing page copy that seals the deal every time.

Do sell the sizzle, not the sausage

Landing pages are a place to tease your audience and pique their interest. What you don't want to do is give away all your secrets and make the resource itself redundant. Hence why you want to sell the sizzle (the excitement and value) rather than the sausage (the content itself). You want to be sharing just enough to make taking the next step seem irresistible. This is especially relevant to downloads, such as reports. Try telling your reader all the ways their life will be better after downloading it. How much they'll improve X, achieve more Y, or do Z faster and better than ever before.

Don't overexplain

But don't overdo the sizzle. Keep your landing page copy simple and to the point. This should be a quick layover for your reader, not a 2-week vacation.

Do A/B test your copy

Chances are you won't get your landing page copy right the first time. But that's exactly what A/B testing is for. If you aren't familiar, you'll want to create two versions of the same landing page, just with slight tweaks. One might be more testimonial-heavy, while the other is more succinct and high-level storytelling, for example. Try each for a week and see which gets the best response. This is also the perfect way to keep refining your landing page copy over time. Inevitably, your audience's needs and circumstances will change, and A/B testing allows you to continually refine your approach to best suit your readers.

And that's landing pages! Short and sweet, just like the landing pages themselves. Don't underestimate how useful they can be at not only pushing what you want, but also for collecting data. Make sure you get them right and they do everything you need them to.

LEAFLETS

Ahh, leaflets. A nice little surprise in our post. Drawers full of them. They're like the ninjas of the marketing world - they always appear when you least expect them. When they work, they're great at keeping customers warm to your business. A nice little reminder that your business exists. Especially useful if you're a smaller business relying on local custom. Whether you're using leaflets to promote your store opening, a product launch, an event, or something else, you need it to:

- Stand out
- Be easy to read
- Make people want to read it
- Look good

Beyond that, well, there's not much to say. They're one side of an A5 page; two sides if you feel you've got a lot to say. In a way, they're a miniature poster - there's only space for the most essential details. So you might need to get creative with what you include. Lay out the essentials first. If it's an event, where is it? If it's advertising a service, what do the audience get and how can they get in touch? As much as you might want to talk and talk and talk, you don't have the luxury. If the space is really confining, consider creating a landing page on your website and including a QR code on the leaflet. This way, they can go directly to somewhere they can get more relevant info.

More than any other content, creating a leaflet might need some trial and error. Write your content in tandem with the layout, and see what works best. With some playing around, you can find something that works well. But before you set off and start making it, here are the dos and don'ts of leaflet writing.

Do write an attractive headline

You only have a few seconds to hook the reader in. Make it exciting. Place the main benefit in your headline. This is if you even choose to write a headline at all. For more information on writing an amazing headline, check out the section dedicated specifically to it.

Don't dawdle

Get to the point. Nice and quick. Whoever reads your leaflet should be able to figure out what it's about at a glance. They don't have to know all the details. Let's say you're opening a restaurant. Readers should be able to figure out that you're having a grand opening, have a feel for what type of food you'll serve, and when the opening is. So keep it concise with the important bits at the front and in a larger font.

Do use the right words

You're selling. Or at least convincing someone to do something or check something out. Use language that resonates with the reader. Here are a few words that sell:

- You
- Introducing
- Imagine
- Value
- Exclusive
- Hurry
- Premium
- Now
- Announcing

If you can fit these words on your leaflet naturally, then do it. And be persuasive. Simply stating facts isn't interesting. Make your product sound sexy.

Don't be shy about proving your credibility

If you've won an award or have been recognised by someone or something that holds authority, you can add this to your leaflet. Anything that demonstrates quality has a place on a leaflet.

Do give them the USPs

Tell them what's special about you. Why should they care if your restaurant is opening? Is it the first and only vegan restaurant in the area? Has it received great reviews? And then add a story element to it. "You'll never have to worry if there's something you can eat - everything's vegan!" or "forget travelling into the city centre, great vegan food is right on your doorstep".

Don't forget the call to action

Your leaflet is no good if it doesn't have any clear instructions. Why did you make it? Are you selling something? Promoting something? If so, then make sure you actually tell people what you want from them. Buy a ticket, buy this product, call us now - something.

Leaflets might seem simple and too short to worry about. But there are still ways you can go about it in the wrong way. Keep these tips in mind and send out the best damn leaflet your community has ever seen!

LETTERS

E ven with the advent of email and instant messaging, letters still have their place in business. You might be looking to send a more formal type of correspondence or you could be communicating with someone who isn't as up on their technology. And despite receiving letters for pretty much your whole life, there's still a way to do them *right*. What's going to matter is how they use them. If you want to use them to get the word out about something you're doing in the local area, that's fair enough. It's a great idea. But you don't want to fall into certain traps when writing them.

Our message of "it's all about the reader" is no less important here. By sending a letter, you're almost a guest in their home. You've arrived through their letterbox, landed on their doormat and... started talking about yourself. Isn't that a bit rude? It's a lesson often forgotten when it comes to letters in particular. So it's worth repeating here. A letter is no different from an advert or a blog in that sense. It has to be about the reader. Because, when you break it down, it's just another way of turning cold leads slightly warmer. It's marketing. Just in a more formal manner.

Because of their more formal purpose, there's a certain expectation surrounding letters. They tend to follow a relatively strict structure, are expected to always be concise and respectful of the reader's time, and have an air of professionalism about their tone. Let's look over the core structure of professional letters…

Your **company address** goes at the top right.

Your **recipient's name and address** is just below this, formatted to the left.

Dear … (ideally, use the recipient's name if you know it. But "Dear Sir/Madam" will do if you don't.)

The **first paragraph should introduce** yourself and the purpose of this letter. This isn't a hard sell though. You just need something there that displays a slightly more human side and shows that this isn't some automated letter (even if it is).

The **second/third paragraphs should bring in more detail and supporting information** about why you're reaching out. This is where you'll justify the importance of whatever you're writing about. Here, you want the focus to be on them. Think about what they want to hear. Are you trying to convince them to sell you their house? Then talk about the high sale prices or highlight the opportunity to move to their next dream property.

The **final paragraph is your call to action** - how you want your recipient to take action now. If this is purely an informative correspondence, with no agenda of an action being taken in return, this will be where you thank them for their time and offer any closing remarks.

And that's it. If you have the right layout in mind when you start, you can ensure you include all the information necessary. Sometimes a tidy mind is all you need! Now for some dos and don'ts of professional letter writing.

Do watch your presentation

Like I said, there's not much room for deviation from the typical letter structure. Now isn't the time to bring out a quirky font and go against the grain. It's useless if you can't read it.

Don't waffle and waste time

How many letters do you reckon go unopened? Or get a quick once over and are put straight into recycling? When writing letters, you want to boost your chances of them being read. This means you need to be respectful of your reader's time. Don't waffle and leave them facing a three-page block of text. No one's going to give that the time of day. Plan for the best-case scenario being a quick scan from your recipient, making sure the core of your message still comes across.

Do keep the content relevant

Similarly, don't deviate from the reason you've already given for your correspondence. Write all that's relevant to that one purpose, and leave everything else for another time. You don't want to cram a secondary point into the close of your letter just because it's convenient.

Don't think all letters need to be formal

Letters are a more formal communication form, yes. But that doesn't mean your brand suddenly needs to adopt a stuffy tone if that's not usually who you are. You can be professional and respectful, while also being warm and friendly (if that's your business's vibe). You can follow the basic etiquette of professional letters while still letting some personality poke through - especially if you're writing to recipients who already know you.

If you're writing letters regularly, now might be the time to check in and make sure you're doing your best to ensure they're actually capturing the reader's attention.

LINKEDIN

LinkedIn: the Facebook of business. Well, close enough. In many ways, it's the ultimate networking platform. Like their website says, this is your professional community. Just thinking about the sheer potential on offer is enough to melt your face off like you've just opened the Ark of the Covenant. You likely already have an account because it's almost a requirement to have one in business. If everyone's on there, you can't miss out. But LinkedIn is about more than making connections and sharing posts. Despite how some people treat it, this is not Facebook. People don't want to see pictures of your dog or know what you had for dinner.

Every part of your account is a potential touchpoint that could make or break your connection with someone. From your profile page, to your posts, to your private messages. That's what we're going to cover in this section; for more on wider LinkedIn strategy, I'm happy to have a chat. Don't underestimate the power of LinkedIn. 93% of B2B marketers consider it to be the most effective site for lead generation. Over 80% of social leads for B2B are generated on LinkedIn. And there are over 740 million members on the platform. So the pressure really is on. But don't let it get to you. And don't freak out on me. Let's go step by step, starting with your profile.

Your profile

There's a lot to say about writing a quality LinkedIn profile, so let's start from the top and work our way down. To start, you should have a recent, high-res picture of yourself. A professional-ish one, too. Not something taken on a wild night out. This should go without saying, but you'd be surprised at how many LinkedIn profile pictures I've seen that look like they were taken on a potato or off your Tinder profile. Your banner image should be high-res too, and contain your business' branding and logo. Now let's look at the actual content.

The **headline**. We have a whole section on headlines, but this one is slightly different. Yes, it is partly there to draw people's attention, but you also want it to be a succinct summary of who you are and what you do so people understand exactly what you're all about. Many people default to putting "CEO of this" or "executive in that". It's not wrong, but it's just a descriptor. There are a lot of CEOs and executives. I also see a lot of "optimising this" and "boosting efficiency in that". It's boring. They're just buzzwords. And it tells me nothing about what you actually do. Here are some of the most overused buzzwords on LinkedIn you should avoid like the plague:

- Specialised
- Leadership
- Strategic
- Experienced
- Passionate

- Expert
- Creative
- Innovative
- Driven
- Skilled

You can't scroll through LinkedIn without seeing at least one of these empty words. Why not try to make it more interesting? Take mine, for example, "helping you achieve your goals through the written word". It's much more exciting than "founder of Coster Content", which tells you nothing. What kind of content? Video content? Graphic design? It could be literally anything. With a more detailed headline, I'm showing my connections how I can add value to them. "Helping *you* achieve *your* goals". This way, the reader instantly knows what's in it for them *and* what I do, because, at the end of the day, people only look for connections that can benefit them.

Next, your **about** section. This is often where people dump every single piece of information they can think of - regardless of its relevance. Where they work, where they studied 10 years ago, what their specialities are. I even saw one person include that they enjoy fishing. Or they do the opposite and put a very brief five lines. Instead, the about section is the perfect place for storytelling about your brand and product or service. Explain why you started your company, where your passion stems from, and what you hope to achieve through your work. Clearly outline what you have to offer and the benefits your connections could expect from working with you. Try to always use a clear, powerful sentence to start. The human attention span isn't what it used to be. You want to hook potential connections in from the get-go. Here's a simple structure you can follow.

Opening sentence:

- A clear, concise summary of what you do and how you add value to others.

First paragraph:

- Who are you?
- What do you do?
- Who for?
- If you're the owner, what was your founding journey? How did you end up in your role if you're not?

Second paragraph:

- Background on your industry (ideally including statistics).
- What problems does your organisation look to solve?

Third paragraph:

- Tell us why your company is amazing and how you've carved out your niche in your chosen industry/market.
- What do you do that others don't?

Fourth paragraph:

- What specific solutions do you provide to the previously outlined problems?
- You might want to include bullet points of your products or services to clearly communicate your value.

Fifth paragraph:

- A call to action. Do you want people to visit your website? Reach out to you in the inbox to discuss working together? Let people know how best to contact you.

This isn't a strict structure - you might find another way that works for you - but it's a pretty solid start, covering everything that's relevant in an organised way. There's certainly wiggle room and space to experiment with your own profile. For example, you might take two paragraphs to explain your founding story because it's especially important and impactful. Or you might skip it altogether. If you're struggling, start with bullet points of the core information you want to share. You can then beef this out once you've established what exactly you need to get across.

And always keep this clean and easy to read. 79% of people scan pages, so you want them to pick up the key information from a quick look. To help with this, split your about section into as small pieces as possible. Avoid any lengthy paragraphs that drone on. Keywords will help your profile performance when people are searching for someone that offers what you do, so it's helpful to weave these in too.

Then there's your **experience**. This is the perfect opportunity to dive into what you actually do. But as tempting as it might be to go wild and write about everything you do on a daily basis and how great you are at it all, don't. Again, we want to keep this scannable. And if you run away with yourself listing off everything, it'll lose focus. The structure for each role in this section should look something like this:

1. Describe the company

2. List your core responsibilities

3. Outline any key achievements in the role

Let's look at each of these points individually. This should be more thorough for your current role, and briefer for any previous ones. You also don't need to list all previous roles in your experience section. Only keep them in if they're relevant and have transferable skills to where you're currently at.

1. Describe the company. You want to cover:

    - What service or product your company is known for.
    - Which team or department you work in.
    - What role your team plays in the wider business and how your individual role contributes to this wider purpose.

2. List your core responsibilities. Go for somewhere between five and ten, keeping in mind our list of overused buzzwords. Try to focus on the responsibilities that will prove most valuable and relevant to the people you're trying to reach through LinkedIn.

3. Key achievements in the role. Choose between three and five, focusing on the value you brought to the company or your clients. But don't just say what you did, tell them *how* you did it. The "how" is the evidence. Without it, you're just making claims.

At some point in this section for your current role, you might want to briefly describe relevant past experience that has led you into this particular position. Emphasis on the **briefly**. So now that your profile is looking fresh and clean, it's time to look at the two-pronged approach to networking through LinkedIn: adding value to your audience on the front-end by creating consistent, engaging posts, and targeting relevant leads with engaging conversation in the inbox. First up: writing your posts.

Your posts

Think of this like your wall on Facebook, or your feed on Instagram. It's where you put your message out to the world. They say you have to make at least five brand impressions to leave your mark, and this is a great way to do it. Your first instinct might be to talk about yourself, but this isn't a marketplace. It's not about selling your service. In fact, you might never mention your product or service. This is what I call the "front-end" - the public image that anyone can read. This should all be about engagement. You want to promote conversation, getting people thinking and sharing ideas. And not necessarily with just you; there's value in facilitating discussion between your connections.

The idea with this is that you want to be a beacon of knowledge. You're *the* person to go to when you want to hear about whatever it is you do. Are you in construction? Then you want to be the person talking about the skills gap, health and safety, and industry trends. You want to look as if you're on the cutting-edge of the industry and have a genuine passion for it. This way, your connections can trust your opinion. You want your posts to come across organically, not like you're trying to be a "LinkedIn influencer". The best advice I can give you when it comes to posting is pulling out your phone, opening Twitter, and searching for @StateOfLinkedIn. Take note of those posts and make a promise to yourself to never write any of those professional-suicide type posts. If it's just self-indulgent, waffling shit that doesn't say anything, you're just wasting everyone's time. And nobody buys into that; you're just going to be a laughing stock. That's not going to help you achieve the goal you hoped for.

Also, let's talk about frequency. I can't tell you to post every single day, as that could encourage a bad habit. You want everything you say to add value. It's far better to do this every few days than trying to find something to say Monday to Friday. If you're finding yourself posting because "you have to", rather than because what you're saying is interesting, educational, or valuable to your audience, it's time to rethink your approach. I could talk about this all day. There are plenty of other rules too, like posting once a day and nurturing that post. Instead of spamming your wall because there's an algorithm to contend with. If you follow my guidance, it shouldn't be an issue, but if you do want to learn more about how this works, you can always reach out to me.

But back to the posts. Where do you start? When writing them, your first few sentences are the most important part.

Why? Because before your reader hits that "read more" button, this is all they'll see. This is the only way for you to hook your reader in and make them eager to view the rest. This isn't to say you should cram as much in there as possible. Quite the opposite, actually. People don't go on LinkedIn to read essays; they go for a quick browse. They're scrolling, only half paying attention to what's in front of them. To notice your post in a flood of others, it needs to stand out and cause intrigue. It needs to be something that's easy to read, to the point, and enticing. Leaving just enough unknowns to encourage your readers to take action and read more.

Crafting the opening sentence of your posts will follow a lot of the same rules as you'll find in the *Headline* section of this book. And the one or two sentences after that - which will also be visible - should be used to add context and supporting information (while also leaving your reader with questions). They have to draw the reader in; two great methods are to start with a question or a shocking stat. Once you've hooked people in with your brilliant opening, they'll click "read more" and LinkedIn will log it as a view. This means your post receives a little boost and others are more likely to see it. For the rest of the post, I have some key dos and don'ts.

Do use short paragraphs

'Paragraphs' isn't even the right word; they're too clunky for LinkedIn. They won't want to read a huge chunk of text, no matter how thought-provoking or life-changing you might think it is. Add some breaks here and there. Keep sections short - one or two lines max. It makes it easier to scan and digest pieces of information.

Don't forget hashtags

Just like all other social platforms, hashtags can be incredibly valuable at boosting engagement. Posts without any get up to 40% lower initial organic reach. Ideally, you want three per post, as recommended by LinkedIn. Although, if there are some you just *have* to put in your post, you can go up to five.

However many you choose, consider the first three carefully. These will be included in the posts URL, making it searchable by Google. Also, don't make them too obscure; you want people to be able to find them by organically searching LinkedIn. #Restaurants is going to get more views than #organicmeat. Equally, think about who you're trying to reach. For my own content, the only person that actually follows #content or #marketing are other marketeers, who aren't necessarily my audience. Business owners are. With that in mind #business or #businesstips make a lot more sense.

#When you're #writing a #post, try putting your #hashtags at the end, and not #lazily scattered #through #the #text. Not only is it bloody annoying, it screams desperation and it's hard to read.

Posts certainly aren't as tricky as they might seem. With that sorted, let's dive into the back-end.

Your inbox

There's only so much brand awareness and networking you can do on the front-end of LinkedIn. At some point, you need to craft real, human relationships. Which is where your inbox comes in. If you've had a LinkedIn account for more than five minutes, you'll know the platform's polluted with messages. People send them all day, every day. Messages are the perfect way to make the most out of your network, discover new opportunities, conduct market research, sell your product, and more. But the power of the humble LinkedIn message is wasted when it looks like everyone else's. Or when it reads like spam.

At any given moment, I have a handful I'm ignoring in my inbox. Not because I'm rude, but because they're bland sales pitches that have been copied, pasted, and sent to dozens of other people. I know they don't really want to speak to me, so why would I message back? People don't want to read a cold, hard sales pitch. We're human. We want real conversations. It doesn't mean you should ask your connections what they're eating for dinner tonight, but your messages *should* be personalised. It shows you actually did your research on this person and prevents you from sounding like an annoying late-night infomercial presenter waffling on about how your product will change people's lives. And not only will this get you on your recipient's good side, but you'll also stand out in their inbox that's probably overflowing with cold, hard sales.

It's easy too, and yet so few put the effort in. All you have to do is click through the links on their profile. Browse their website, check out their socials, or even just read one of their latest LinkedIn posts. This is how you begin to craft your message. Lead with something you saw. It doesn't have to be complicated. It could look like:

> "Hi, I saw your Instagram post about being a people pleaser. I know the struggle all too well! Recently, I've been trying to overcome it by not shying away from difficult conversations. It's a struggle, but I'm getting there. How did you find X?"

And build from there. Relationships take time to build. No-one owes you a conversation straight off the bat. Don't expect too much from people. Instead, by taking a step back, you've given them a reason to open your message and **engage**. You stand out from the "Hi, I'm getting in touch to see if you're...". Yawn. A personal touch really makes a difference. Then you can keep the conversation rolling. Ideally, you want a two- to three-message funnel. Your goal is to take the conversation off LinkedIn as soon as possible, opting instead for a meeting, phone call, or Zoom, which are far easier for building genuine relationships. It should be similar to an email funnel, just shorter; read the section on *Email marketing funnels* for more info.

Give a brief overview of why you think a working relationship would be valuable with this person. Perhaps a few lines about what you do and what you offer, and why they should care. Then ask if they have time to talk to you this week. But LinkedIn messages aren't just about the big sell at the end. They're also great for keeping connections warm and building relationships. You're simply having a friendly conversation - with no hidden agenda. Although this *could* be setting the foundations for a proper business relationship further down the line. Simply asking their opinion on something they're familiar with or passionate about is a great way to do it. Like:

> "Hi, I was wondering if I could get your opinion on something. I see you work in the X industry. Personally, do you think email marketing is

worth it in this space? Or should businesses
focus on other mediums of marketing?"

Then sign off with a thanks and your name. Simple.
There's no reason this can't count as one of your five brand
impressions. And having this prior interaction - coupled
with your engaging, inspiring front-end posts - puts you in
this person's mind. And, should the time come where your
services would be beneficial, they're far more likely to come
your way. Whichever you're trying to do, you end up with
someone who knows who you are, what you're all about,
and why you're the best person for the job. It isn't a hard sell;
it's a soft introduction, and it's the best way to get someone
to warm up to you. Now for some dos and don'ts of LinkedIn
messages.

Do write like a human

Nothing will turn the engagement off in your recipient
than a scripted message. If a message is clearly copied and
pasted, and has no specific reference to me whatsoever,
I'll archive it quicker than you can say "hi". You're a human
being talking to other human beings, which so many people
on LinkedIn seem to forget.

Don't over explain

Often in LinkedIn messages, less is so much more. You want to share enough information for the other person to recognise and understand your value, but leave enough questions unanswered to make a phone call sound enticing. If you show me all your cards in the inbox, you might rid yourself of the opportunity to wow me in-person or over the phone.

After mastering your profile, posts, and messages, you'll be in a great position to harness all of LinkedIn's incredible potential for networking and generating leads.

LONG-FORM CONTENT

f you've got a lot to say and a 500-word blog just won't cut it, then you're in the right place. Long-form content actually outperforms short content, helps your website rank higher on Google, increases the time a visitor spends on your site, and is more likely to be shared on social media. What form it takes is up to you. It could be a much longer blog, a white paper on a particular topic, or even an entire book. Ironically, this might end up being one of the shorter sections in the book. That's because many of the lessons you've learned in the other pillars - and in other chapters - are applicable here. Those pointers on blogs? Yep, they're relevant here. Want to choose the right headline for your piece? There's a section on that too.

But if one factor separates long-form content from other pieces, it's just how much planning you need to put into it. With a 500-word blog, the chances of you going off-piste are small. But when you have hundreds of points you want to make, ensuring these are in a coherent order is key. And unlike some of the other content I talk about, long-form content should be much more focused on being educational. It's about asserting yourself as the expert by helping your audience. Through helpful content, you win their trust and then - if all goes right - their business. There are other benefits too, depending on the format. For example, if it's a digital piece, you can create a landing page for it and have people enter their email to get it. This way, you can add a prospective client to your mailing list (in a GDPR-compliant way, of course).

Your content has to be discreet, though. You don't want a white paper that just says "come to us, we're the best". No one wants to read a whole white paper full of someone patting their own company on the back. You want to offer value and solutions, while nudging the reader in the direction of your company. When it comes to your long-form content, you need to follow four key steps:

1. Research
2. Plan
3. Write
4. Edit

Do they sound familiar? That's because three out of the four are chapters in this book. We'll touch on those briefly, but for more information, check out those specific sections. There are plenty of tasty tips in there!

Research

Since you've read the chapter on research, you know all about your audience. This is great, because it'll shape what you write about. The only extra information I have for you is to research your topic well. Say you're a dog food company and you want to write a white paper on dog nutrition that teaches owners how to adjust their dog's diet. If you're giving out advice like this, it better be backed up by science. When it comes to long-form content, there's an expectation that it's more academic than your average blog. Not to say your blog shouldn't be as thoroughly researched; just that your audience is going to expect a real education from a book or white paper. So your research time should be spent collating information from reputable sources and moulding your content around these facts. I recommend organising everything you find on a document so you can easily jump back and forth while you're writing.

Planning

Some people like to think of long-form content as blogs stitched together. This approach is fine if it helps you break up the writing, but you need to ensure it doesn't read that way. It needs to flow from section to section, so make sure there's something that links them together. Your language may also change slightly without you noticing, so it pays off to go back and look over it to correct those seemingly minor details. It might be easier for you to give titles to your chapters so you have a clear idea of what the contents of each will be. So that might look like this:

Chapter one: how a dog's digestive tract works

Chapter two: essential vitamins and minerals a dog needs

Chapter three: how to ensure your dog gets the nutrients they need

Chapter four: common misconceptions about dog nutrition

And so on. This way, you're less likely to lose track and accidentally write bits that belong in chapter four in chapter three. Chapters should be in a logical order. Explaining how to do something before introducing the concept is bamboozling and you'll instantly lose your audience's attention. Check over your plan to ensure the order you've chosen makes sense. Then write bullet points under each chapter. What are you going to cover? How do you want to explain it? Do you have examples? Then organise your bullet points into the most logical order. Do this for each chapter and you've built a solid plan.

Writing

The next step is actually writing it. I won't spend too much time on it because there's an entire section dedicated to helping you with this part. The only piece of advice I'll add is don't feel pressured to write it all at once. If it helps you to step away and come back to it later, then go for it. Don't rush yourself if you feel it's going to create a worse final product.

Edit

Editing is arguably the most important part of writing. When you edit, you'll notice typos, little mistakes, and sentences that you thought made sense but now realise aren't landing. As tempting as it may be, do not skip this step. Ever. Oh, and you should do it *at least* twice. Your writing will thank you for it. Once you've finished with it, someone else should edit it too. And then, *finally*, it's done. It's a multistage process, so check out the *Editing* pillar for more information. Before we wrap this part up, let's look over a couple of dos and don'ts.

Do ask yourself if it needs to be long form

Before you launch into writing it, there's one question you need to ask yourself: does this *have* to be long form? If you can say what you're going to say in fewer words, do it. This rule extends to all content. Every sentence should be new and exciting. If you try to drag out what could be a 700-word blog into a 2,000-word white paper, no one will read it. Or rather, they will until they notice that you're just waffling to make it longer than it needs to be. If you're struggling to tie all your points together, it could be better suited to a series of blogs you can post on your website over the course of a few weeks

Don't forget to mine it for content

Do you know what you can do with all those lovely words? Use them for different types of content! If you've written a 3,000-word behemoth, it could become multiple blogs, emails, or social media posts. All that hard work you put into it can save you a massive amount of time in the future.

This might have been a short section, but that's because all of the advice you need is found throughout this book. It can be a big undertaking to write something so lengthy, but all you can do is start with the first word. So get going!

MENUS

Looking at a restaurant's menu before we even arrive at the venue is such a strange human habit. Yet plenty of people do it. Why? Who knows. But it's satisfying nonetheless and I'm not inclined to question it. And they'll be wanting to take a look at yours too. While the food might be the star of the evening, the menu is how you're going to set the tone. Even before it begins. Making it a special part of the experience will largely come down to the language you use.

Food is sexy. Just thinking about eating a juicy steak or a creamy carbonara gets me salivating. That's the feeling you want to capture with your menu. You want guests to be spoilt for choice simply because everything sounds so effing amazing. More than that, your menu is an insight into your brand. Are you a demure, five-star, exquisite experience? Or are you an edgy, trendsetting fusion restaurant? This character is something else you want to bring to life. Where to begin? Let's look at some crucial dos and don'ts when it comes to your new menu.

Do let your brand personality shine

The colour scheme, layout, and font of your menu should be reflective of your brand's personality and aesthetic. It should serve as an extension of your actual restaurant or bar. For example, the classy establishment I just mentioned might opt for a more traditional font and classic menu layout, whereas the vibrant, modern fusion restaurant might choose a more energetic, brightly coloured vibe.

This isn't just the design; it's the play on words you use too. Agonising over which meal to choose is an addictive first-world problem I enjoy. Spending time pondering "what's a Triple Nom 2.0?" or "ooooh what's a Liberty Island?" Before finally deciding on a "Blame It On The Whiskey Burger" with a side of "Phoenix Fries" is certainly a lot more enjoyable as a customer than a plain ol' double cheeseburger and chips. And you can guarantee people will be coming back for the other choices in a few weeks. Well, that one's on you, actually.

Don't overcomplicate the layout

Research suggests that guests will only spend around 109 seconds looking at a menu, often ending up choosing one of the first dishes they see. It means you don't have time for your guests to hunt around for the specific section they're after. Put burgers with burgers. Keep meats and fish in their respective groups. Keep it logical and scannable, so visitors can quickly identify the parts of your menu that are most relevant. This way, you free up more of their 109 seconds to read your captivating food descriptions. But more on those later.

Do invest in your menu

You don't want your menu to look like it could've been created on Microsoft Paint, circa 2004. Equally, on a recent trip to Wales, I was handed a hand-written drinks menu. Nothing fancy. Just an old school book with the cover ripped off with blue biro scrawled randomly all over it. You're ideally looking for something with a touch more effort put into it. Graphic designers and photographers will be a worthy investment to create logos and photography that's in keeping with the wonders of your establishment. It can be easy to disregard these as unnecessary expenses. But, for a menu design that stands the test of time, the initial investment will pay dividends in the long-run.

Don't get too fancy with the fonts

You might think a fancy font will perfectly pair with the upscale design of your bistro. But if no one can read what you actually have on offer, because the font is almost impossible to read, what's the point? Sometimes, less is more. And just because you *can* change up the font, doesn't mean you should. Don't overlook the power of the basic fonts we all know and love. You can talk to your designer about this, but our tip is serif fonts (that's something like Times New Roman that has strokes to cap off letters) tend to fit more formal locations, while sans serif suits informal.

Do add enticing detail to your menu descriptions

No matter the nature of your business, you want your menu to include evocative descriptions that make your audience feel something. You want to pique their interest and get their mouths watering. Using food description words has been shown to boost sales 27% more than without. While longer food descriptions - meaning a few lines, not a full page - sell 30% more food. Let's look at an example for this. Which would entice you more?

Standard: Steak and chips

Elevated: A flame-grilled, responsibly sourced sirloin steak with thick-cut truffle chips and garlic aioli.

When it comes to adding detail, preying on your guests' senses can be powerful. For example, words to denote texture or flavour, like tender, crunchy, rich, creamy, or light. Another example of good descriptive words for your menu are those that describe the food's preparation. For example, toasted, stuffed, slow-roasted, glazed, or smothered. You also want to use them to show why you're different. While people will obviously want to know what's in the pasta dish they've ordered, or what's involved in making it, you need to be sure to also differentiate yourself from others. For example, highlight the 'locally sourced ingredients' or your unexpected, unique spin on a classic dish. Incorporating more of these into your menu descriptions will make your already tasty dishes even more irresistible. And they help you win your customers over before they even dig in.

Don't overdo the adjectives

Saying that, don't be OTT. No restaurant needs to write a full paragraph of description for a house salad, outlining the entire recipe from start to finish. You want to entice your guests, not bore them with unnecessary waffle. Keep it concise, with just enough details peppered throughout to get mouths watering.

Do give your menu to a sample audience to proofread

By recruiting a sample, unbiased audience, you can test drive your menu and make sure it's as strong and guest-friendly as possible. Questions to ask include:

- Does the layout make logical sense?
- Is the font legible?
- Do they understand your descriptions?
- Are there any key questions left unanswered?

This is also a great time to A/B test it. You just need to create two versions and see which lands better.

Don't forget about your online menu

Like I said at the beginning of this section, people *love* browsing menus online. Myself included. In fact, 77% of diners will check a restaurant's website before dining in or ordering takeaway. The simplest way to go about it is to upload your physical menu online, though this means you have to consider this during the design. If you opt for a web-based menu as opposed to a PDF, the same rules apply. Keep your brand personality and vibe, use clear and enticing language, and be easy to navigate. You'll also need to consider the different devices people might be using to view your digital menus and test this from a UX perspective.

And there you have it. Some key tips for elevating your menus and enhancing your guests' experience. You could have the best decor, chefs, and customer service around, but if your menus are lacklustre, unclear, or uninspired, you're never going to see the full-fledged success you desire.

NEGATIVE CONTENT

Imagine the world if everything went according to plan. Everyone was always in a happy, upbeat mood, errors never happened, and life was a consistently positive, uplifting place. If only, right? The truth is: nothing is ever going to go our way 100% of the time. We're going to make mistakes. Other people will, too. And that means we'll face unpleasant situations we'd rather not be a part of. So our communication isn't always going to be positive or easy.

That's right. We're going to be talking about negative content. The difficult conversations where you have to deliver bad news, a telling off, or anything else that could ruffle some feathers. No matter what the situation is, there is one absolutely solid piece of advice that I can give you. Remember that the recipient of your communication is a **person.** They're a living, breathing, beautiful human being just like you. They are fallible, they have emotions, and - most importantly - they're not beneath you. So before you tell off an employee in the heat of the moment, think to yourself: "if I read this onslaught, would I respond calmly and to the best of my ability?"

When approaching negative correspondence, start it how you intend it to end: peacefully. My favourite way to address this is with the shit sandwich. It's always a winner. It works in emails, texts, social posts, letters, you name it. If you're not familiar with the premise, it's simply two positive statements (your bread) sandwiched around your bad news (the shit filling in the middle). The positive statements aren't supposed to be lies or contrived false niceties; they're truths you use to cushion the blow. If the person you're messaging isn't the real source of the complaint (i.e. a customer service advisor), then the first positive could simply be something like *"I'm aware it's not your fault, that doesn't make the situation any less pressing, but I recognise the issue does not lie with you."* Or, if it's criticism of a colleague and this is an isolated incident, you might want to lead with an overview of what has been great about their performance leading up to this point.

Then, tactfully, deliver your shit, AKA your negative message. Take their personality onboard and adapt your message accordingly. To close off your sandwich, end it on a high - perhaps with a suggestion of a resolution and invite the other person to contribute to the conversation. No one in this world is perfect, you and I included. But if you're candid with people in a way that lets them know that something hasn't worked as it should have, you give them the opportunity for personal growth without causing shame and embarrassment. By working together on a solution, you can move on without too much stress or set back on either party. Now for some general dos and don'ts for any negative content you might have to write.

Don't send negative communication in the heat of the moment

Nobody wins if you approach a conversation angry. Your recipient will be quick to hop on the defence, you won't be able to accurately get across what you want/need to say, and everyone will leave the exchange feeling even more tense. Instead, try to stay cool. And if you're struggling to do this, leave the situation alone and return to it once you're feeling more zen. The best negative communication will be clear, concise, and respectful. All of which become almost impossible when your inner Hulk is bubbling away beneath the surface.

Do offer solutions

Wherever possible, you want to already have potential solutions for the situation in mind. Doing this ahead of time is preferable. This way, you'll come across as organised and professional in the moment. And, if the exchange becomes emotionally charged, you won't have to think of anything new on the spot. It's easy to assume the worst when on the receiving end of negative communication - thinking "I'm going to lose my job" or "they hate me now". Instead, offering solutions helps show them that you're focused on moving forward and gives them permission to look past the mistake. It instantly puts you back on the same team and can be a life-saver for easing tension for everyone involved.

Don't make it personal

When we're on the receiving end of bad news or negative feedback, the last thing we want is someone else's unsolicited advice. Where possible, try to keep your own opinions and feelings out of the exchange. This is a professional situation, and for the cleanest possible outcome, it's best to keep it that way. Always aim to deliver the message as an impartial outside party. Even if the situation does impact you directly.

Say you're speaking to a colleague about a mistake they made. How you feel about the situation is irrelevant. What you would have done differently is also irrelevant. Sharing your own views and advice, while probably well-meaning, runs the risk of your recipient taking the exchange personally and channelling any frustration to you instead.

Do anticipate any questions

To make your exchanges as smooth as possible, you want to anticipate any questions the other person may have. After all, the more clear and informative you can be from the get-go, the sooner you can move on to more positive topics. So before hitting send, have a read through your message carefully, looking out for areas that could be misinterpreted. The other person isn't going to be at their most grounded if they think you're coming at the hard. Anticipating their questions can be a respectful, helpful way to approach your communication.

Don't beat around the bush

You know when you can just tell someone has something to get off their chest? But instead of just coming right out with it, they make all this small talk and play nice to try and ease you in? Annoying, right? Well-written negative content is no different. You're sending this email, message, text, or letter for a reason. So let's just get straight down to it. It'll be far more respectful of the other person's time. You want this to be like ripping off a plaster - over before either of you know it. There's plenty of time for small talk once the issue at hand is resolved.

Do keep your communication open

This exchange isn't just about you getting your frustrations off your chest. As humans, we all want to feel seen and heard. And the other person will no doubt have something to say after receiving your feedback or complaint. So make sure you're closing off your message openly, encouraging them to respond and have their say. Even if they can't say anything to change or excuse the situation, feeling the space and opportunity to speak their mind will likely leave them feeling a lot more positive about the exchange.

Don't crack any jokes

Sometimes, humour can be a great way to lighten the mood. This, however, isn't one of those times. Any half-baked attempts to make the other person laugh will be jarring, and likely to come across as insensitive or disrespectful. I know you might feel uncomfortable, and I know humour might be your favourite way to handle unpleasant situations, but please try your best to avoid the dad jokes.

Do talk like a human being

When we feel uncomfortable, delivering bad news we'd rather avoid, it's easy for us to become a little bit distant and detached. But while this exchange should stay professional, you also don't want to sound like an uncaring, cold robot. Like I said before, it's a human you're talking to. So show them the respect and decency of treating them as such.

Negative communication is never going to be the most enjoyable part of your day, but there are ways to make it far easier for everyone involved and more effective and productive for your organisation.

NEWSLETTERS

Often, as business owners, we feel pressured to stay in touch with potential or existing customers, and a newsletter is the perfect way to do that. But, just like everything else in this book, there are some crucial steps you can't afford to miss. Whether you just started firing out newsletters in the past few weeks or if you've been at it for a while, now's the perfect time to take it up a notch and create newsletters that your recipients just *have* to open. Before we get into writing the newsletter, there are some points to consider. It's also worth mentioning that if you're sending it by email, you might also want to read the advice in the *Emails* section. There are some juicy bits in there!

What are your goals?

Are you trying to educate, get sales, or keep customers warm? This will influence the content. For example, if you're trying to generate sales, you might put deals in your newsletter or a link to a short blog introducing a new product, highlighting the benefits. If you want to educate your audience, you might add a video tutorial or a handy list of stats.

Have you gathered all the information you need?

Now you have your goals set out, what specific content are you going to include? Newsletters can contain a wide range of sections, such as:

- New blogs
- Social posts
- Job listings
- New products
- Sponsored content
- Company news
- Events

And that list is far from exhaustive. It's your space to talk about what you want, so don't feel you have to hold back. Once you've figured out what to include, you'll want to consider the layout. It should flow from one section to the next, making for an enjoyable read. It's no different than any other content in that regard. Here's a structure that works well:

- Subject line
- Introduction
- Main sections
- Outro
- Call to action

So what do you need to think about before writing each section?

The subject line

I mentioned some similar advice in the *Emails* chapter. Ideally, you're looking for ten words or less. Any more and the recipients won't see it all. They'll be hit with the good old "…". You want something that makes the best first impression. Hit them with a big bang. It doesn't matter if the content of your newsletter will change the readers life, if the subject line is average, they won't read it. Spend some time crafting a solid subject line that'll stand out amongst the dozens of unread emails that have gone stale in their inbox. It's a good idea to write the subject line last as you'll have a better idea of what it should be once the content is written.

The introduction

No messing around, get straight to the point. Newsletters have incredible potential but only if your reader actually hangs about long enough to give it a chance. They need to understand what it's all about at a glance. Get their attention with a statistic, story, quote, or something else interesting.

Main section

These are the parts you planned to include, be they blogs, new features, or any big news. You don't want them to run on too long as a newsletter is supposed to be more of a snapshot of what you're up to right now. If you're planning on releasing it, say, monthly, you'll be touching base with them enough that you don't have to dive in too deep every time. Where possible, you can link to a larger piece. For example, if you're referencing a blog from that month. Then the recipient can always read more if they wish.

Outro

In many ways, this is a mirror of your intro. Summarise, keep it brief, and wish the reader well. If you have any last points that don't fit elsewhere, stick them here.

Call to action

Like any call to action, give your reader the means to get in touch. Maybe reference something from the newsletter - such as a new product, and say they can find out more by getting in touch. The easier you make it for them to contact you, the more likely they are to try. And that's it. All in all, it doesn't have to be much longer than your average blog - 500 to 600 words would work well. But you might be wondering if there are any specific tricks to *how* you write newsletters. Let's check some out...

Personalisation

Add their name! Personalised emails deliver six times higher transaction rates. And 52% of customers say unpersonalised emails turn them off. It's so easy, it'd be daft not to do it.

Show, then tell

Many people determine if an email is worth their time based on how it looks, which can be a bit frustrating, but that's the truth. So lead with enticing images and keep a clean, clear, spacious layout. *Then* go into the written content.

Choose your words carefully

There are a *lot* of words that send your email straight to the spam folder. And words that trigger this tend to fall under six categories:

- Needy - anything that sounds desperate or exaggerated.
- Cheap - "everybody's a winner" type emails.
- Far-fetched - think "get rich for free" type spam.
- Dodgy - anything that seems shady.
- Manipulative - "you have ONE HOUR to collect your WINNINGS".
- Pushy - you probably know how this one feels.

Some words that'll send your email straight to the spam folder include:

%	Expires
Act	Extra
All-new	Free
Amazing	Guarantee
Apply	Hello
Bargain	Important
Best	Limited
Cash	Now
Certified	Offer
Cheap	Opportunity
Click	Risk-free
Compare	Spam
Congratulations	Urgent
costs	Winner/winning/
Exclusive	Won

There are *a lot* more but if I put them all here I'd run out of paper, and I love trees. Another point to note is that all-caps and all-lower-case subject lines can look spammy. Stick to sentence case - that is, a sentence that starts with a capital letter and doesn't capitalise any other words (unless needed). Emojis can also catch the eye of the reader. If it fits your brand and the content, add one. But don't go wild. So now you've got the basics, here are some dos and don'ts that will help you shape this into the best newsletter around.

Do track your newsletters

Many analytics tools are free and easy to use. You can track your newsletters to check for open rates, bounce rates, and conversions. Analytics will expose areas for improvement or confirm that what you're doing is working. They'll also show you what kind of content your audience views the most, which is valuable data that could result in a change to your content strategy and a boost in views and conversions.

Don't just share your products

Sure, you might be using newsletters to boost sales, but your audience didn't sign up to be pestered with deals, offers, sales, and new products. They want interesting, valuable content too. You can mention deals every now and then, but it shouldn't be the primary focus of your newsletter as it'll just result in people unsubscribing. About 90% educational content to 10% promotional works well.

Do choose the right moment to send

This should be part of researching your audience. It might be the case that a huge chunk of them live in America. They could be hopping out of bed when you're tucking into your lunch. You need to find out where your audience is, what time they check their emails, and send it to them at the best time possible. You don't want to put in all that hard work just for your email to be ignored because it landed in their inbox at 2 a.m.

Don't forget about mobile

We do almost everything on our phones now and that's not going to change anytime soon. An email newsletter that can't be read on mobile devices is pointless. Mobile opens account for 46% of all email opens. That's way too many people to miss out on. Especially when optimising for mobile has never been easier.

Do use an email service provider (ESP)

Such as MailChimp, for example. It makes everything much smoother and your emails will look more professional. This will also give the reader the option to unsubscribe. If you send your newsletter from your personal email, they'll have to ask you specifically to remove them from your database, which you'll then have to do yourself. It just saves you and your audience a lot of time. As well as this, ESPs have a 90-99% deliverability rate, so more of your audience will actually receive your email.

Don't forget about the design

I touched on this earlier, but it really is important. Each piece of content needs to sit comfortably in its allocated slot. It shouldn't look crammed in; there should be breaks between each piece of content so that it's easy to read. Be mindful of pictures too. They work great in most emails, but some make the mistake of adding too many and the result is a busy email that confuses the reader.

Now you can create newsletters that your customers will love that will get you tangible results. Before long, your audience will be frothing at the mouth to open it. Okay, maybe it won't be that dramatic, but at least they won't roll their eyes when they see it!

ONLINE COURSES

During the COVID-19 pandemic, the search volume for "free online learning" shot up by a whopping 367%. While it certainly took online learning up a level, it's been a steadily growing trend for some time now. And it'll only continue to grow in popularity at an estimated CAGR of 8.56% in the lead up to 2026. It's the perfect timing for anyone looking to pass on their wisdom. Sometimes, blogs don't cut it. There's not enough time or space to educate your audience via this medium. Even long-form content like white papers might not suffice. They're also great because it's a more direct way of educating your audience.

So online courses seem like the perfect answer. But make no mistake, it's a big undertaking. It can be difficult to know where to start. Though if you can get it right, you can assert yourself as the expert while creating valuable content for your audience. Not to mention all that juicy potential to attract new customers. Now, before we get into it, this is worth saying: if you're going to create an online course, you need to be an expert on the topic. It may seem obvious, but I don't want anyone to be under the illusion that this is a get-rich-quick scheme. It's going to take a lot of your time and it's going to push the limits of your knowledge. That's not something you can half-arse. But if you **are** an expert and have a lot of knowledge to share, then you're in for an exciting and worthwhile journey. Let's dig in!

Organise yourself

Some of what I'm about to say is going to sound similar to pillars 1 and 3. But out of every section in this chapter, writing an online course is going to be your biggest challenge. Only because there's so much to it. So when I emphasise researching and planning, it's because you're not going to get very far without it. You **could** fly by the seat of your pants as you write. I know that's what I'm like too. But if you do that with your online course, you're just going to be making more work for yourself. So to start with, let's make sure your head's on straight.

The work on your course is going to start well before you begin to write it. You're going to need to organise your thoughts and feelings. The first question: what is the course about? This seems like an obvious one, but stay with me. I don't just mean this in a generic sense, like "it's an online course about graphic design". It's more about what journey are you taking your audience on. Where are they at the start of the course, and where do they end? Sticking with the graphic design example, the answer to the question might be: "it's a course about starting with zero graphic design knowledge and becoming an intermediate". You could go even further: "the course is about logo design" or "the course focuses on graphic design in a corporate setting". The more specific you are about the topic, the easier you will find writing it. It gives you an idea of where to start, and planning each lesson is simpler when you know what your audience's goal is.

Next, you need to think about what to include. For this part, I recommend getting a new notebook or starting a blank document. This is going to be your brain dump for all your ideas and research. Any time you find an article with a stat you want to include, dump it in there. Thought about a cheesy opening line for a lesson? Dump it in. It's going to be a living document that you add to over time, and will be a foundation for the next step. You have to plan out each lesson. First, think about how the course will be structured and how the information is meant to be absorbed. Is this going to be a 30-day course where people are expected to check in every day? Or is it more of a "pick up and go at your leisure" kind of deal? This will affect how you structure your lessons; if it's made for people to learn as they please, you're going to have to consider how each lesson stands on its own. You don't want too many references to previous lessons they might have forgotten.

Then, you want to plan your lessons. How many you include is up to you. If you feel you've got a mountain of education, it might be 50 lessons or more. But if it's a smaller topic - something like "a crash course on QuickBooks" - it might be more like 7 or 8 lessons. I strongly suggest you start by creating a lesson template. Key to any good online course is consistency. They should follow the same structure and include the same sections. To show you what I mean, here's an example:

Lesson title:

Objective of this lesson:

Key takeaways:

Activities:

Quote:

This is a simple way of organising what each lesson will be.

Lesson title is what it says on the tin. This will be the name of the lesson as the audience sees it. It'll likely be the last part you write and will probably change a lot as you write and edit.

Objective of this lesson is for you. You want to go into each lesson knowing what it needs to accomplish. If you don't have a clue, you'll just end up waffling.

Key takeaways is similar. This is what your audience will learn in this lesson. Because if it doesn't teach them anything, what's the point?

Activities is a section most online courses have. This is the "homework" of the lesson and usually comes at the end of the lesson. It should tie into the objectives and takeaways and make them reflect on what they've learned.

Quote is an example of something you might include, but it isn't mandatory. I've seen some courses start with an inspirational quote, which is a nice idea. But if you include it once, you want to include it in **all** the lessons. As I said, you want to be consistent. Whatever quirks you decide to include - be it a meme, video clip, mindfulness exercise, or anything else you can come up with - include it in your template so you don't miss it.

Your template is your starting point for each lesson. What you write here won't be anything your audience sees. It's more about reminding yourself what you need to imbue each lesson with. That's the organisation done. After this step, you should have a plan for all your lessons, meaning what's left is the writing.

Writing your lessons

I won't spend too much time here as pillar 3 is dedicated to exactly this point. BUT... there's something that needs saying about online courses. And it affects how you write them... This isn't like any of the other sections in this pillar. In those, you're writing content that's meant to be read. But when it comes to online courses, you're writing content that's meant to be **said**. Most courses are delivered in a video format. Meaning you're technically writing a script for yourself (or whoever presents it). This is going to change some aspects. How you read something out loud is different to how you read it in your mind. As you read in your mind, your brain does a lot of filling in the gaps. You don't have to read every word to know what's going on. And if I wanted to,

I could ramble on and make really long sentences, knowing full well that I don't have to stop to catch my breath.

But when you're reading out loud, you have to consider these aspects. You're not going to want run-on sentences or too many multisyllabic words. That's a recipe for disaster - you'll spend most of the recording tripping over your words. So when you write your course, think about how you can make it easier to read out loud. Use shorter sentences and words.

And shorter paragraphs too. Like this.

The reason you want to do this is to create some white space between sentences. If you have a seven- or eight-line paragraph, there's a chance you can lose where you're up to, meaning you might have to start again. It might also affect your grammar. If it helps, include extra commas where you know you'll take a pause. This will help you regulate your breathing as you speak. Does all this mean your writing can be a bit messy? After all, as long as you understand it, no one else is going to see it, right? Not quite. For accessibility reasons, it's great to have closed captions - i.e. subtitles. Most online course platforms will allow you to add these in. And, like with any writing, you want them to be perfect. You also might want to provide a text version of your lessons for people who prefer to learn that way.

You want your online course to be professional, and perfect spelling and grammar is part of that. It'll be a reflection of you as an educator, and they may feel that if you can't get that right, then who's to say the value of your content is right too. So be clear, be concise, and above all, be amazing. Before we close out this section, here are some dos and don'ts to keep in mind.

Do treat your plan as a living document

As you organise your lessons, you'll probably come up with some new ideas. Or you might change your mind about a certain lesson. That's fine! Your plan is something you can go back to and tweak if you want. In fact, I'd say it's mandatory to a degree. Say you're writing lesson 10 and realise it would be much more effective if you introduced a certain concept back in lesson 1. In that case, of course you'd want to go back and make some changes. It's going to be a fluid process, so embrace that.

Don't take your knowledge for granted

Something you might find hard while writing is explaining your lessons in a simplified way. When we write about a topic we know a lot about, it's difficult to put it in words that people less familiar understand. Be mindful of this fact. If you're writing a graphic design course and mention layers in Photoshop, ask yourself if you've explained the concept of layers enough. Or it might be about spreadsheets and the best formulas to use. But you have to think if your audience needs a crash course in what formulas even are. Write for the layman and increase the difficulty of the lessons as you go.

Do think about extra resources

It's rare to find an online course that doesn't include supplementary resources. PDFs, worksheets, infographics - all of these and more will come in handy at some point. This means you have to a) think about where these fit into your wider lesson plan, and b) how you're going to write them. Once you've thought about what you want to include, check out some other sections in this chapter for advice.

Don't forget to promote it!

Once you've created your online course and put it online for the world to see, you need to market it. Sure, people might find it, but they'd have to be searching for that particular topic. By marketing it, you ensure it reaches people who **want** to see it, and those that don't yet realise they want to see it. Again, how you do this is up to you. It could be an email funnel (if you have a pre-existing audience) or social media ad copy. Check out the appropriate sections for more tips.

It's not easy being a teacher. They work hard and aren't always appreciated. That's kind of what you open yourself up to when you write an online course. But do you know what else you get when you're a teacher? Satisfaction. Knowing you've taught someone a new skill or passed on your wisdom is a great feeling. So let that idea drive you as you create your stellar online course.

PACKAGING

You know the age old saying "you can't judge a book by its cover"? Well, when it comes to product packaging, you kind of can. All business copy has a similar purpose: to capture attention and win people over. And this is *especially* important when it comes to packaging. It's like The Hunger Games on shop shelves. There are hundreds of similar products on offer. But, somehow, your products have to sit there calling out to customers like an enticing siren song.

Your visual branding and design may capture initial customer interest - stopping people in their tracks as they power walk down the aisle. But it's your written copy that has to seal the deal. You have to **assure** customers that you're their best fit. That picking your product up was the best decision they've made all day. That their hard-earned pennies should be spent on your product, over the countless others out there. In short: it's your words that turn a curious consumer into a dedicated customer.

"What's in it for me?"

If I were to summarise the goal of packaging copy in one simple sentence, it would be this. All any potential customer browsing your products is going to want to know is what's in it for them. It really is that simple. I want to know exactly what you're going to give me or how you're going to make my life better. I want to be able to make a quick and easy comparison between you and the 10 other products in front of me. Which offers the most relevant benefits to my life? What problem will your product solve? How will it fit into my life?

The sooner you can answer the "what's in it for me?" question, the better. Some of the best packaging out there does this in the headline on its front-panel copy. This way, a customer doesn't even need to pick up your item to figure out the answer. A face cream isn't just a nourishing face cream. It's a face cream that turns back the hands of time. A hot sauce isn't just a hot sauce. It's your one-way ticket to flavourtown! The goal is to answer the question in such a way that you make the purchase irresistible. The work you did in pillar one will be invaluable here. Based on your audience, what's the one pain point you could emphasise on your packaging that would have the greatest impact? Drilling down into the **one** problem your product solves will allow you to write really snappy, powerful copy for your packaging.

Less is always more

This goes for your packaging as a whole, as well as individual sentences. So many brands overdo their packaging copy in an attempt to give their customers *all* the information. But, the truth is, they don't need all the information. When writing for packaging, you want to cater to quick reading. By keeping it short, sweet, and to the point, you do all the hard work for your customer. I don't want to use my skills of deduction or spend five minutes reading tiny print to figure out the value you'd add to my life. I just want you to tell me in simple, direct terms.

When you distil all your value into one or two easy-to-read sentences, all you leave your customer to do is decide whether or not to buy. Confusing language and droning sentences will only distract from this core decision, and often won't work in your favour. Here are some additional dos and don'ts to keep in mind when writing for packaging.

Do let your personality shine

In concentrated industries, the quality of your product won't always set you apart. Perhaps there are many high-quality products out there. Now what? In these instances, it's up to your brand personality to help you stand out. Aside from figuring out which product suits their lifestyle best, customers will ask which brand's personality and tone of voice speaks to them most. We like brands who share our values and outlooks on life. It's why a gen-Z brand will sound **very** different from one marketed towards boomers. How does your ideal customer speak? How can you tap into this in your copy? How can you use your brand personality and values to attract your people?

Don't forget about storytelling

When it comes to the back of your packaging, where the majority of your copy will be, storytelling allows you to maximise impact by tapping directly into reader emotion. Use all you know about your audience to paint a relatable picture that helps your customer imagine themselves already owning and using your product. The more personal and specific you can be, the better.

> *You know when you wake up in the morning wishing you could have an extra few hours of sleep?*
>
> *Well... we can't turn back the clock. Yet. But, our calming lavender pillow spray can help you drift into a deeper sleep each night, leaving you feeling more refreshed and ready to shine.*

An opening section like this shows your audience that you understand them and their struggles. It helps you set the foundation for a more familiar, emotional bond between customers and your products.

It's easy to overthink your packaging copy. But the simpler you keep it, the better it will land with your customers. So long as you're clear about who your products are aimed at, and the core pain points you solve for them, snappy, engaging copy will soon be falling right off your tongue.

PITCH DECKS

You've spent months (or even years) creating the business of your dreams. You're finally ready to make all the hours of blood, sweat, tears, and hard graft worth it by pushing forward to market. And so we come to the pitch deck. It's a mandatory document for any company looking to get to that next level. If one thing you write has to be as near to perfect as possible, this is it. No pressure. I'm only joking. Kind of. It does need to be excellent. After all, the people reading it are serious, profit-oriented people looking to get the most value out of their investment.

So this pitch deck should be about getting an investor excited about the **potential** of your idea. It's **not** about regurgitating everything you know and are passionate about. Or sharing every single detail that's great about your product or service. It can be tempting to dump everything on them. But when it comes to your pitch deck, investors just want to know you've got a unique idea, that it's profitable, and how long they can expect to see a return on their investment. Anything else will just be white noise, distracting from this core message. On average, investors fund around 1% of the pitches they receive. And they spend fewer than 3 minutes viewing the decks that hit their desks. No investor will want to work hard to understand your business idea or hunt down the relevant information from a block of text. Whether or not your business garners the interest it deserves comes down to you doing all of this work for them. Let's go over the basic structure of a pitch deck. We'll start with the non-negotiables.

Opening slide

Now it's important not to overthink this - or any other slide in your deck for that matter. Always remember, less is more. For this first slide, you simply need your business name, a logo, and a 5-10 word tagline that perfectly captures your business proposition. If you were to drill down into the problem you solve, or the value you offer, what does this look like? Here are some examples:

Airbnb - *Book rooms with locals, rather than hotels.*

Uber - *Next-generation car service.*

YouTube - *Broadcast yourself.*

See what I mean by less is more? In a matter of a few words, you know exactly what each of these businesses is about. And this is what investors want from your opening slide. It should demonstrate you have no doubt what your brand's core purpose and value is.

The problem

Investors don't want slides upon slides of preamble before you get to the heart of your business. You should provide all the context they need as soon as possible. Talking about the problems you address outlines the specific pain point you're trying to solve for your audience. You can start to bring in some storytelling - but more on that later. Uber's pitch deck in 2008 centred around the ageing and inefficient technology of current taxis, a lack of two-way communication, and GPS coordination between driver and customer. How does your business innovate similar to this? What burning problems is it solving?

Your solution

Next up is your solution. This is your core value proposition. No matter what your business is, how are you going to make people's lives easier? Or change the present market for the better?

Completing your pitch deck

These first three slides are critical. But which others you include , or the order they should follow, will vary largely depending on the nature of your business, its greatest assets, and how far along on your startup journey you are. Some other slides to consider include:

- **Your target market and demographic** - Include statistics on why this is a profitable market to tap into and demonstrate your success in already reaching this audience.
- **Revenue/business model** - Clearly evidence how your business idea will be profitable.
- **Traction and funding roadmap** - Outline your journey so far, including any successes and future goals. This is what really separates an interesting business idea from an exciting proposition with real potential.
- **Marketing and sales strategy** - What's the plan to reach your audience and take your business to the masses?
- **Team** - If you've got great people at the helm of your business, take the time to show investors the business is in great hands.
- **Financials** - Clear charts that demonstrate sales, customers, expenses, and profits.
- **Competition** - Show who your main competitors are and how you're differentiating yourself from them.
- **Investment** - Why you want it, how the money will be used, and the time frames for returns.

Which you include will depend on what information you think is vital for any investors. My number one rule for writing your pitch deck no matter the section? Be clear and informative, without overwhelming your reader with information. Investors are time-poor, predominantly interested in money and profitability, and preoccupied with the bigger picture, rather than nitty gritty details. Will they care about how your business came to be? Probably not. Will they care about how it will make them lots of money? Absolutely.

It sounds harsh, but it's true. If they want to know the finer details, they'll ask for them. But in this pitch deck, you're here to wow them. Unfortunately, it's not going to receive the thorough attention it deserves. If investors are going to receive hundreds of pitch decks to rifle through, they will always appreciate a business that's respectful of their time. With this in mind, keep it short, but sweet. The average length for pitch decks is 10-25 slides. But even the larger end of this scale is reserved almost exclusively for later-stage startups. This isn't the moment for bells, whistles, and cherries on top.

When it comes to the actual words you write, it helps to anticipate what questions they might have. Imagine that any investor reading your pitch deck will be asking the following:

- "Why you?" - Why are you the best choice for solving this problem?

- ✎ "Why now?" - How are you in the strongest position to make this a success in the current market and climate?
- ✎ "Why me?" - What's in it for them? Why should they back you and take a chance on this opportunity?

If your pitch deck isn't making the answers to these questions glaringly obvious, you've still got some work to do. Along a similar note, pay attention to the visuals you use. Always opt for easy-to-understand diagrams or graphs. Investors don't want to have to 'figure out' your slides. They want you to tell them exactly what they want to know. If you're using graphs, also include text to explain what they're looking at, if it isn't abundantly clear. Is there a sharp plateau? Explain why. Otherwise, you're only leaving space for uncertainty and doubts. Diagrams should always enhance your point and complement your writing, not overcomplicate matters. Before you actually sit down to write your pitch deck, let's run through some quick dos and don'ts that you need to know.

Do tell a story

Remember when I said everyone loves a story? Investors are no different. The best pitch decks take their reader on a journey. Which is why it pays to have your problem and solution slides right at the beginning. To win investors over, you want to make them feel something. And those few opening slides are the perfect place to start. It's slightly different to how you would normally tell the story though because of how brief you need to be. Find a way to distil your messaging into just a few sentences. How can you quickly grab their emotions? Some hard-hitting stats at the start would work great, something like: "Did you know it takes consumers X hours to do this simple task? With us, we have it down to just 5 minutes."

Don't regurgitate everything there is to know about your business

This one is easier said than done. It can be tempting to prove just how knowledgeable, passionate, and qualified you are. But that's not what investors care about at this point in time. You're not the one being judged; your business proposition is. So leave your ego at the door and focus on the task at hand. You'll have plenty of time to win them over with your passion and keen interest at later meetings.

Do revisit your pitch deck

Across competitive markets, it's not uncommon to receive more rejection than interest. But don't get disheartened by this fact. Take each no as an opportunity to grow and evolve. And bring your pitch deck along on this journey with you. View your pitch deck as a living document that will constantly be altered as you learn from experiences and evolve as a business. Revisit it after every meeting or rejection and you'll be surprised by how quickly things will change.

Don't be afraid to ask what individual investors want/expect from you

Sometimes you're blessed with the chance to chat with a potential investor ahead of submitting your pitch deck. For example, if you were to meet someone networking. If this is the case, take advantage of the opportunity to feel them out and gauge what they most want from potential investments. A quick 5-minute conversation can be incredible for tailoring your pitch and communication. Investors *want* to find great businesses that align with their interests and priorities. So don't be afraid to ask questions about what they're looking for.

Do make sure it can stand on its own

Step one of this process will be to win an investor over during a quick flip through. And you won't necessarily be there to add your two cents for this. As such, your pitch deck should work by itself, able to get you in the door without you being there to present it. You want to keep it concise, but you also need to make sure *all* the valuable information is there and easy to digest.

That's all the secrets of the pitch deck I have to tell you. Be clear, be concise, and you'll be on to a winner for sure.

PRESENTATIONS

Ever sat through a boring presentation while someone drones on through each slide? Your mind probably wandered miles away from the room you were in. And when you snapped back, you had no idea what they were talking about. You definitely have. We all have. But presentations don't have to be boring. They can be inspiring. They can galvanise your audience into action. But it's easier said than done. It's easy to make mistakes, such as creating a presentation that's too long, losing the audience's interest. Or a chaotic one that doesn't seem to follow any structure, which is just confusing. So here's how to take your presentation up a notch and transform it into the kind that knocks your audience's socks off.

The feature presentation!

Start by asking yourself what its purpose is and what style you want it to be. The answers will influence your presentation. You'd present differently to a group of kids than you would to experts in that field. And outlining your purpose will ensure your presentation stays focused and to the point. Now, there are various methods you can follow to create a presentation that will wow your audience instead of lulling them into a peaceful sleep.

The first is Guy Kawasaki's 10/20/30 method. Guy Kawasaki is a marketing specialist and Silicon Valley venture capitalist. His method states that your presentation should have a maximum of 10 slides, last no more than 20 minutes, and contain text no smaller than 30 points. But why? Ten is the optimal number of slides because, as Kawasaki insists, a human being can't wrap their head around more than ten concepts in a single sitting. So if your presentation is a pitch, it might look something like this:

1. Problem
2. Your solution
3. Business model
4. Underlying technology
5. Marketing and sales
6. Competition
7. Your team
8. Projections and milestones
9. Status and timeline
10. Summary and call to action

You might have half an hour or even a full hour to deliver your presentation. But you should be able to talk through your ten slides in twenty minutes. You'll also need to ensure there's plenty of time left at the end to answer questions. And the thirty point text. Let your words breathe. Any smaller than thirty points and text looks crammed in and leaves your audience squinting to try to make it out. Or, if there's lots of text, they'll be more focused on reading than listening to you. If they bother trying to read it at all. The text should summarise points, not be a teleprompter for you to read off.

By following this method, you cut down on waffle, keep your presentation short but sweet and leave plenty of time for questions, which is one of the most important parts of any presentation. Let's look at another popular method - Monroe's Motivated Sequence.

Monroe's Motivated Sequence was developed by American psychologist Alan Monroe in the 1930s. It outlines five steps to grab someone's attention and inspire them to take action. And it goes like this:

1. Hook
2. Need
3. Solution
4. Future
5. Action

Hook - There are infinite ways to grab your audience's attention. You could start with a joke, say something shocking, tell a relatable story, or use facts and figures. Knowing your audience is how you'll know what will hook them in.

Need - Now you've got their attention, you need to introduce a problem they're experiencing and convince them it needs to be solved.

Solution - The solution is your product or service. Go into detail about what your solution is and how it'll fix that problem. If possible, back it up with evidence such as case studies or testimonials.

Future - Ask your audience to imagine the future. This could mean the future where your solution saves them time, meaning they have more to spend with their family. Or it could be a glimpse into the future without your solution where they're constantly battling against the clock. But don't over-exaggerate. They'll see right through you and, at the very least, using fear to drive sales is unethical.

Action - You've made your case, you've stirred up all this energy in your audience, now tell them what to do with it. Otherwise, they won't do anything, meaning you wasted your time and theirs. What do you want them to do?

Both methods are widely trusted and used, as they're captivating, to the point, and memorable. Before you set off to create your five-star presentation, here are my dos and don'ts.

Don't write in full sentences

Okay, maybe you can a *little*. But your ideas will come across much clearer in bullet points than sentences, for example:

Pros of cloud storage:

- Low cost
- Secure
- Easy recovery

Is much clearer than: "Cloud storage is an incredibly secure, cost-effective way to store your data. Not to mention the…." and so on.

Do stick to one idea per slide

Too many ideas on one slide can detract the value and importance of each idea. One idea per slide keeps them uncluttered and makes it easier for the audience to focus and follow.

Don't use diagrams and graphs that require a lot of explanation

Anything visual should be easy for your audience to understand with little to no explanation. If it needs a lot of explaining, it needs simplifying. Make sure it's clearly labelled and, if you have to, draw attention to it and explain the concept. You might have figures from a recent audience survey and could preface it by explaining what it is and where you got the data from. Then you can leave the numbers on screen for people to digest. Done right, these will speak for themselves.

Do practice your presentation

Ideally, you should film yourself too. This way, you can identify areas for improvement. And, if possible, give it a whirl at the venue you'll be giving your presentation in. You can get accustomed to the room and it might make you feel more confident when the day to deliver your presentation comes. Studies have also shown that practising in the right location can aid in memorising it. So it should come more naturally to you if you're in the same environment.

Don't forget about body language

Adopt a power stance, walk around the space you have, smile, and make eye contact. Obviously you don't want to stare anyone down. But choosing a handful of people to switch between means you can maintain eye contact without making anyone uncomfortable.

Presentations are crucial in business. But a presentation must captivate the audience to be successful. By following these steps, you'll be ready to get out there and deliver a killer presentation that leaves your audience hungry for more.

PRESS RELEASES

What's the opening line to New York, New York by Frank Sinatra? I believe it's *"start spreading the news"*. I didn't know he worked in marketing! Bad jokes aside, if you have news you want to get out into the world, you're going to turn to the trusty press release. It's about getting your message to as many people as possible across as many channels as possible, well outside your own bubble. That's exactly what makes them so tricky though. They need to be well-written, engaging, and informative enough to attract the attention of people who might not usually care. Not only that, they have to catch the eye of journalists and publications in the first place to get your story out there.

It's a lot more pressure than your average blog so needs special attention to get it right. So where do you start?

What's its purpose?

You need to think about what you're trying to achieve with your press release. As I said above, it's to attract attention. But to what? A press release can be used in multiple situations. It could be a new product or service launch. Or you might have some huge business news to share, such as a merger, acquisition, or change of executive positions. You might be hosting an event, opening a new location, shaking up your whole brand, or just getting the word out about an award win. Basically, it's you shouting from the rooftops about your company. It's marketing.

What you're talking about might slightly change what you're hoping to accomplish, but all roads lead back to putting yourself on a pedestal. You want people to know about your company, though that doesn't mean it should purely be a sales pitch. It should still tell a story, just one that's - as I said before - **well-written**, **engaging**, and **informative**.

That's why you need to consider the secondary audience: the journalists and publications. They decide whether to run your story. If it's just a dispassionate run-through of Mary stepping up as your new CEO, why would they care? They're a hurdle to getting your message to the masses. And they'll want a story that gets them clicks. So in everything you write, think if it's appealing to them. Or better yet, build a relationship with them and *ask them directly.* If what you say adds value to the reader and improves their publication, why wouldn't they want to work with you? But if you're approaching them with the same regurgitated garbage you took to all the newspapers/magazines, what makes a piece unique to them? Why would they want it?

This will affect how you write it. Some of the work is up to them to tailor the story to their site or newspaper. As such, you don't need to do much of the editorialising; they'll fill in those blanks. They want the information. Just the facts. It's your job to hype them up. Let's look at how to structure your press release and get the maximum interest in it.

Your structure

There's no strict structure, per se. But there are some elements that are expected. Before we look at the specific text, there are some details you need to include somewhere in the press release.

Contact details - This is a given for any document, but especially here. Let them know who they can contact to find out more information if they need it. So don't include a generic number or email. Send them directly to the person who can help them, be it a PR manager or the business owner. These typically go at the top, similar to what you would find on a letter.

Release statement - By this, I mean a line that either says "for immediate release" or a date when it should be. Keep it simple, nothing extra, and put it towards the top in bold so they can't miss it.

Location - This is likely the location of your business or where the story is relevant. If you're based in Manchester in the UK, it would simply say "Manchester, UK" before you start your press release. This gives the publication an idea if it's relevant to them.

Ending mark - In the past, press releases would include "###" at the end to signify the end of the information. Nowadays, it isn't needed, but many still use it as a courtesy.

Those elements should be somewhere in your press release, but when it comes to the main body, here's my advice.

Headline

Like any good blog, you need a killer headline. Something that distils what the story is about and why the reader - both your audience and the journalist - should care. If you want more advice on this part, check out the *Headlines* section!

Paragraph 1 - your introduction

Unlike a blog, you want to start with the most important information. Usually, my advice would be to set up the story and explain the problem. But as I mentioned, that's the job of the journalist. They want to know, up front, what this story is about and why they should care. If you spend a paragraph waffling on, they'll throw your press release in the bin. To start, you want to answer their immediate questions: what's the story about, who's involved, and why it's important. So let's say I was writing a press release for my dog food company. Maybe it's just been stocked in a major supermarket. I might start like this:

> "Manchester, UK - Today, the UK's leading supermarket announced it would be the exclusive stockist of an up-and-coming, high-quality brand of dog food. The supermarket giant will start stocking the product across 1,000 stores from April 1st, providing a fresh approach to pet nutrition for dog owners up and down the country."

With that, you answer the three main questions:

- What's the story about? - A major supermarket chain stocking my dog food brand.
- Who's involved? - The aforementioned major supermarket chain with 1,000 stores.
- Why is it important? - Because it's a fresh approach to dog nutrition.

You're setting up the story you're about to tell. Think of this paragraph as the summary at the top. You're including a few juicy details to draw the journalist in. Don't worry that you're being brief; there's still time to get the rest of your messaging across.

Paragraph 2 - the details

Now you can get into the meat of it. Your next paragraph should be where your story really comes to life. You want to use this space to build on what you just wrote. Why should the reader care? And what extra information is necessary? So, going back to the previous example, the second paragraph might go like this:

> "This dog food company recognised a need for uncomplicated dog nutrition that's transparent about what ingredients it uses. There are no artificial nasties included; only all-natural flavours and quality protein sources. The major supermarket chain loved what they saw and, following a trial in 100 stores, decided to up it to the full 1,000."

With this, I've given the reader more context about why the dog food is needed, why the supermarket chain was attracted to it, and what circumstances led to this moment.

Paragraph 3 - a quote

No press release is complete without a quote or two. These should come from the most authoritative voices involved. Usually business owners, C-suite executives, or heads of departments. And if two parties are involved, it would be best if you had a quote from both sides. So in my example, I as the business owner would give a quote talking about how amazing it is to work with such a big name, and my future plans for the business. And the other party might talk about what attracted them in the first place and that they hope it will be a fruitful partnership. The most impressive name would go first. So as a representative of a big-name supermarket, their quote would go before mine.

Paragraph 4 - the outro

This is just a short one- or two-sentence closer. It would summarise the press release and sign off in a clean fashion. There really isn't much to it. It might look like this:

> "Both the dog food company and the supermarket are looking forward to their exciting new partnership and can't wait for the food to hit the shelves soon. In the future, new flavours and treats are sure to follow."

That's all you need. Everyone's happy and there's even a hint to the future.

Paragraph 5 - about you

Every press release will end with information about the company who wrote it. This is likely going to be extremely informational as its purpose is to provide some background about your company to the journalist. It gives them an idea of who your company is, and they can use this information in their own article if they wish. Now, just because I said it was extremely informational doesn't mean it has to be boring. It's your excuse to sell yourself. Some details you might want to include could be the founding year, sales figures (or other impressive numbers), relevant award wins, ethos, or general service. For my example, it might go like this:

> "This dog food company was founded in 2020 by X who wanted to change the face of dog nutrition. Not happy with her own experience as a dog owner, X set out to give dogs the high-quality food they deserve. With over 20 different recipes - along with a range of sensitivity tests - the company has sold over 100,000 units."

You want to put a lot of effort into this part as it can be used in all your press releases. Do make sure to tweak it each time to add the most relevant information, but for the most part, it's evergreen content. You also might want to end it with some more contact details, just for reiteration, but it doesn't need to be a full call to action. The journalist reading it isn't likely to get in touch in that way. And that's your general structure. Let's finish by running through my top dos and don'ts for press releases.

Don't go on too long

I might have written a lot about press releases, but the irony is they don't need to be long. You're probably looking at 300 to 400 words, and most of that will be the quotes. The truth is, it doesn't need to be long. As I said, it's for journalists; they just want the facts. It's up to them to bulk out the word count. The shorter you make it, the easier it is for them to digest, see its value, and get the story out there.

Do make your quotes snappy

Quotes are great, but do you know what makes them even better? If they're snappy. Quick, effective soundbites work wonders. That's not to say the whole quote should be one line. What I'm saying is that you want a part of it to really shine on its own. Going back to my example, it could be something like: *"Dog food never tasted this good."* It's an attractive snippet that can be used out of context yet still gets the point across. It would look great isolated and used to break up paragraphs.

Don't lean on opinions

Stick to the facts. Avoid adding your own opinion to it. Look back at the examples I wrote. Sure, you could say some of them were dramatic, but they weren't wrong. An opinion would be a statement like: *"This dog food is going to change the world."* Of course it isn't and of course the owner of the company would say that. Leave the editorialising to the journalist. If all you do is big yourself up, they're just going to roll their eyes.

I know it can feel like a lot of pressure. You want this press release to spread as far and wide as possible. You want every publication to pick it up and run with it. And I know this makes it tempting to oversell yourself. But let the facts do the talking. Let your merits shine through and watch as publication and publication takes the story. And even if not everyone does, don't fret. As long as someone uses it, it's done its job. And you've done yours. You've got this.

PRODUCT DESCRIPTIONS

The best product descriptions are the ones that bring an item to life. They don't just say what a product is; they explain **why** a customer needs it. They unlock the power of persuasion to make it impossible for your audience to imagine their life without hitting that 'add to basket' button. What's the secret?

Well, the goal of any product description is to persuade your customer to take action. To buy whatever product it is you're describing. And this means, as with any other persuasive writing, your product descriptions need to appeal to two things: Your customer's **emotions** and their **logic**. As humans, we're led by emotion. We see an item, it makes us feel a certain way, and we want it. That pair of low-rise, flared jeans remind us of our childhood and we're overcome with a wave of nostalgia. Or we have a particular affinity to a certain brand and so will happily buy an item we could get for half the price elsewhere.

Then, we talk ourselves out of the purchase because we've already got 14 pairs of jeans and why would we need more? This is where our logic comes in. Our rational mind spoils all the fun. But our rational minds can be bargained with. At this point, we either abandon the sale or, if done right, the product description will predict this obstacle and start appealing to our logic. We have 14 pairs of jeans, but *these* jeans are sustainably made. Or *these* jeans will last me a lifetime and therefore I'll never have to buy another pair again. And before you know it, you're stalking the Hermes tracker like it's going out of fashion. All of this is to say that the best product descriptions are those that take a two-pronged approach, appealing to both your customer's emotions and logic. Let's look at the emotional aspect first.

Set the scene

Writing product descriptions is all about tapping into the emotions of the customer through storytelling. You're selling to real people. So you want to be selling real situations and experiences. Even something bland like a rolling pin sounds so much more appealing when you add a story to it. But don't take my word for it. See for yourself. Which sounds better?

"This rolling pin is:

- *High-quality*
- *Features revolving handles*
- *Made from beech*
- *Hand-wash only"*

Or...

"What's cookin'? This beautifully made beech rolling pin with revolving handles is a must-

have for any kitchen. Whether it's gooey chocolate cookies that melt in your mouth or a homemade pie to tantalise the taste buds of your loved ones, this is the perfect addition to any home chef's arsenal."

The second option sounds much more appealing, even though it's describing the *exact same* product. Why? Because you can imagine it. You put yourself in the scene. You can almost taste the cookies you'll make with your new rolling pin. You can feel them comforting you after a long day at work. Bullet point lists aren't sexy. Stories are. Product descriptions are about more than telling people what something is and what it does. They help you relate to your audience, establish trust and familiarity, and allow your audience to imagine the product in their lives. And all of this can be incredibly powerful for generating sales. That being said, your product descriptions *do* also have to share what an item can do. Which brings us onto the logic portion.

What's in it for me?

To appeal to your customers' logic, you need to offer them all the ammunition needed to justify their purchase. You have to let them know why they absolutely **need** to buy this spatula, pair of socks, computer, or whatever else. Three core questions to address in your product copy are:

- What pain points does this product solve?

- What will they gain?
- What makes this particular item better than any others out there?

In any product description, you want to reel your reader in with storytelling, before sealing the deal by circumnavigating their logic. Answering all of these questions helps you play devil's advocate on your customers' rational, money-saving thinking. Depending on the products you're selling, you may also need a paragraph explaining what a product actually is. Because while a spatula needs no explanation, a piece of computer software will likely need a little more detail. Now you get the idea of what writing product descriptions involves, it's time for some dos and don'ts!

Do be specific

There are many product descriptions out there that don't really say anything at all. They're vague and use bland descriptions just to fill space. The type that will say a piece of software is amazing and efficient without actually explaining why that is. If your product descriptions ever leave your reader wondering "so what?", you're not being specific enough.

This internet solution is fast. How fast exactly?

This piece of accounting software is secure. How is it more secure?

340

This photo-editing app has a wide variety of filters. How many filters?

This body butter contains a powerful cocktail or nourishing ingredients. What are those individual ingredients and their benefits?

You get the gist.

Don't sell to everyone

You could waste so much time and energy trying to sell your products to the whole world. When in reality you only want to be selling them to your ideal customer. The more specific and personal you can be, the better. All the work you've done to come to market will help. Who are you selling to? What kind of language would they use? Is humour appropriate or not? What kind of storytelling will land the best?

Do use the word 'you'

Using the words 'you' and 'your' increases the emotional stakes of your copy and helps bring your reader into the narrative. Rather than being a random rolling pin I might never meet, it becomes *my* freshly-baked cookies, using *my* rolling pin, in *my* kitchen. If something already feels like mine, why wouldn't I want to hit the buy button?

Don't just list the features

Focus on the benefits of a product, not just its features. For example, if you're providing fibre-optic broadband, you need to put it in the context of your customer's life. They'll already know it's fast. But if you told them they could stream their favourite TV shows while their son games online and their daughter watches YouTube videos with zero loading time, it lands a lot better. Fibre optic broadband is the feature. Doing all the things you love online with no loading time is the benefit.

Do inject product stories

Who doesn't love a good story? If relevant, behind the scenes stories can help increase your reader's emotional response to a product and your brand. They remind your customers that there are humans behind your business. And that there's love and care behind your products. Who created a product? What was your inspiration for it? Why do **you** love the product?

Don't forget about your personality

Product descriptions are the perfect place to let your personality shine. If you're a funny brand, be funny in your product descriptions. Hit me with all the puns and dad jokes you've got. If you're more on the serious side, honour this in your descriptions, too. The ultimate goal is a consistent customer experience across your entire online website and online presence.

Do include social proof

Not everyone will scroll through pages of reviews before making a purchase. But customers *are* more likely to believe other customers than a business itself. We're sceptical folk. And of course you're going to think your products are the bee's knees. Featuring a short, snappy quote from a review in your product descriptions can help you overcome this. You benefit from social proof, without relying on customers going looking for it. This will go a long way in building brand trust and authority.

Top-quality product descriptions aren't going to write themselves. And if you have a lot to write, they can seem daunting. But just take your time, write them when you can, follow our advice, and they'll come together in no time!

PROPERTY LISTINGS

There's no shortage of bland, two-dimensional property listings out there. You know the ones. They view the written description as a simple means to an end. Usually filling it with simple bullet points of basic facts and features. *3-bedroom. Large, spacious kitchen. Beachfront property with a large, private garden.* These descriptions are all accurate, yes. But they don't pull at my heartstrings and transport me to the scene. I can't instantly imagine waking up to that beach view or entertaining my friends in that large, spacious kitchen. In short, it doesn't put me (the prospective buyer or tenant) or my life in the picture at all.

You'd think it's more important today than ever. With so many estate agents and easy access to property listings online, you know you need to do everything you can to stand out. Not just for your company, but for the homeowners you represent. With this in mind, let's look at how you can unleash your creativity and produce captivating property listings that make taking action irresistible for your prospective buyers and renters. For the sake of ease, I'm only going to refer to buyers for the rest of this section. But rest assured that all the guidance rings true for stealing the attention of renters too.

Who are you selling to?

In the *Research* pillar, I talked about knowing your audience. That's vital here, of course, but when it comes to property, you need to dig into it a little deeper. Before you put pen to paper, ask yourself: what kind of people is this property likely to attract? Developers? Investors? A family? A solo, first-time buyer? Who have you dealt with while selling similar properties in comparable areas? Without fully understanding your buyers' needs, you can't tailor the content to what they're looking for. If you know a property in the city centre is going to be a hot ticket for investors, what qualities are you pushing versus a semi-detached in a suburb that's going to attract families? One might be looking for rental potential, the other outdoor space or transport links. It's only once you get under the skin of your buyers and their motivations that you can communicate with them in a meaningful, direct way.

What components make up a listing?

So what are you looking to include in a listing? Outside of the main selling points, that is. Property listings will usually contain the same core written elements, but it's how you use them that'll make the difference. Let's go through how you can improve each part.

Property information

This is the simple facts of a property, usually laid out in a bullet-point list. The bedrooms, bathrooms, square footage, asking price, whether it has a garden, estimated rental income, or any other key features. Rather than just covering the basics here, such as a home having central heating or being double glazed, create this list based on what you believe your prospective buyers will prioritise most. And always lead with what you consider to be most important. Are buyers likely to commute and value proximity to a train station? Could it be a young family who care about the schools nearby? If so, you want these features seen as quickly as possible, so don't wait until the full description.

The opening line

As with any other content, you want your descriptions to start strong, with an attention-grabbing opening statement that piques interest and encourages further reading. In one succinct sentence you want to hone in on your prospective buyers' motivation. Think of it as an extended version of your headline, where you're able to mention one or two key features to win your reader over. For example,

"Recently refurbished, this charming 1-bed home is finished to an exceptional standard and well situated in a lively up and coming neighbourhood." Or, "Achieving an average monthly rental income of £1,150, this 2-bed flat is refreshingly modern and located in a popular city-centre area."

The first of these might be tailored towards a young couple looking for their first home together. The second would be more suited to an investor looking to expand their portfolio.

Property description

You've covered the basic features and selling points in the content so far. Now it's about filling in the details and telling a story. In your description, you want to complement your images, building a vision of what living in the home might look like to a buyer. Use the power of storytelling to help your reader imagine themselves already there. To achieve this, you'll want to focus on both features **and** benefits. A kitchen island is a feature. Ample counter space to wine, dine, and entertain your loved ones is a benefit. A bay window is nice enough. But a bay window that floods the spacious living room in afternoon sunlight? When can I move in?

These specific visual images will encourage an emotive response from the reader. They help you sell a lifestyle, not just four walls. Through the power of words, you can tap into the individual desires of your audience and create a strong desire to own the property, before they've even scheduled a viewing. To bring that to life, it's time to grab those thesauruses, ladies and gentlemen. Is the fireplace beautiful? Or is it bewitching? Is the living room well-sized? Or is it roomy, while also retaining a cosy and inviting quality?

Every other listing out there will use the same old basic adjectives - beautiful, really, unique, and spacious (to name a few). Where possible, try to use something different. This is how you ensure your listings stand out and unleash your prospective buyers' vibrant imagination. And when it comes to property, you're never just selling a home; you're selling an area too. What would matter to the buyer most in a local area? Are their shops, parks, bars, restaurants, or a beach nearby? What kind of life could they build here?

As an example, if an area is up and coming and seeing a lot of interest at the moment, say so. This will help create FOMO and a sense of urgency to take action. Now that we've covered the basics, let's look at dos and don'ts for writing your property listings.

Do talk directly to your reader

'You' and 'your' help your reader form a direct connection. Rather than talking about a distant property, you're placing them directly in the narrative. By speaking as if a property is already theirs, you raise the emotional stakes. Similarly, if you're talking to individuals and families - rather than investors or developers - opt for the word 'home' instead of 'property'. It has a far more personal, intimate feel.

Don't be vague

Being specific helps you to be more believable. Is it a quick walk or drive to the nearest train station? Well 'quick' could mean anything and doesn't tell your reader anything. Something could take 30 seconds walking along, but with six kids and a dog, just getting to the end of our road can take ten minutes! Passages of time are subjective and unique to the individual so pointless when used as 'context'. Instead, share exactly how many minutes it'll take. And if there are a lot of amenities on the doorstep, what are they? Again, be specific. Hairdressers? Cafes? Pubs? Restaurants? Supermarkets? Think of what someone might want on an average day.

Do highlight anything new or branded

A recently refurbished bathroom or popular brand of fridge are both examples of big pros in property. They can seal the deal for buyers who are going back and forth. Anything you feel will be the cherry on top of an already great property should be shouted out directly.

Don't shoot yourself in the foot

People are always looking to save a few pennies. And property buyers are no different. The words you use in your listing can actually impact the offers you receive. Suggesting an owner wants a quick sale, that a property needs some TLC, or that it's a fixer-upper could all encourage prospective buyers to try their luck at lower offers. Which, if you're looking for above asking-price offers, will get quite tedious. An exception to this is if you've got a seller who does *really* want to rush a sale, even if that means getting lower offers. I suppose this could be a do or a don't, depending on the circumstances.

Writing powerful property listings requires you to focus on quality over quantity. And I won't lie, this does take a little more time. But once you start, I promise you won't ever turn back. By producing detailed, buyer-led copy for your properties, you'll never run the risk of selling them short again.

REPORTS

Being able to take a specific event, topic, or issue, research it thoroughly, and condense your findings into a succinct, fact-based deep dive that's easily digestible and, dare we say, enjoyable to read? It's not an easy feat. But that's the conundrum you face when it comes to writing a report. Reports are all about making other people's lives easier. You're gathering all the information and evidence on a certain topic and laying it out in a structured, accessible way that saves someone else the time and energy of researching it themselves. Perhaps you're analysing and applying data or information to help them make a decision or to understand something new.

As a general rule of thumb, any report you write should be well-structured, detailed, clear, and concise. It's a delicate balance. You can't simply word-vomit all your thoughts and findings onto the page and call it a day. There needs to be some method to the madness. There are plenty of varieties of reports out there - including those written for academic, business, or scientific purposes. But, for this book, I'm going to break down reports as a whole. So feel free to take or leave the tips and tricks that suit your particular brief. Let's jump right in.

What's your objective?

You need to begin with a really firm understanding of your objectives. What have you been asked to write about? Who are you writing for? What are the parameters of your research? What's the end goal of your audience after reading? Take some time to sit with your brief and make sure you're super clear on what's being asked of you. If anything in the brief is unclear, it's better to get clarification before you start putting in the hours of research and writing. Then, once you've made friends with your brief, I always suggest writing one single sentence that summarises what your report will achieve.

For example: *"This report will explore whether social media is ruining humans' attention spans."* Or: *"This report will educate readers on why fried chicken is more popular than other types of chicken."*

This sentence isn't for anyone else but yourself. So don't feel pressured or overthink it. The goal is to challenge yourself to distil all your thoughts into one clear idea. It'll help you drill down into exactly what you want to say. This is then something you can revisit while writing to stay on track. When it comes to deciding whether or not a certain piece of data deserves to make the final cut, you can judge it alongside this sentence and see if it earns its place.

Plan your structure

The purpose of your report will determine what sections you'll need to include. But generally, reports will contain a combination of the following:

Title page - Nothing complicated, just the name of the report and perhaps some contact details in a footer. Along with your logo. It'll likely be the last page you put together.

Table of contents - An important addition that helps your readers find relevant sections quickly. Depending on the length and breadth of your report, this might include sub-headings too.

Executive summary - This should be a quick summary - emphasis on the 'quick' - that introduces the purpose and goal of your report, as well as summarising any key findings. It should follow the title page and give the reader an idea of what to expect.

Introduction - As well as introducing the topic, this section will also touch on any relevant background information, your aims and objectives, and why the following report will be valuable for a reader.

Methodology - A summary of the methods used to gather your data. For example, did you use a survey? Who were your respondents?

Findings - This is fairly self-explanatory. What were the findings of your research? This is less about analysing or explaining them, more about laying them all out in a clear, easily digestible way.

Analysis - Now you can analyse and discuss your findings. What do your findings actually *mean*? What do they show about your industry or business? Why should your reader care?

Conclusion and recommendations - These might be individual sections or combined as one, depending on how much you have to say. This is where you'll bring together all the information you've gathered in a succinct way, offering a holistic, definitive interpretation. As well as offering guidance for any next steps.

Bibliography - Including the information of sites or references you've used is important for giving credit where it's due. But it also allows your reader to do any additional reading they feel necessary.

There's no hard and fast rules about what your report should contain. Take it on a case-by-case basis. If you've collected all your research and facts from Google, for example, you won't need a methodology.

Create an outline

Before you actually get to writing, reports feel a lot like a puzzle. You have the overarching goal of the piece, and now have to find all the individual pieces to fill it out. Using the basic reporting structure above, you've decided which sections are relevant to your individual brief. It's time to put your thoughts to paper. Now is when you'll begin gathering and organising all the relevant data, information, and research you want to include. This could be a combination of your own perceptions, online research, or primary data.

Getting all your data and information onto the page - even in messy note form or bullet points - is helpful at uncovering gaps that need further attention. You can easily see areas that are light on content, or places where you're lacking evidence to support your claims. With a thorough outline that houses all your thoughts and reference material, writing becomes so much easier. Rather than flitting between the document, Google, your survey tool, and anywhere else, you can methodically move through your outline and expand your notes, confident you're covering all bases. Now you've got all your rough ideas onto paper, here are some dos and don'ts for writing the first draft of your full report.

Don't write your executive summary first

The purpose of your executive summary is to provide a topline overview of the report to follow. As such, you can't write it - at least not very well - until you've written the rest of your report. It might come first in your report, but I always recommend tackling it last. This is the same with your introduction. You'll need to get a feel for what your research is saying and any final conclusions before you can accurately summarise what your audience will gain from reading it.

In a similar vein, write it out of order if that helps you. Since sections like the results or methods are objective facts, not something you have to express your opinion on, these should come easier. Plus, it always feels good to get some words on the page and makes it easier to push through with the rest.

Do check your formality

In general, reports err on the more formal side. Who your audience are will determine just how formal you have to go. If you're putting together a quick report for your boss to skim read ahead of a big meeting, you'll likely be fine keeping your tone and formatting more laid back. You might even include quick bullet points to communicate a lot of information quickly.

But if you're writing a report that'll be shared around the big executives of your organisation, or released externally, you'll want to keep your tone on the professional side and follow all the conventions of formal reports. And if it's a public-facing report, you'll likely want to balance the weight of the subject with your brand identity. So if you're usually a cheery, positive face but you're doing a report on mental health, you need to balance your cheery nature with the sombre subject.

Don't forget the visuals

You could spend five hours producing an in-depth written account of your survey results. Or you could spend five minutes turning them into a brightly-coloured, eye-catching pie chart. I know which I'd rather. Not only will this save you valuable time and effort, but it also makes your report more engaging and your findings **a lot** easier for your reader to understand.

Do stick to the facts

Unlike essays, reports have no place for opinion. They're all about cold-hard facts. While your conclusion *might* contain your own perceptions of an event or situation, steer clear of including any direct opinions throughout. If a point can't be supported by research, you probably shouldn't be making it.

Don't overcomplicate

Reports should be easy to read and digest - both for a fellow expert on the subject, as well as someone with little experience or knowledge. As such, you want to keep your language simple and succinct. Offer explanations for anything you feel might need it. And aim to make your writing as accessible as possible. Which reminds us...

Do avoid jargon

Unless you know categorically that everyone reading your report will share the same knowledge as you, it's best to avoid jargon. Or, at least, explain what any jargon means if and when you use it.

Reports play a huge role in information sharing across an organisation. But not all reports are created equally. Without the proper preparation, report writing can feel like trying to wrangle a very large tiger into a very small cage. That is, until now.

SIGNAGE

N ow I don't know if all of you get as triggered by badly written signs as I do. But it's a real problem I've noticed. On roads, shop fronts, in shopping centres. The list goes on and on. Despite the great responsibility signs have, there are **a lot** of questionable ones out there. We use them to sign post our businesses and secure custom, to navigate people from A to B, or to literally keep them alive - yet we can't use a comma to actually make them readable? Or proofread to make sure readers know they'll be 'fined £100', rather than 'find £100' for parking illegally? We've all seen bad examples.

"CAUTION SLOW KIDS ON ROAD WITH NO SHOULDERS DEAD END"

I'm sorry... what? Writing copy for signage challenges you in new ways. You're not aiming for the sexiest sounding sentence, or trying to evoke vivid images in your readers' minds. Instead, you're hunting for the perfect formula of as few words as possible. Your goal is to capture attention, communicate a clear message, and inspire action. All within about 2-10 seconds.

A sign from above

The best signs are short, snappy, and easy to remember. This is how you get them noticed and make sure your reader retains the information. If you walked past a 5-foot sign full of size-11 text on the street, would you stop and read it? I'm going to guess not. The purpose of your signage is going to determine its length. For example, a small sign to let passersby know that out-of-this-world sandwiches are just around the corner will be far shorter than one letting your staff know what to do in the case of a fire. But no matter the amount of content on a sign, the more you can condense the message, the better.

In the case of shorter signs, where you're aiming for around five to seven words, it can be helpful to work backwards. What **one** takeaway do you want readers to have after reading the sign? This forces you to go back to basics and stop overthinking what to include. We have this tendency to try and say **everything**, when signs are far more effective when you stay specific. By first drilling down into the key purpose, you can reign in any waffling or over-explaining you might have a tendency to do.

Let's use the sandwich shop example above. If you're hoping to capture the attention of people on their lunch break with a sign two streets over, your reader won't need to know the ins and outs of your business or what sandwiches you have on offer. They'll just need to know you make tasty sandwiches that have the power to brighten their lunchtimes. So, if that's the core message, how can you produce an engaging, memorable sentence that'll stick with them? "Sandwiches like you've never seen before - next to the Waterstones". You get the idea.

With larger signs, such as those for health and safety, you're going to need more than a headline's worth of text for compliance purposes. This will be a big test in condensing your message. Start by identifying everything you **have** to say. Then see how you can condense it. How can you describe the evacuation procedure in as few words as possible? Can you use bullet points to streamline the copy? Are there two scenarios that require the same response? Can you group them together? Don't be afraid to split the content into multiple signs if this makes them more eye-catching and easier to digest.

Consider what the overall message of the content is and create an attention-grabbing headline for it. Or pick out the most important pieces of information. How can you condense these into a line or two that will sit in a bigger font at the top of the sign to capture attention? And let's all take a vow right now to **always** proofread our signage. While going viral on Twitter for a sign littered with typos could get people talking about your brand, it'll be for all the wrong reasons.

As the writer, you can't rely on the printers or whoever is making your sign to catch and correct your grammar. And if they don't catch the errors, you've just wasted a lot of time and money on signs that you can't use. Or, worse still, signs that you'll use without realising and take the reputational hit for. To finish off, here are some additional dos and don'ts of writing the perfect sign.

Do aim for consistency

I recently saw a sign that burnt my brain. It was three words. The first word began with a capital letter - standard. The next had no capitals - fair enough, I suppose. The final word? All caps. Please make it make sense. With signage, always aim for consistency. Consistency in terms of font, font size, and capitalisation. Otherwise, you risk making your reader work harder to understand your message. Or them ignoring your sign altogether.

Don't overlook the power of numbers

Numbers are great for signage because they take up less space. They're easy to understand and can portray a message far quicker than words ever could. Some examples might be including prices or discounts. After all, who doesn't want a good deal on their lunchtime sandwich?

Do embrace white space

Cramming writing onto a sign isn't conducive to the sign ever being read. It only becomes harder for anyone to read or understand. This is where borders and white space come in. When I say white space, it isn't necessarily literally white. Whatever the colour of your sign is. As long as each word has some room to breathe. It's far easier for your reader to focus and absorb the information in front of them. If you're able to strike a balance of writing and background space, you'll find your signage lands far better.

Don't forget images

You know what they say: a picture is worth a thousand words. And this is true for your signs too. Images are far easier to digest than words. They get to the crux of your message quicker, instantly orienting your reader. Plus, they're a lifesaver for fitting more information into your sign, while also keeping it readable.

Do use personality and humour

Now I'm not saying you have to sprinkle jokes into your health and safety signage - although, this *would* probably improve readability. Nor am I expecting the local council to start making the little stick figures on pedestrian crossings look like clowns. But injecting some personality and humour into your sign copy where appropriate is a brilliant way to help them land. A great example would be including a funny pun on the chalkboard you leave outside your shop or cafe. This highlights your business's personality and will leave an impression on passersby - even if they don't visit you on that particular day. The next time they're around and need somewhere to grab a coffee, they might actually remember you.

Similarly, internal signage can be the perfect opportunity for some personality. If you consider yourself an upbeat, lighthearted business, make this known on all the instructional signs on-site. It'll help you provide a more well-rounded, cohesive customer experience.

Signage is a challenge in saying more with less. But when done right, it can lead to big boosts in brand awareness and customer retention. Follow these tips and you'll be off to a great start.

SOCIAL MEDIA POSTS

D id you know - at the time of writing - over 58% of the world's population uses social media? Or that social media users have grown at a compound annual growth rate of 12% over the past decade? It's become essential for businesses to prioritise their presence on social media. But, to get eyes on your pages, and to turn those views into tangible business outcomes such as sales or leads, you need to be producing high-quality content that helps you stand out.

For the purposes of this section, we're going to focus on the big three social platforms: Instagram, Facebook, and Twitter. But do bear in mind a lot of the guidance will also apply to any other social channels that contribute to your weekly screen time. First up, some general rules of thumb to follow when writing your posts...

Keep them short and sweet

People don't go on social channels with the intention of reading an essay; they go to browse. If we're being really honest, most of the time, we're just sitting there aimlessly scrolling while procrastinating at work or killing time before we go to bed. Your social posts aren't going to be catching your audience at their most focused or invested. So you want to make sure everything you publish is easily consumable. That what you're saying is engaging - providing value, education, or entertainment - in a succinct way.

Instagram captions driving the most interactions were between 1 and 50 characters. That doesn't give you much space at all. It's similar on Facebook. Posts with 80 characters or less received 66% more engagement. While marketing leader at Hubspot Dan Zarrella believes 120-130 characters to be the sweet spot. And 100 characters is commonly known as the ideal character count for a tweet. However, tweets with even less than this have been shown to see 17% more engagement. So when it comes to your social media posts - irrespective of the platform - you want to say more with less.

Adapt to the platform

Just like you wouldn't use the same copy on your social channels as you would your website homepage, your social media copy should vary across platforms, too. Many writers fall into the trap of writing a great piece of copy and putting it **everywhere**. Open Twitter, copy, paste. Open Instagram, copy, paste. You get the gist. But as great as that piece of content may be, it needs adapting for different channels. What makes a brilliant Instagram caption won't necessarily gain any traction on Facebook. And vice versa.

Each platform has its own USPs that make it unique. For example, Twitter is *the* platform for discussion. That's its entire premise. People go on Twitter to voice opinions, engage in debate, and discuss current affairs. This lends itself well to more off-the-cuff, stream-of-consciousness type content. The 'hot takes' which are likely to grab people's attention and inspire replies, likes, or retweets. On the other hand, you see far less back and forth on Instagram because the platform is primarily visual. And the way it's built just isn't as suited to long threads of conversation.

With Instagram, it's mainly your visuals that will promote engagement. But a witty, relatable opening line in your caption could make the difference between someone pressing 'read more' or scrolling right past to the next cute dog. Text within images is also a popular way to shape your Instagram content. After all, who doesn't love a meaningful, inspiring quote?

Facebook posts are generally best for videos, blog posts, or curated content. Copy that's informative and directly addresses an audience's need or pain point. Why is this all important? Well, you need your content to match the platform you're on.

Understanding what makes a platform tick and what feeds its algorithms should always shape the content you produce. It's how you make sure you receive good engagement and avoid getting lost in a wave of other posts. Even your own audiences will vary in demographic and interests across the different platforms. So, with that in mind, let's look at each of the three main platforms.

Twitter

Twitter tends to have the snappiest, least manicured content of all the channels. While other platforms force you to be more modest in your frequency of posting, they welcome everyone's every thought at any given time. Unfortunately for you, this means you're fighting a load of mundane and (often) grammatically incorrect posts just to see the light of day. Here's what you need to keep in mind when it comes to Twitter.

Post length

Thanks to Twitter's 280 character limit, you don't have the luxury of writing a long post. Though this isn't necessarily a bad thing. Readers will be browsing for short and sweet content that makes them laugh, gets them thinking, or makes them form an opinion on something. And this character limit forces you to get straight to your point. It can be a challenge to condense a large, important message to a measly 280 characters (including spaces), but it can be done. The best way to do it is to get really specific.

Being specific allows you to milk every idea/topic/piece of content you have for what it's worth. Instead of covering a broad topic in one post, you can split it into multiple. However, if you really can't squeeze your message into such a tiny box, there are ways around it. Try putting your key point or take away in an eye-catching, branded text graphic. Again, people don't want to read an essay, so keep it concise. Then, use your tweet space to introduce the point or reiterate the key take away. Or you could create a thread, posting the first part of your tweet and then responding to it. Then respond to the response and so on. You can use threads to deliver more information in a neat, digestible way, while keeping the topic in one place.

The goal of tweets

Twitter was created for conversation. So start one! Ask your followers a question or explicitly state that you're looking for opinions on a topic. Sometimes, people just need an open invitation to spend some time indulging their own thoughts. When people respond to your tweet, it gets a little boost from the algorithm. More so than when you receive a "like". Meaning more people will see it. Discussion plays a huge role in keeping users on the platform, which is why the algorithm values it so much. Twitter is also the place a lot of people go for their news. In fact, according to a survey by the American Press Institute, this is **the** most common reason why people use Twitter.

What this means for your content is that attention-grabbing headlines will work a treat. Then, you can link through to a blog post relating to the topic, post it alongside a text graphic like above, or a video. This way, you're catering to both those having a quick scroll, as well as those looking for more information.

Instagram

Despite being a predominantly visual platform, high-quality written copy still has its place on Instagram.

Post length

Unlike Twitter, you don't face a stringent word count on Instagram. Well, unless you're a major waffler and struggle to keep your thoughts within 2,200 characters. BUT Instagram captions only show the three lines (or 125 characters). This means people will have to click "read more" to see the rest of your caption. So you have to get good at piquing readers' interests quickly. Post length is something you'll likely want to mix up. Give your followers some variety. Sometimes, a quick one liner with emojis is all you'll need to bag a lot of likes. Other times, you might want to educate your readers. In this case, writing a long-form caption might be more appropriate - with a scroll-stopping opening line, of course.

The goal of Instagram posts

As we said, Instagram is a visual platform. While a great caption can do *a lot* for keeping your audience interested, it's always going to come second to the visual element. Luckily, professional-quality photos aren't the only way to secure high engagement on the platform. Text graphics, inspirational quotes, and other visual representations of text are becoming more and more popular. Writing engaging captions to educate, then stripping out a particularly powerful quote to create an accompanying eye-catching graphic, might be your secret to success here. However, you want to also play the game and mix your feed up with actual imagery, too.

Facebook

To this day - in 2022 - Facebook remains the most used social media site. So even if you no longer use it, sometimes, your market will.

Post length

Facebook is the platform most compatible with long-form content. You can have over 63,000 characters in standard posts. However, just because you can, doesn't mean you should. At least not all the time. Like we said, it's still the shorter posts that perform best. Similar to Instagram, your written posts will be capped after the first few lines, with your audience having to physically click to see more. So always make sure your posts start by building anticipation and enticing your reader in. There's no point having your funniest line before the cut off point.

The goal of Facebook posts

The most engagement on Facebook tends to be on posts that add tangible value - whether that's by educating or entertaining. And the most popular form of content tends to be videos, receiving up to 59% more engagement than other content forms. This doesn't mean you have to spend hours creating brand new ideas for video content. You can easily strip out existing blogs and create a quick two-minute instructional video to help your audience improve their recruitment efforts or debobble a jumper. Then, for the corresponding copy, go to town selling the benefits of this content. Instantly let the scrollers know that their life will be heaps better in just two minutes' time.

The next most popular content on Facebook are blogs and curated pieces. This would be targeted, insightful content that addresses the unique pain points and needs of your target audiences. It's about striking the balance between being educational and entertaining your reader. There's such a breadth and depth of what you could write about that it's hard to cater for everyone reading this right now. Take what lessons you can and see what you can apply to your social channels. Another great place to look at is the *Blogs and social media strategy* section, which has some helpful advice on pacing your content.

In addition to standard posts, don't underestimate the power of groups and communities within Facebook. Where appropriate, consider where you may add value to certain groups by sharing regular content. As long as you're not spammily selling, you're not depending on a following that you've had to cultivate yourself to get your message across. To wrap up this part, I have some extra dos and don'ts to keep in mind.

Do use hashtags - sparingly

The point of hashtags is to help people find new, relevant content and accounts to follow. To join conversations that matter to them. So as long as you keep your hashtags relevant and don't overdo it, you could significantly expand your reach. You can use branded hashtags too. This way, when people tweet about your brand or product, someone who hasn't already heard of you may stumble upon it. They also make it easier for you to respond to and engage with customers. Hashtagging anything and everything under the sun isn't advisable though. Keep it to a few here and there. In fact, they can help your posts reach more people. Posts that use between one and ten hashtags tend to perform the best.

Don't ignore your external content

Your social posts don't exist in a vacuum away from all the other content you produce. In fact, they can be a great way to promote your external content - such as blog posts, white papers, or even your other social channels. Add a link to a video, blog, or report with some short, attention-grabbing text to introduce whatever you're linking. This way, you're building a self-sufficient web of content.

Do be relatable

Social media posts are a wonderful way to humanise your brand. Don't shy away from unleashing more of your personality than you would on say your website or emails. By nature, social media is a more relaxed, natural form of communication. So while we don't recommend doing a complete 180 on your usual business persona, adding a few more relatable anecdotes or quick-witted jokes can help your content land easier with your reader.

Taking your business's social media content to the next level can feel like a big ask. But so long as you remain authentic to your brand, endeavour to educate and entertain your audience, and have a basic understanding of what content performs best on which platform, there's no reason you can't start racking up the engagement in no time.

TENDERS

The tendering process is a pivotal moment for your business; a key part of growing and securing new revenue and opportunities. But the competition can be fierce. Some buyers will have hundreds of tenders to scan through for just one contract. Which is why writing the strongest possible tender responses is essential in order to boost your chance of selection. When it comes to writing one, we're going to focus on your answers to the qualitative questions, as these are where sloppy or half-baked writing will let you down. The actual content that your responses should include will vary depending on the individual contracts you're bidding for. So, for the purposes of this book, we're going to look at how to nail your qualitative tender responses - no matter the nature, size, or scope of the project at hand.

Being able to write valuable tenders succinctly will come from clearly understanding and clarifying the criteria you'll be compared against. The better you understand what's expected of you, the easier you can drill down into the key, relevant information. So, before you get to writing, make sure you understand exactly how you'll be assessed and scored. Have you been supplied with documentation outlining how you can score highly? If not, have you had a conversation with the buyer directly to clarify exactly what they're looking for?

Address each and every point of the question

One of the quickest ways to lose out on contracts is to overlook aspects of the question. This one is so important. It's like the cardinal sin of tender writing. If something's been put into a tender question, it's because the procuring team deem it essential. Let's look at an example.

A question might ask you to provide details of any asbestos awareness safety training you've carried out. And to include stated dates, names of recipients, names of trainers, and any of their associated qualifications. While it might be a lot of work to gather all the dates, names, and qualifications, if it's been explicitly asked for, it's imperative that you make the time. The fact of the matter is that you can get **so** much guidance on writing strong, high-scoring tender responses by simply deconstructing the questions you're being asked.

Use the structure of a question itself to help you. Let's say a question is broken down into five subsections. You can shape your response similarly, methodically breaking down each and adding the subheadings in to assist the buyer in reading your tender. This way, you can be confident you're touching on every aspect of each question. It can be more difficult when faced with vague, open-ended questions that don't really give anything away. In this case, you'll want to lean back on the corresponding specification and, if necessary, get clarification from the buyer directly.

Along a similar vein, make sure you're **only** answering questions with the information requested. Now is not the time to dump all the USPs of your business or the information **you** consider impressive. You're writing for your reader only. That's going to be the crux of your tender. It's a small piece of advice, but one that will have a massive impact. Before we round off this section, here are some dos and don'ts.

Do expand where necessary

Rather than answering a question by listing what skills your team has, go further. Tell the reader exactly what benefits they'll get from choosing you over anyone else. By going through the tendering process, you clearly believe you'd be able to complete the project appropriately. But this is about demonstrating exactly how and why you'll be able to do so faster, better, or easier than anybody else. Have you done similar projects to this one in the past, and therefore are able to offer additional guidance and support? Do you have niche industry experience on your team that elevates your offering? Look at everything you can bring to the table.

Don't be too colloquial

This is a business proposal. You need to maintain a professional tone - even if this is a business you know well and have worked with before. Out of every kind of content discussed in this chapter, a tender might be one of the most formal. If anything, it's the one where you don't want too much personality, either. Just state the facts, bring forward your best qualities, and let those speak volumes.

Do provide evidence

I could tell you that I once won the World Record for eating the world's largest burrito in two minutes flat. Or that I once went axe throwing with (and beat, might I add) Dwayne "The Rock" Johnson. Would you believe me? You probably shouldn't.

And you should expect the very same scepticism from the readers of your tender responses. You can say you've done a lot and drone tirelessly about certain skills you bring to the table. But if you can't back these up with concrete evidence, you're going to struggle to make the strong impact needed to win competitive contracts. In every question, support what you're saying with evidence. Use facts, figures, quotes from client testimonials, dates, and qualifications wherever possible.

Don't ignore the word count

Sometimes, writing a lengthy, detailed response is actually the easy part of writing your tenders. The difficult part is trying to fit all you want to say into 500, 200, or even 100 words. This is something you'll want to be wary of when initially putting your thoughts and ideas together. For example, if you know a question only has the space for a 100-word answer, you're not going to list twenty different points you'd like to cover. Bullet points can also really help here, allowing you to say more and cover a lot of ground, while still conforming to the word counts.

The reason this is such a big deal is that they won't take kindly to anyone who breaks the rules. With so many tenders to run through, they'll look for any reason to throw your submission in the bin. They want partners they can trust to follow the rules and do the work right. Going over the word count subconsciously shows you're not that.

Do care about the details

In a similar vein, pay attention to every detail. This is about more than your basic spelling and grammar mistakes, but also the formatting requirements of the tender. They might want answers in bullet-point form. Or they might want you to put certain answers in certain boxes. And some questions will come with stipulations of **how** they want you to answer it. I've seen some that ask for details such as award wins or key staff. When they ask for something like that, you can't miss it. Once you've written your tender, check how the buyer is accepting submissions. Some prefer mail while some prefer email. These are simple boxes to tick off, but will help minimise any barriers between you winning the contracts you want.

Armed with these top tips, you have all the insight needed to produce relevant, high-quality tender responses and put your organisation in top contention for competitive contracts.

WEBSITE CONTENT

It goes without saying that there are a lot of websites out there. About 1.93 billion (at the time of writing), if you want to be precise. And yet there are so many that just aren't... great. They're not appealing to look at, they're hard to read, they're boring, the list goes on. But with 75% of consumers saying they judge a business' credibility based on their website, you really can't afford to let it be lumped in with the bad ones. Your website is everything. It sounds dramatic, but it's true.

It's often the first trace of you that potential customers will see. And it can make or break their perception of your business. So it needs to be the best it can be, and that starts with the content. Most people approach website and blog content in a similar fashion. However, website content is a beast all its own. Above all else, the finished product should be scannable, all about your reader, and easy for them to understand. You want to be at your audience's fingertips, answering questions they haven't asked yet, and providing solutions they don't even know they need. You want to be succinct and engaging, showcasing exactly why you're the best fit for their unique circumstance. Sounds simple, right? Well, it actually sort of is. So let's look at where to start.

Take stock of what you have

The first place to start is to look at your existing website. If you have one, that is. But whether you're building one from scratch or want to elevate what you already have, my advice is the same. So start as you mean to go on. How do you take stock? I find it's best to organise every page you have, and for me, a trusty spreadsheet is a good place to start. List every page in a Microsoft Excel or Google spreadsheet, along with either links to the pages on the site or on a separate document. This is important because you need to get your head straight.

What you don't want is to be shuffling through countless documents trying to find web pages and putting them together like a jigsaw. Don't overwhelm yourself like that. Lay them out so you can see what you've got, and from here, you can assess what you need to do next. In the case where you **don't** have a pre-existing website, do the same, but list the pages you want to include. There are some that every site will have:

- Homepage
- About us
- Products or services
- Contact us

And some others that you might want:

- Blog or news
- Your company ethos
- Testimonials

- Case studies
- Terms of service
- Delivery and returns policy (if you provide a product)
- Individual pages for each product or service

At this point, look at what you have and ask if there's anything you want in your new version. If you have pages missing, add them to your spreadsheet so you know to fill in the gaps later. Next, you just have to take it one page at a time. This is where you will begin to rewrite the content. It means you're not darting back and forth between pages and can concentrate on one idea at a time. The chances are a lot of what you already have is fantastic, it just needs to have some of the lessons of this book applied to it. Does the tone of voice reflect who you are as a company? Are you putting the audience first? All of the questions you'll ask yourself throughout the other pillars.

Think about the layout

Another aspect of rewriting your content is thinking about how it will be on the page. How you approach this will depend on what you're doing with your site. If you're not planning on whipping up an entirely new site, instead using what you already have, you still need to keep the layout in mind. How is it set up at the moment? If, for example, your homepage is split into four sections, your new content will need to be in four sections too. And, as another example, if you're not planning on adding a scrolling list of features, there's no point in writing one.

But if you're building an entirely new one, you have free reign over the design. By this, I mean that you can think of the layout as you write, picturing it in your mind as you go along. Make notes of this as you go, so you can pass these ideas on to the person building the site. Don't get too attached to the ideas as they might not work in practice, but considering the layout at least makes you think about what you write and when.

Unlike blogs, websites cannot be large chunks of text. Nobody's going to want to read that. Each page needs to have a flow to it. Different sections that break up the monotony of reading. Pictures, graphics, and colours to make it a more pleasant experience. With this in mind, there are plenty of engaging ways to display your text. Banners with snappy slogans (which you'll find on almost all website homepages) or sections separated with images. You might use iconography, tables, charts, videos. Your options are endless. There are a number of ways you can lay text on a page to make more of an impact. You can have:

- A carousel banner
- A static banner
- Centralised text
- Left-hand image, right-hand text
- Right-hand image, left-hand text
- Two colour text

- Iconography (with or without text)
- Videos
- Blogs
- Tables/charts/graphs
- Testimonials
- Calls to action

The list really goes on and on, but those are some examples to get the gears turning in your head.

Tell a story

One way in which your web pages are similar to blogs is that they both need to tell a story. Not literally; rather, each page should have a flow to it. Each section should connect to the next, guiding the reader through a number of steps. An easy way to break down each of the pages is to think about the PAS system. This stands for:

- Problem
- Agitate
- Solution

You start by addressing the **problem**. What issue are you solving for the client or customer? For a dog food company, the problem might be complicated dog nutrition. Pet owners who don't have the time to read every single label and just want high-quality food for their pooch.

Then you **agitate**. Why is the problem worse than they think? Using the same example, you could state that dog foods use terrible ingredients and that most of what's on the shelves aren't the best.

Finally, you bring in the **solution**. What your product or service does to solve all their woes. It could be that your food sources the highest-quality ingredients and makes the labels as transparent as possible.

This approach can be applied to almost every page on your site, but especially your homepage. What you're doing with PAS is creating the story. You're going from A to B to C, with each point linking to the next. The problem and agitate parts are there to show you know what your audience's problems are, and it puts them firmly in the driver's seat. Bookend the above with a banner containing a slick opening statement and a strong call to action at the end, and you have the makings of a pretty good web page.

My final tip is to **always write your homepage last**. As is the case with any headline, how are you supposed to summarise something you haven't written yet? Instead, starting with your story and services will get you super clear on what particular information needs highlighting on the homepage. For specific tips on certain pages - such as product descriptions - there's a relevant section for you if you flip back a few pages! To cap everything off, here are my do's and don'ts for writing your website copy.

Do make it scannable

The way we read content online is different from how we read print. When we're online, we want information fast. Reading a website is usually a means to an end. We read it because we want to buy, learn, or hire someone to do something. Therefore, you need to keep your content scannable. This way, your readers quickly find the section they're looking for and read more in detail if they want to. Using bullet points is a great way to keep your website copy brief and snappy. While subheadings help readers to quickly locate individual sections.

Don't abuse SEO

A huge part of modern-day websites is playing the SEO game. It's hard to avoid. Entire companies exist to make sure your content is jam-packed with SEO buzzwords. And rightfully so - it's how your website makes its way up Google's ranks. But that doesn't mean you can use them indiscriminately. Search engines are getting smarter. They can tell when you're using SEO terms for the sake of it. And, more importantly, so can the reader. So if you're a **plumber in Bristol** and you want to show up as the premier **plumber in Bristol**, and want everyone to know you're the best **plumber in Bristol** whenever anyone searches for a **plumber in Bristol**... Do you see how annoying that is? You have to be smarter about when and where you use your SEO terms.

They have to blend into the copy, not stand out. So don't pack them in there just because you can.

Do use pictures to complement your copy

I touched on this slightly when I was talking about the layout. But it's worthy of its own section. I've seen too many sites that have one picture at the top of a page and that's it. At heart, we're all still like kids who love to skip to the pictures. Why do you think Instagram is so popular? We expect pictures on websites. It's a great way to break up the text, add some colour, and keep people's brains engaged. You can also use it to showcase your products or services. Investing in some professional photography might not be a bad idea if you can use the photos to elevate your site. Companies with a tangible offering, such as construction businesses, can show people how good their work is, rather than just telling them.

Getting your website right is essential for your business. And these tips will make sure you get you started on the right foot.

PILLAR THREE:

WRITING

> *Your writing is ugly. Do you know how I know? Because so is mine.*

Writing and editing are two peas in a pod. If writing is the hyperactive toddler that's OD'd on blue Smarties, running around the house causing chaos, editing is the nanny frantically trailing behind, putting out fires left, right, and centre. In short, the first without the latter is a recipe for disaster.

Often, we feel this immense pressure to write perfectly from the get-go. To put pen to paper and make pure magic happen straight off the bat. Now, I'll take a stab in the dark and assume no one is capable of such mastery. I hate to break it to you. And setting ourselves up against this impossible standard is futile. The debilitating pressure to get things right often leaves you unable to start in the first place, wasting your own precious time. And/or you find yourself frustrated at the end when you inevitably never reach that promised land of perfect writing. Let's agree to stop with the unrealistic expectations from now on.

Now you've got a clear idea of structure, and you've switched your focus to what the audience wants, it's time to get your unfiltered, messy thoughts out and start writing. The cleaning comes during editing, but we'll get to that soon enough. Let's start with that first annoying hurdle: writer's block.

THE TRUTH ABOUT WRITER'S BLOCK

M any of us set our minds to a writing task - no matter how big or small - confidently crack our knuckles as we stare at the screen, go to type, and…. Well, nothing. After a few painstakingly silent minutes of bugger all creativity, you stare at the ceiling while swivelling in your chair. Wait a minute, is that a cobweb? I must hoover that *immediately*. The vacuum cleaner comes out and, before we know it, the rubber gloves are on, and the house is cleaner than it's ever been. You finish the end-of-year accounts five months too early, alphabetise every piece of paperwork you've ever owned, organise all your clothes in colour and season order, prep food for the next 12 years, and turn into an ironing machine. Ah, now to get that proposal started. Gee, would you look at the time? Oh well, guess it's off to bed. You'll get to it tomorrow.

First, it's time to hire a cleaner. Second, let's sort that procrastination out. We love to make our procrastination sound sexier by calling it 'writer's block'. Doesn't "I've got writer's block" sound far better than, well, *"I can't be arsed"*? We blame the temperature of our office, the noisy construction going on across the road, a bad night's sleep, lack of inspiration, the absence of noughties hits egging us on - literally *anything* to explain why we're not in our writing groove. But here's the harsh truth: writer's block? *Total myth.*

There's no such thing as the perfect setting to write in. Mentally or physically. Even the pros aren't perfect. When people imagine a writer, they think of this romantic, tortured genius with a typewriter, effortlessly delivering quips about comparing thee to a summer's day. Oh, if only it were that quaint or easy. At some point in your life, you've probably sat pulling your hair out, staring inches from the screen because you can't think of that one word you need. We've all been there. You spend all that time worrying about whether your writing is even interesting enough to read: now, **that's** what a writer is.

Writer's block doesn't exist. Most of the time, you're letting your lack of certainty about what to write or how to write prevent you from writing anything at all. If you wanted to, you could force some words out. Sure, they might be crap, but isn't a page with jumbled sentences and half-finished thoughts far less overwhelming than an entirely blank page? You'll be glad to hear you're not alone with these struggles. Writing feels hard at first because it's a skill you have to learn and continually practise. This is good news, though; it means you can learn to strengthen that muscle.

While writer's block is a myth, there are common stumbling blocks you might face while writing. And if there's anything Aries Merritt, the greatest hurdler in the world, can teach us, it's that hurdles are for jumping over, not awkwardly waiting behind. So if what you're feeling isn't a 'block', what is it? You're simply facing writing anxiety. The fear of the unknown. *How long will this take me to write? What will the finished product look like? Will it land well with people?* I get it. It can be a lot to juggle.

Sometimes, we write, bursting with ideas that we can't wait to put into words and upload for the world to see. And then we realise - *for the world to see? The WORLD?* Anyone can see your writing, and if you let it, that can be a scary thought. *What if it's terrible? Am I even qualified to write this? Have I ever been good at writing?*

You question everything you do and wonder if you should give up and leave it to the experts. But the truth is, even the experts feel that way. In his memoir "On Writing", Steven King professes shame and a lack of confidence in his writing until he was 40. It was a belief instilled in him by a teacher who once branded his work as "junk". He later read between the lines and understood that she was not his intended audience. So of course it didn't resonate for her. You're never going to please everyone. But you're also not writing to everyone. Once you've established who your audience is, everyone else is unimportant.

If you want to get better at writing, start today by simply writing and applying the lessons learned in the research and structure pillars. Contrary to popular belief, writers don't work by becoming overcome with spontaneous inspiration. Stephen King is a perfect example with his daily writing quota of 2,000 words. This is a bit extreme if you want to make your emails land better with people, but it highlights how King sets an expectation for his day before he gets started, as you should. If you have an important email to write, set aside 20-30 minutes of your morning to plan and draft your key points. If you're struggling to get your words out, start with a bullet-point list of what you'd like to say. Can't find that perfect first word to start with? Change the sentence. No one knew what you were going to say anyway.

Even when you feel blocked or anxious about the result, writing *something* will always be better than writing nothing. After all, how do you improve on something you actively avoid? Shakespeare's first-ever draft probably wasn't all that, but he's written some of the most iconic plays that are still adored today. He didn't achieve that without practice. With a consistent writing routine, our confidence and writing skills will only improve. It means less of that 'writer's block' negativity and more hideous first drafts we can turn into masterpieces - but more on that later.

With your own professional writing, any hesitation will often be a case of not knowing where to start. Then, finally, perfectionism sets in, and we decide to put the task off until the perfect opening appears in our minds as if by magic. The thing about perfectionism is that 'perfect' doesn't exist. It took me years to accept this myself, but you need to hear it. **PERFECT DOES NOT EXIST**. Don't take my word for it - let's look at the science. There are about 7 billion people in the world. That's 7 billion opinions and 7 billion perspectives on what 'perfect' is. With 7 billion versions of what perfection looks like, how are you going to convince me that this esoteric illusion exists?

With this in mind, whose yardstick are you measuring yourself against? Give yourself a break. It's time to get comfortable with being good enough and accept that most writing pieces will start half-baked and pretty shit. You don't even have to start from the beginning. If you have an idea for a powerful paragraph but don't know where it belongs yet, write it down. Write the last line first if you like. Your final version needs a winning structure and audience-led message, but it doesn't have to start there.

Which leads me to the next critical lesson.

YOUR WRITING IS UGLY

D o you know how I know? Because so is mine. You're not supposed to churn out 500-word masterpieces off the cuff. I can't, and I read and write all day, every day. So next time you think badly of what you've put together, cut yourself some slack. Writing is **supposed** to be messy. Editing, on the other hand, is where you crack out the microscope and look for every little error. It's what turns first drafts into audience-ready content. But they aren't the same, and they need to be completed in order.

Remember the analogy about laying individual bricks until you have a house? This is what we're doing now. You're no longer aiming towards writing a finished piece. You're not focusing on getting every line right before moving on to the next one. That's boring and exhausting.

I want to introduce you to something I like to refer to as the FUFD, otherwise known as the 'Fucking Ugly First Draft'. It's long, it drones on, it's indulgent, it's every "brilliant" idea you've ever dreamed up and spewed onto your page. And it **isn't** great writing. The only difference between knowing about the FUFD and what you've potentially been doing until this point is that you don't send or share your FUFD. There's more work to be done in the last pillar. But the lesson here is to be gentle with yourself, and it's okay to brain-dump.

There's something so freeing about accepting that writing will be ugly at first. Once you embrace separating writing from editing and acknowledging the difference between a FUFD and an edited, finished piece, you'll find the process a lot easier. It takes a lot of the pressure off and frees up space for you to get to work.

THE MAIN BIT: THE WRITING

The long and short of the writing pillar is this: get on with it. When you're clear on your communication style, the structure of the piece you need to write, and have an audience-led attitude, you're ready to go. The biggest tip I can give you at this stage is to write, write, and keep writing. It's going to be messy. The grammar is going to be shit. Some of it won't make sense. It's going to be out of order. And unfinished thoughts will pepper the page. But keep going anyway.

If you feel the urge to groan and blame your inability to start on 'writer's block', shift your perspective. And your expectations. Stop tripping yourself up worrying about the result. Stop expecting yourself to write a perfect opening paragraph. If you're looking for a place to start, try writing out a bullet-point list of your key messages instead. Then, one bullet point at a time, expand until you find your feet.

Steven King quotes: "To write is human, to edit is divine". Well, to be human is to be fallible. Divinity is pure. So give yourself a break and permission to be as clumsy and messy as you please when writing your FUFD. Bullet points, a nonsensical block of text, one unnecessarily long sentence? All fine for a FUFD. You'll quickly discover what process works for you.

Let your e-number-high toddler run wild and don't stop until you're finished. Then you can piece your thoughts together like a jigsaw into the plan and structure you made earlier. When you're done and have nothing more to say, it's time to get murderous.

PILLAR FOUR:

EDITING

If I were Michelangelo setting out to create my famous statue of David, I wouldn't start hacking into marble and hoping for the best. I would begin by taking a step back to admire the rectangular block that I'm working with. Whatever you're writing will come together in the same way.

O nce your FUFD is ready, you're in the home stretch and there's only one step left. The editing. Mark Twain simplifies the process: "Writing is easy. All you have to do is cross out the wrong words."

But I prefer Steven King's more melodramatic version: "Kill your darlings."

In your content, that is. Now you've allowed yourself to cause absolute carnage, it's time to step up and regain some order, turning your beautifully messy FUFD into something you can share with your audience. It's time to kill your darlings - all the parts of your writing that you cherish, but threaten the readability or value of your work. When I ask most people how many times they check over their work, they more often than not say once or twice. What they mean is they've produced a FUFD and ran with it. It's time to change that.

To jumpstart your editing process at this stage, I need you to give your work the time to settle. I don't mean "leave it" as in abandon it and hope it magically transforms into the best thing you've ever written, but let it (and you) rest for a short time. Perhaps go on a quick walk with the dog around the block, have a snack, or pop the kettle on.

When you come back, any emotions, negative or positive, will have subsided and you can be more objective. Separating yourself from your work - even for a few minutes, although in an ideal world a bit longer - is crucial to see it for what it is. Not only that, but when you're reading a piece over and over, you eventually transition from reading it to simply remembering it. Of course you're going to remember what you wrote: you agonised over it! So take a step back to allow yourself to move forward.

Have you had a rest? Good. Let's get to work.

EDIT FOR YOUR AUDIENCE

---

warned you I was going to go on about this one. We all know people who won't stop talking about themselves. They've bought a new car, got a promotion, they're thinking of getting their hair done, are having MAJOR relationship issues every day of the week, or they're doing something else that you couldn't care less about. And, after listening to all of their talking, do you like these people any better? Probably not. Do you want to hear more? Please, no. Are you over the conversation? Most definitely.

In this same way, talking too much about yourself is killing your communications. But why do we do it? According to research, talking about ourselves produces a similar neurological reaction as tantalising our tastebuds with decadent food, taking drugs, or having sex. In other words, it feels good. But, of course, you think your message and purpose are the mutt's nuts, so you're addicted to the buzz of shouting this from the rooftops. You're helping people, after all. If your writing isn't landing though, are you helping anyone?

There's nothing wrong with being passionate about your message. But you shouldn't allow this to get in the way of adding value to your audience. No matter what you're writing, the key is to do it with them in mind. When you write your FUFD, all your points are likely from your perspective. After all, you're not trying to write complete sentences; you're looking to put your thoughts to paper. Now you've brain-dumped and are ready, you can shape your content from the perspective of adding value to their lives.

This will look slightly different depending on the type of content that you write. If you're writing persuasion-based content that we covered in the structure pillar - such as emails, CVs, pitch decks, and presentations - you're typically focused on the one individual you're writing to. In which case, you can specifically tailor your content to them, their colour personality, and their needs. If you're writing informational content that's more likely to be wider spread - such as social media posts - then you need a strategy that puts your audience in the driver's seat. For example, Nike doesn't focus on sportswear and shoes. They talk about working hard, achieving your goals, and the impressiveness of the human mind and body. Maybelline doesn't hammer on about makeup. They talk about self-confidence, friendships, and individuality.

I often hear from people who are worried about boring their audience. You might even feel there's no point in posting a blog because no one will even care about the topic. If, after you've digested the pillars, you genuinely feel like the reader won't like it, then you're probably right. Working through the pillars highlights what you should be writing **and** what you shouldn't be writing. Throw the idea in the bin and write about something that will interest them. If you're bored by it, and they're going to find it boring or pointless, what's the point of writing it in the first place? Don't fall into the trap of being a post-for-the-sake-of-it type of person.

Once you have your FUFD ready, it's time to edit your content with your reader in the driving seat. So what does putting the audience first look like? I took a real email thread as an example of persuasive writing to show you the difference between the two. Writing for the audience doesn't mean losing your message or not having a goal behind it. You're refocusing your approach, with your reader at the forefront of your mind. Let's explore that.

Email one
Writer led

Hi [THEIR NAME],

As someone who manages X within X sector, I think you'd be interested in our X. Essentially it is [ELEVATOR PITCH].

There is no standardised X. This often means organisations like [THEIR COMPANY NAME] are left having to X. As I'm sure you're aware, this is a waste of X!

[YOUR COMPANY NAME] is different. We are [FIVE LINES OF TEXT INTRODUCING THE COMPANY].

For example, [FURTHER FIVE LINES TALKING ABOUT A CASE STUDY].

We support a number of X providers, like [COMPETITOR] and [COMPETITOR] with their X and I believe you would also be a great fit. Could we arrange a time for a brief chat, and I can explain a bit more about us, our history, our product, and how we can make X easier for you?

Thanks, [THEIR NAME]

[YOUR NAME]

Audience led

Hello [THEIR NAME],

I hope you're well.

There is a lack of X in the X sector that needs to be tackled. As this affects you, I wanted to reach out.

As a result of no blanket way to X in the X sector, most organisations are frustratingly left with [CHALLENGE 1]. The process becomes [CHALLENGE 2]. Does this sound familiar?

We found businesses like [THEIR COMPANY NAME] were looking for a solution that removes X. So we created one.

[CASE STUDY EXAMPLE].

I made you a 2-minute overview to show you how we're helping the likes of [COMPETITOR] and [COMPETITOR] with their X.

Are you open-minded to getting a date in the diary to see how you can make your X easier too?

Warm regards,

[YOUR NAME]

Both examples use pretty much the same information. They both share a brief case study. They both talk about the sender company. But example one is written to benefit the sender, and example two, the recipient.

- "I think you'd be interested in X"
- "Paragraphs of text about your own company"
- "I believe"
- "Could we arrange a time for a brief chat, and I can explain a bit more about us, our history, our product…"

It's the language you use that puts you first as the writer. Telling people why you think and believe they need you is a big no. Put yourself in their shoes - who are you to them? And why should they care what you think or feel? They don't know you from John or Sally to value your opinion in the first place. This is a busy person you're emailing. They don't care about paragraphs of text about you. They definitely don't want to sit on the phone and listen to you talk about yourself.

It MIGHT be true that what you have - even if it's free and takes minimal effort to integrate - is a benefit to them, but your content won't land if you frame yourself as the most crucial person in the room. Instead, take those same elements and reframe them. Ask them to weigh in by talking about their experience. Is this something impacting you? Do you agree this is a problem?

When reaching out to anyone, identify their colour personality and write content that prioritises what they're interested in. For this thread, we're talking to a red. Let's break down what we wrote and why.

"There's a lack of X in the X sector that needs to be tackled. As this affects you, I wanted to reach out."

Instead of telling the reader that they'd be interested in you, we've done the research and made a broad industry statement. By doing so, you create one of two opportunities. Either this problem doesn't impact them, meaning they're not your potential customer and won't pay attention anyway. Or they are, and you maintain their attention to read on, which is what you're looking for.

"As a result of no blanket way to do X in the X sector, most organisations are frustratingly left with [CHALLENGE 1]. The process becomes [CHALLENGE 2]. Does this sound familiar?"

Again, you're making a point, but instead of talking at them, you're giving them something to relate to. You address a potential pain point that they may be well aware of. It shows them that you know what you're talking about and understand their concerns. We end with a question because we can't assume they've gone through it. We've reverse-engineered what problems we can solve, and by asking this, we're funnelling the people we want to be talking to further down the email.

"I made you a 2-minute overview to show you how we're helping the likes of [COMPETITOR] and [COMPETITOR] with their X."

An additional resource is an excellent way to pique their interest and speak to their personality colour. If they're red, they don't want to miss out on benefits going to a competitor (and will appreciate the shortness of it). If they're green, they'll appreciate data and statistics. If they're blue, they're curious to see what others are doing. If they're yellow, you can highlight how it's helping the people they care about, be it staff, students, clients, and so on.

"Are you open-minded to getting a date in the diary to see how you can make your X easier too?"

Instead of making the call so you can talk about you, focus it on how they can make their life easier. It's the same message as the first email but has an entirely different meaning. Let's take a look at another example email. This is a possible follow-up to the previous ones.

Email two
Writer led

Hi [THEIR NAME],

It's [YOUR NAME] again. Did you have a chance to look through my previous message? I strongly believe [YOUR COMPANY NAME] can transform the way you go about X. We've made a brief 20-minute video that explains at a high level how we work.

Here's a summary of the main features:

- [FEATURE 1]
- [FEATURE 2]
- [FEATURE 3]
- [FEATURE 4]
- [FEATURE 5]

If you're not the right person to speak to about this, I would appreciate it if you could forward this to the relevant person(s) and let me know so I can pick it up with them directly.

Thanks,

[YOUR NAME]

Audience led

Hi [THEIR NAME],

How are you?

Thank you for taking the time to view the video on how [YOUR COMPANY NAME] works. I thought I would share some of the main features that are making X easier for the likes of [COMPETITOR] and [COMPETITOR].

[FEATURE 1]
[BENEFIT PUTTING THE AUDIENCE FIRST]

[FEATURE 2]
[BENEFIT PUTTING THE AUDIENCE FIRST]

[FEATURE 3]
[BENEFIT PUTTING THE AUDIENCE FIRST]

[FEATURE 4]
[BENEFIT PUTTING THE AUDIENCE FIRST]

I have availability in my diary next week to discuss how this can benefit you. When suits you best?

Warm regards,
[YOUR NAME]

How would you feel if you received an email from a stranger? *"Hey, me again. I still think we're amazing; here's a bullet-point list why. If it's not you, what's your colleague's name so that I can bombard them too and then they can be mad at you for it?"* It's not the most endearing, is it?

I often see the words "brief" and "thirty minutes" together in a sentence when discussing resources. What an oxymoron. Half an hour is not quick. It's 1/16th of the average person's workday. If you've ever walked down the high street, you'll see fundraisers trying to interrupt people hustling about their day. Think back to their success rate and the kinds of reactions they receive. Now consider your communication. Why are you expecting any different? Would you give someone twenty minutes if you didn't know them? Of course, you wouldn't. Start with a teaser version of what you want to show them, pique their curiosity, and then you can ask for more time.

I'm sure many of you reading have sent emails like this in the past. I know because my inbox is full of them. So is yours. I'm not here to shame or embarrass you, but let's turn this around into a positive habit that makes your life easier - and your readers' lives too.

Let's be brutally realistic here. A stranger does not care who you are. They're not interested in what you believe. No one owes you a favour. Why are we expecting people we haven't built up a rapport with to give their colleagues' details out willy-nilly? If my staff members started giving my phone number to every cold caller, I wouldn't be happy. Why are we putting people in that position? Do your research. Jump on Companies House. Be a little more proactive, and don't expect strangers to help you when they don't owe you anything. Instead of rattling off a list of features, show them why they should care about it. An example could look like this:

No more death by spreadsheets

Make it simple for your off-site staff. Instead of them drowning in hundreds of different spreadsheets that are impossible to decipher, wouldn't it be easier if they could access just the information they needed at the click of a button? One that's uniform and accessible for not only staff in the office, but also remote workers, contractors out on a site, and wider supply chain partners?

This approach would appeal well to the reader as you're outlining how you're making it easier for their team without ever mentioning yourself. Now let's look at what the last email might say.

Email three
Writer led

Hi [THEIR NAME],

I've not heard back from you, so I'll assume you're happy with the way you're currently handling X. Nevertheless, my colleague has just published an article about X which you may find useful going forward.

If you're still interested but haven't had the time to respond, just let me know the best time to reach you for a quick chat. Alternatively, you can book an online demonstration here.

Either way, let me know.

Thanks [THEIR NAME],

[YOUR NAME]

Audience led

Hi [THEIR NAME],

I hope you're well.

X should be simple, but in the world of X sector, it isn't. Our latest infographic proves how difficult it can be; do you find you face the same challenges?

I wanted to check in with you and see how our features are landing for you. As you know, by X, you can transform the way you X.

I'm curious. Of the four features I've shared with you:
- [FEATURE 1]
- [FEATURE 2]
- [FEATURE 3]
- [FEATURE 4]

Which stands out for your company right now?

It would be great to talk about your current situation; when suits you to get a call in the diary? Why don't we show you how we can bring you the same results as [COMPETITOR] and [COMPETITOR]?

Click here to book your online demonstration.

I look forward to speaking to you soon.

Warm regards,
[YOUR NAME]

An easy rule of thumb to know who you're prioritising is your use of I/we or you/your, especially when starting an email, sentence, or paragraph. Whichever you use the most is where your focus is. It's a good idea to avoid trying to rub people up the wrong way. Sweeping statements like "I've not heard back from you, so I'll assume you're happy" can come across in a way you didn't intend them to. And they don't paint you in a particularly positive light.

Instead, try focusing on making broad, researched points and relate them to the reader by asking open-ended questions. It invites them to the conversation by presenting the chance to feedback with their own experience:

- "Do you find you face the same challenges?"
- "I'm curious. Of the four features I've shared with you, which stands out for you?"
- "It would be great to talk about your current situation."
- "Why don't we show you how we can bring you the same results as [COMPETITOR] and [COMPETITOR]?"

These are all excellent examples of relaying your points back to your audience. You're not making any assumptions. By wording it in this way and **asking** for their input, you're being much more humble and effective than pushing your beliefs and opinions.

When you only think and write from your perspective, you're stifling yourself. Taking the lessons learned from the research pillar, you can reverse engineer your message to find subject matters and angles that appeal to them. Make your life easier. Instead of trying to win your audience over to your way of thinking, find **their** way of thinking and use your words wisely to draw them in. You could have some pretty amazing messages suffocating under self-indulgent waffle. By editing for your audience, you transform your content into something meaningful that inspires action.

Once you've put your reader in the driver seat, you can get to work transforming your FUFD into reader-ready content.

EDITING WITH A PICKAXE

With editing, I consider myself a sculptor of sorts. If I were Michelangelo setting out to create my famous statue of David, I wouldn't start hacking into marble and hoping for the best. I would begin by taking a step back to admire the rectangular block that I'm working with. As a writer, this is my FUFD. Before you get into the finer details, you want to look at the bigger picture; consider the entire piece. Michelangelo didn't start with David's eyebrows, after all. Let's make sure you've not got a leg where a head should be.

I'd first take out my pickaxe and hack out the outlines of all my limbs. In my writing, this is making sure all my points are in the correct place, in keeping with my structure and plan. Before you get into the nitty-gritty of asking yourself if there's a better word, statistic, or analogy you can use, you need to observe your work as a whole.

There are five simple questions to ask yourself when you have your pickaxe in hand. Scan your work and ask yourself each one. If the answer is no, swing that pickaxe until you're happy with the results.

Are you saying too much?

I talked about this earlier: killing your darlings. Yes, you might have an amazing paragraph that you want to marry, but if it isn't adding to the wider piece, why is it there? But hold on, you don't have to delete it. That's still useful to you; you can repurpose it. If you're writing a blog and there's way too much information, why not cut out the fat **and** save these for later? They could work well as a social media post.

If you're talking too much in your CV, repurpose some of that content for your cover letter. If your proposal is getting lengthy, strip out the summary page and make that an accompanying email. Even though not everything in your FUFD will stay, it doesn't mean you have to kill it outright. Instead, consider the role of this particular piece in your wider plan, looking for ways to use it elsewhere.

Is this written for my audience?

By now, you're probably sick of me talking about it, but I can't make the importance of talking directly to your audience any more clear. This is your final reminder. Imagine that they're standing in front of you. Read the piece to them. Are they loving life? Are they nodding their heads enthusiastically, looking grateful for the information you're imparting? If not, something needs to change.

Is this enjoyable?

If it isn't, how can you bring it more to life? Is a story or anecdote missing? Typically, something that's boring to read is something that's also hard to read. Overcome this by saying more, yet writing less. Be concise. While a long, flowing sentence might look more impressive on the page, as you wax lyrically, as we're doing now, all it achieves is increasing the word count while damaging the overall impact of what you're trying to say, as you lose the attention of the reader with each and every word. Like those last 52 words of drivel. Sentences that have a point and get to them sooner rather than later make for far more effective and engaging written communication. This is also an important principle to apply to your headline. 80% of people will read the headline, but only 20% will read the rest. How can you keep your readers' interests piqued?

Am I making my point?

If not, you need to continue digging deeper until there are no questions left. An easy way to do this is to state your key idea as clearly as possible near the start. Cut down any unnecessary waffle that precedes this. We love to prepare our audience for our main points with an unnecessary preamble. Don't ask me why. I do it, too. But axing these parts will work wonders for improving the readability and clarity of your writing. And like I said before, if they're helpful and interesting, you can always use them elsewhere.

Keep your main points your focus, slashing anything that doesn't support them, distracts from them, or doesn't enhance your argument. It'll be helpful to put yourself in your audience's shoes (again) for this part. Play the cynical reader to pick apart your work. The 'so what' method that you'll adopt in the chisel section will help with this.

Does it flow?

Read your piece aloud. If it's hard to read to you, how is your poor audience going to feel? Are you darting from point A to B to Z to P to A? Is everything in the right order? Does one point flow into the next? Does every paragraph contain a new point? Or do they restate what you've said before? Are the paragraphs Frankenparagraphs? Are they made up of disjointed sentences awkwardly pushed together? They shouldn't be.

Sentences should build on one another and every paragraph should earn its keep - adding distinct, new value to the wider piece. It might be as simple as changing around some sentences and paragraphs to ensure everything follows a logical order.

With that said and done, you can put down the pickaxe. After one hell of a shoulder workout, it's time to switch it out for your chisel. Let's add the last few flourishes to bring that masterpiece to life.

EDITING WITH A CHISEL

C hisel work is your true Dexter moment. Those pesky darlings that thought they got away with it are about to meet their demise. Sneak up on them with a chisel and take them out one by one until there's nothing left other than your very own David proudly erected on your page, ready for the world to see.

But how do you know how to spot a darling? Well, there are hundreds of them. Some you'll find yourself falling victim to more than others, some you'll already be a master of avoiding. Once you become aware of them, they're more obvious on your killing spree.

Waffle vs storytelling

You want to start as you mean to finish: strong. Back in 2013, Microsoft conducted a study into our attention spans. Comparing results from 2000, where the average attention span stood at 12 seconds, the average had dropped to only 8 seconds. You don't need to be a mathematician to see what this trend might mean for our attention spans *now*. And when you also take into account that SimilarWeb found the average time spent on websites - predominantly on mobile devices - went down by 49 seconds between 2017 and 2019, it looks even worse.

This shortening of attention spans will inevitably affect how your readers engage with your writing. You have even less time to win your readers over, so you've got to make your writing work harder. Openings need to grab your readers. Your first few paragraphs should draw people in and make them enthusiastic to read the rest. This is one of the most important places to check for darlings. Remember how I said we all *love* a pointless preamble? They're acceptable enough in our FUFD, but now it's time to trim them down. Often, you'll find you can remove your whole first paragraph and it won't take anything at all away from the wider piece. If that's the case, kill it.

Consider this chapter. What would happen if we did just that?

~~Chisel work is your true Dexter moment. Those pesky darlings that thought they got away with it are about to meet their demise. Sneak up on them~~

430

~~and take them out one by one until there's nothing left than your very own David proudly erected on your page, ready for the world to see.~~

~~But h~~How do you know how to spot a darling? Well, there are hundreds of them. Some you'll find yourself falling victim to more than others, some you'll already be a master of avoiding. Once you become aware of them, they're easier to spot as you embark on your killing spree.

Does the second version get to the point quicker? Absolutely. In this particular case, considering my audience - and I know you guys have a sense of humour - I opted to build up the scene and paint a story. But this is also a book - so there's more leeway for tangents and waffle.

In a blog post where I have 500 words, I would have trimmed the fat. The extended opening doesn't add value and takes away space for words that will. In an email, where no one wants to be sat reading forever, I would have made it shorter still. Write appropriately for the medium of choice and cut sections of your writing using the same judgement.

Your closer should be strong, too. After reading what you have to say, you don't want your reader to feel let down when they finish. You want people to finish your piece wishing it hadn't ended. Or wanting even more. If it's a blog, they might then be tempted to look for more great blogs you've written. In the case of an email, a strong close could make the difference between them taking action or not. With any professional correspondence - be it emails, blogs, proposals, or anything else under the sun - you want to make a lasting impression. How can you make like Obama and drop the mic?

Use stronger words

In our FUFD, we're freestyling and using the first words that come to mind. It's when we go back and take a deep dive into each line that we start to spot sentences that can be developed further or made more impactful. Staying on the start of this chapter, *"Once you become aware of them, they're more obvious on your killing spree"* became far more impactful when it evolved into *"Once you become aware of them, they're easier to spot as you embark on your killing spree..."*

You're better than the shit words you use. Don't be lazy. There are a minimum of 50 synonyms for "thing" and over 20 for "stuff". By simply changing a few words in a sentence, you can transform your writing from good to great.

Say it with less

Ah, filler words - the Japanese knotweed of the written world. Basically, a filler word is just a word that doesn't really say very much. In your text, they are actually highly meaningless. Needless to say, they really slow down the pace of what you're trying to say. For what it's worth, they feel quite natural to write, but they add no value. Have you ever recorded yourself and recoiled in horror at the amount of errrms that you've unknowingly dropped? In my humble opinion, this is the impact your filler words have on your content. Despite the fact they seem helpful, when it comes to your business writing, they need to go. Oh, hang on. Let's try that again.

A filler word is one that doesn't say much. In your text, they're meaningless and slow down the pace of your writing. They feel natural to use but add no value. Have you ever recorded yourself and recoiled in horror at the amount of errrms you've dropped? This is the impact filler words have on your content. They seem helpful, but in your business writing, they need to go.

Do you see what I did there? Any:

- Basically
- Just
- Very
- Actually
- Really
- Despite the fact
- When it comes to
- Highly
- Needless to say
- For what it's worth
- In my humble opinion

Are filler words, and they need to go. Used correctly, **basically** is used to summarise complex matters. If what you're explaining is already simple, as it should be to improve readability and audience engagement, indicating you have to make it more simple for people is condescending.

Very, **despite the fact**, **really**, and **when it comes to** are all as useful as the silent D in handkerchief. Delete them and your sentence remains exactly the same. **Just** is similar, though it can be useful for emphasis (e.g. describing something arriving "just in time"). Using **needless to say** is shooting yourself in the foot. Because if it truly were needless to say, why are you saying it?

For what it's worth is like using **may**, **might**, or **could**. It screams uncertainty and a lack of confidence. Unless you're legally obligated to not commit to promises and absolutes - typically in the medical, legal, and financial sectors - be confident in your language. Finally, **in my humble opinion** is my favourite fail of all time. We already know it's your opinion, you wrote it. Calling it humble doesn't make it so.

Making our point and making it twice

Have you ever been one foot out the door, or with your finger hovering over the red button to get to your next meeting, waiting for someone who knows you're in a rush to finish saying something they're repeating for the 3508943 time? Even though you understood what they said the first go around? That's how it feels when you're flogging a dead horse, repeating the same point in different ways. And it makes your reader lose faith in you. You're not Santa. Make your point once and move on. Kill, kill, kill.

Keep an eye on your sentence length

Have you ever read something and been exhausted halfway through because the writer forgot to give you a comma so you can breathe? It's not awesome. Make sure you're not doing this to your reader. A 25-word maximum per sentence is a good rule of thumb.

Avoid obvious statements

'Obvious statements' are subjective to your audience and subject matter. This rule needs your common sense. If you were writing to me, a writer, and you're a full stack developer explaining what Python is and why it's worth considering for my business, 'obvious statements' to you would be like deciphering Mandarin for me. Jargon would leave me confused and probably a little overwhelmed. In this case, I would appreciate you explaining it to me like I'm a five-year-old.

However, if you were talking to a fellow developer, writing a piece titled "Python 3.10.0a7 and all you need to know" and you start breaking everything down into layman's terms, you're being condescending. Other obvious statements might take the form of cliches or positive statements. They sound good enough but are emptier than we realise. And they aren't always as apparent as "the sky is blue" or "we need air to survive". In your professional writing, they usually look like "we work hard for our customers", "we're pleased to have won the writer's of the year award", or "we care about our staff".

Well... duh? A good way to identify an obvious statement is by reversing it. No one's going to think you can't be arsed to work hard, that you're pissed about the award, or that your staff don't mean anything. You're pitching the bare minimum when I'm sure there are *plenty* of unique selling points you could be shouting about.

Adjectives aren't sincere, exciting, or credible

The quickest way to transform your writing from cliche to sincere is to drop adjectives. Adjectives tell us what something is. They are the hypeman in your text, gassing up whatever you've got to say. Here are a few adjectives that are commonly overused in business:

- accessible
- accurate
- adaptable
- aesthetically pleasing
- agreeable
- available
- balanced
- candid
- capable
- certified
- clear
- compliant
- cooperative
- coordinated
- credible
- detailed
- different
- diligent
- distinct
- economical
- efficient
- focused
- functional
- futuristic
- good
- hard-to-find
- harmonious
- helpful
- holistic
- hybrid
- important
- inexpensive

- inquisitive
- intelligent
- knowledgeable
- large
- lean
- long-lasting
- long-term
- momentous
- necessary
- new
- next
- optimal
- organic
- outstanding
- painstaking
- parallel
- perfect
- perpetual
- popular
- possible

- powerful
- premium
- productive
- proud
- quick
- real
- real-time
- relevant
- reliable
- resilient
- reusable
- scalable
- secure
- simple
- sincere
- skilful
- small
- smart
- sophisticated
- special

- spectacular
- stable
- standard
- steady
- strategic
- strong
- substantial
- subtle
- successful
- succinct
- talented
- tangible
- tested
- thoughtful
- timely
- unbiased
- unique
- unknown
- upscale
- workable

When differentiating between two options, adjectives do have their place. Knowing that a training session is full-day and off-site, rather than being a half-day and on-site avoids catastrophe. Comparatively, telling me it's your new, innovative, premium, hybrid course doesn't add anything. It sounds more desperate than compelling. Instead, tell me about what value it'll add to my life. Sell me on the person I'll be after completing it.

Embrace the "so what?" method

It's time to embrace your stroppy teenage self and start asking "so what?" more often. Put yourself in your audience's shoes. When reading your piece, read it as them. With all their detachment and scepticism. If anything you're reading leaves you saying "so what?", "why do I care?", or "how does this help me?", then you haven't dug deep enough into your point. Keep pushing and repeating "so what?" until you've clearly articulated yourself and can't answer any further. Adjectives are typically the culprit for any lingering 'so whats?'

Take 'exciting' for example. Calling something exciting is like calling your opinion humble. "We've launched our exciting new course!" So what? Why is it exciting? By answering your 'so whats', you uncover the true essence of your message. You anticipate your audience's questions or protests, creating a more enjoyable, valuable experience for them.

It's likely that adjective-ladened sentences are showing up in your content a little like this: *"Our SaaS platform is an intelligent and insightful tool for your organisation." "Our professional team has years of technical experience and are motivated to deliver our services efficiently and safely."*

They look good, don't they? The problem is you're not **saying** anything. If your website conversions are low compared to website visitors, or people aren't messaging back on LinkedIn, it's likely because your words have no meaning. Efficiency is great, but what does it mean? It varies largely in meaning and value depending on the reader. Einstein was intelligent. But so is an ant. See how we're left with another 'so what' moment?

Instead, *"Our SaaS platform combines 100,000 terabytes of big data per second, auto-deletes incomplete files, and predicts potential next steps based on learned behaviour patterns."* Or *"With three decades of experience, our team can overcome any technical challenge, helping you to solve the most complex of problems. Our commitment to efficiency means we complete each job on time, keeping your projects on track. Always."*

Now your audience knows that your platform is intelligent and insightful and that you're efficient, as well as knowing what this means for them. You've taken your content from empty to something that holds weight.

Get good at using verbs

Now you're uncovering the essence of what you have to say, it's time to get good at using verbs. Verbs are the elegant storytellers of your sentences. Your own Charles Dickens on the page. Even he says the pain of parting with adjectives is nothing to the joy of meeting verbs. Well, he didn't. But he should have.

Instead of bloating your writing with empty adjectives, you can start leveraging verbs to pack a bigger punch. I could tell you how I took my dog George for a walk through the woods. Or, I could tell you how we strolled, flew, torpedoed, cantered, sprinted, or ambled through the woods. Thanks to a simple word choice, you know exactly what kind of mood Big G was in that day.

End of the line

Punctuation is essential. Period. Mastering it is key to clearer writing. Knowing how to use more complicated punctuation doesn't mean you should; semicolons are impressive, but ending sentences sooner rather than later can make text punchier and more effective.

Be active, not passive

Your content is worse if it's written in the passive voice. Writing content in the active voice is more engaging. Do you see what I did there?

Passive: Your content is worse if it is written in the passive voice.
Active: Writing content in the active voice is more engaging.

Using the active voice gives a sentence more impact and improves flow, whereas the passive voice makes them longer and vaguer. You need to bring the active subject of the sentence to the beginning. In this case, the subject is the writing.

Spell check yourself before you wreck yourself

Do you remember that White House tweet about then-President Donald Trump's bilateral meeting with Teresa May? Teresa May is a soft-porn actress/glamour model. *Theresa* May was the UK's Prime Minister. Details matter.

While your business content is unlikely to end up as the next Clinton-Lewinsky sexscapade, mistakes can have a lasting impact, and likely not the one you're hoping for. Asking someone to bare with you *(instead of bear)* is asking them to get naked with you. Unless that's what you meant, knowing to use bear instead will pay dividends. You can save yourself the embarrassment and the unintended reputational damage.

Does tihs make sens? If a hole email or blog was writen like this, wud u trust it? I'll take a stab in the dark and assume no, and rightly so. Often, these aren't representative of your abilities, but a result of writing in haste. It's still not a valid excuse though.

Always scan your writing before hitting send or publish. It doesn't have to take you long and it saves you the annoyance. Particularly when texting. Autocorrect is a bitch for making up words. As a writer myself, it's infuriating. But ultimately, it's you, not your phone, that the recipient will judge.

Spelling mistakes can cause your professional image to plummet, especially if it happens regularly. They're also the easiest writing mistakes to rectify because all you need to do is proceed with a little more caution. I get it, you've been working on the proposal all day and you want to get rid of it now. But trust me, the few minutes it takes to proofread will be worth it. It could be the difference between you winning work or not, after all.

Spice it up to spot mistakes

It's all well and good me telling you to re-read your work before you send it. But I know from experience there's a little more to it than that. When you've spent hours working on a piece of writing, you struggle to pick up on little mistakes because you're too aware of what the piece is. You'll likely skim through as you read and be less able to spot slight mistakes.

When you're looking at what you've spent time agonising over, you're no longer reading - you're remembering. Your brain is naturally going to fill in the gaps. But your audience hasn't been through the same process as you, so you need to put yourself in their shoes and whip out the fine-toothed comb.

Try taking a break between each round of proofing. Distancing yourself from the piece, even if only for a few minutes, will help you look at it with fresh eyes. Looking at your writing in different formats can also be helpful when trying to spot mistakes. I know a lot of people like the traditional method of writing, printing, and taking out the red pen. Personally, I love the rainforest and prefer keeping it digital. Instead, on your screen, you can play around with different fonts, sizes, and colours. It's like wearing a wig. You can transform your look effortlessly. And when it looks different, your eyes are forced to see it in a new light and are more likely to see those pesky typos or spelling mistakes.

Another method for tightening the readability of your writing is to hear it back in someone else's voice. You could pester your bestie, partner, or work wife, but an easier method would be to search for a free text-to-speech reader. You'll be surprised how many times you'll wince while thinking "well that doesn't make sense". It'll also highlight areas that are still too wordy or convoluted. Or those moments where you realise an entire paragraph is one, impossibly long sentence.

SO THIS IS THE END...

Well... that's it! There's no long-winded conclusion. No last-minute advice. I've been through everything there is to know, and all that's left is for you to go out there and start writing the amazing content I know you can. There's nothing else to teach. With these four pillars, you're ready to transform your writing. So, as Stephen King says: "Kill those darlings. KILL. THEM. ALL." There might be some slight paraphrasing of the quote.

Your writing can reach beautiful new heights by researching your audience, structuring your content in the right way, writing everything you can think of, and editing into a work of art. Once you've been through it at least three times with your pickaxe and chisel and listened to it back, make sure you're confident your reader will love it. After that, you're ready to take the plunge.

With practice, practice, practice, you'll soon hone your skill and become a writing machine. You'll have your days where the right words don't come to you, or an error slips through the cracks, but keep at it.

It's brutal, but you've got this.

Resources

- https://onlinelibrary.wiley.com/doi/epdf/10.1002/he.36919771703?purchase_site_license=LICENSE_DENIED&show_checkout=1&r3_referer=wol&purchase_referrer=onlinelibrary.wiley.com&tracking_action=preview_click
- https://www.digitaldoughnut.com/articles/2019/september/the-80-20-rule-of-headlines#:~:text=Think%20about%20these%20interesting%20statistics,important%20element%20of%20your%20content.http://dl.motamem.org/microsoft-attention-spans-research-report.pdf
- http://dl.motamem.org/microsoft-attention-spans-research-report.pdf
- https://www.similarweb.com/corp/reports/2020-digital-trends-lp/
- https://alejandrocremades.com/interesting-facts-and-data-around-pitch-decks/
- https://www.campaignmonitor.com/blog/email-marketing/email-copywriting-technique-results/
- https://zety.com/blog/hr-statistics
- https://www.linkedin.com/pulse/how-use-misuse-hashtags-linkedin-greg-cooper/
- https://www.gloriafood.com/menu-writing
- https://www.restaurantdive.com/news/77-of-diners-visit-restaurant-websites-before-going-survey-finds/562008/
- https://www.campaignmonitor.com/blog/email-marketing/email-copywriting-technique-results/
- https://blog.hubspot.com/sales/the-ultimate-list-of-words-that-sell
- https://www.meltwater.com/en/blog/how-to-write-more-effective-press-releases-with-6-examples
- Steven King - On Writing
- Will Smith - multiple inspirational videos
- https://class-pr.com/blog/attention-grabbing-headline/
- https://neilpatel.com/blog/write-better-product-descriptions/

- https://prowly.com/magazine/press-release-examples/
- https://corporatefinanceinstitute.com/resources/careers/how-to-job-guides/monroes-motivated-sequence/
- https://guykawasaki.com/the_102030_rule/
- https://alejandrocremades.com/interesting-facts-and-data-around-pitch-decks/
- https://markinstyle.co.uk/elearning-statistics/#COVID-19_Elearning_Statistics
- https://www.prnewswire.com/in/news-releases/elearning-market-to-reach-usd-370-billion-by-2026-at-a-cagr-of-8-56-valuates-reports-886649451.html
- https://www.paldesk.com/how-to-write-a-good-newsletter/
- https://coschedule.com/email-subject-line-tester
- https://journeys.autopilotapp.com/blog/email-spam-trigger-words/
- https://instapage.com/blog/personalization-statistics
- https://www.linkedin.com/pulse/how-use-misuse-hashtags-linkedin-greg-cooper/
- https://www.forbes.com/sites/jiawertz/2019/08/31/the-number-one-thing-marketers-need-to-know-to-increase-online-sales/?sh=246f286b7fed
- https://sproutsocial.com/insights/social-media-character-counter/
- https://buffer.com/resources/10-new-twitter-stats-twitter-statistics-to-help-you-reach-your-followers/
- https://buffer.com/library/the-ideal-length-of-everything-online-according-to-science/?utm_content=buffer72e0e&utm_medium=social&utm_source=twitter.com&utm_campaign=buffer
- https://blog.hootsuite.com/ideal-social-media-post-length/

Printed in Great Britain
by Amazon

39612730R00255